365 DAYS

KINGDUIT™

SOUND MIND POWER

The Wonderful Counselor!

PHEBE FIRE

Master's Mental Health Counseling

CONTENTS

KINGDUIT

This book contains decades of wisdom from the author. All stories have name changes. Using faith-based information is at the risk of the reader. It is designed singularly for personal, Christian devotion, educational, and informational purposes only. If you have questions about the mind/body health connection, consult relevant professionals before you begin implementing mental healing. The content should be used in a natural, Holy Spirit-led context and shall never be regarded or compared to seeking professional medical, psychiatric, psychological, or professional therapeutic treatment.

Due to the complex nature of the mind, memory, historical recall, emotions, trauma, and the process of thought, you should consult a Christian-based health practitioner before seeking Biblical self-improvement in mental health. Mixing any substances, either natural or synthetic, can alter your consciousness levels and put you at risk. Being sober-minded and alert is a must.

Liability for any damages, losses (personal or financial), or conflicts related to contents of this publication shall not be the responsibility of either the author or the publisher.

Any published contact numbers or addresses may be changed at the discretion of the author or publisher.

ISBN: 979-8-9892755-2-6

DISCLAIMER

Biblical Mental Health is a natural approach to the healing of the soul, mind, intellect, heart, and emotions. Jesus Christ is the self-proclaimed burden-bearer, that means Jesus will take and remove trauma from the soul by faith. The promises of freedom from burdens are for those who are willing to go to Jesus Christ the Nazarene! In other words, you won't let yourself continue to be burdened repeatedly because you are ready to seek help from the Lord Jesus.

Faith-based natural healing is possible via self-will in partnership with the promised Holy Spirit helper. The Bible clearly states that Jehovah Rapha is the God of Healing and the Wonderful Counselor. Since the beginning of mankind, God Almighty has made Himself available to His people along with the world of humanity.

With mental wounds, suffering and pain can be a part of the healing process. Therefore, to pursue KINGDUIT presented by Biblical Mental Healing, one should carefully assess their own willingness to take seriously the encouragement from this daily read. Either guard the heart and read the information for educational purposes only or open your heart to the God of the Bible alone!

A faith-based natural healing remedy shall not be compared to or regarded as seeking professional medical, psychiatric, psychological, or professional therapeutic treatment. Due to the complex nature of the mind, memory, historical recall, emotions, trauma, and the process of thought, consulting a Christian-based health practitioner before seeking biblical self-improvement related to mental health can provide professional support.

Mixing any or all substances, either natural or synthetic, can alter your consciousness levels and put you at risk. Therefore, the benefits of natural mental remedies are negatively altered. Being sober-minded and alert is foundational to seeking faith-based mental healing.

This servant is using her freedom with humility. "May God himself, the God of peace, sanctify you through and through. May your whole spirit, soul and body be kept blameless at the coming of our Lord Jesus Christ" (1 Thessalonians 5:23).

Dedicated to: MY BELOVED BRIDEGROOM, Jesus of Nazareth

PROLOGUE

A Biblical Natural Healing Approach

There is no one that wants you to be blessed with super abundant mental health more than the Lord God Almighty! He's not just the Lion King of Kings; He's the knitter of your soul! He doesn't want to sew a diagnostic problem patch on you; He wants to color weave you with unconditional covenantal love.

He is a yarn lover who puts a hem around your life behind and in front while keeping the palm of His hand upon you. His invisible hand has never left your invisible soul. When He knit you together, it was like a poetic tapestry with designs of eternal artistry unique to YOU! God's workmanship is marvelous and complex. You already know this because even you can't trace God's awesome purpose over your life. Yet you can testify that He's done enough wild things that you are ready to trust Him with your mental health.

The thoughts the Lord has for you are vast, they cover the creation of your physical body, your thoughts, your coming and going, your words, your sleep, your good times, your lost days, your dark days, and your future days (from Psalm 139).

The best way to approach mental healing from a biblical perspective is to investigate the historical biblical narrative of how God started delivering people from psychological torment. This goes back to the garden snake.

God doesn't change; His methods still work to provide healing and deliverance. The Lord is still a Wonderful Counselor and Mighty God. As we review the biblical narrative, He will start knocking on your heart's door hoping you will trust Him. Then, if you are willing, God is all-knowing, so He is ready to review, WITH YOU, your personal historical narrative.

Since mental health is a soul place, the best way to approach this devotion is to be childlike. "But Jesus called the children to him and said, 'Let the little children come to me, and do not hinder them, for the kingdom of God belongs to such as these. Truly I tell you, anyone who will not receive the kingdom of God like a little child will never enter it'" (Luke 18:16-17). When you approach Jesus like a child, sometimes words aren't necessary. Just showing up in your prayer closet and saying "Abba" (God as Father) is enough. You can even grab the crayons and draw. The room at the end of each day is for you to "ART THERAPY DRAW," which is drawing biblical images to help understand the concepts of healing. The artwork is to write something out to understand a concept and/or bring clarity in your soul if you don't have words. That means it can be basic, and Jesus will receive it like a child seeking the kingdom of God. Your King can do it! KINGDUIT!!

When you are prompted to draw or write, it is a form of communion between your human heart and God. The healing connection awaits you in this devotion. "You show that you are a letter from Christ, the result of our ministry, written not with ink but with the Spirit of the living God, not on tablets of stone but on tablets of human hearts. Such confidence we have through Christ before God" (2 Corinthians 3:3-4).

JESUS DECLARED, "COME TO ME" (Matthew 11:28).

"THESE ARE THE WORDS OF THE AMEN, THE FAITHFUL AND TRUE WITNESS, THE RULER OF GOD'S CREATION. . . HERE I AM! I stand at the door and knock. If anyone hears my voice and opens the door, I will come in and eat with that person and they with me" (Revelation 3:20).

When the reader first encounters Jesus due to a divine knocking on the door to their soul, I wonder if your mind can comprehend that the "ruler of God's creation" is close. Yes, the King of the Universe stands ready to counsel you!

Who has the answers to life mysteries? I went to a counselor and got tagged, diagnosed, or identified with extra problems. I went to a pastor and got a piece of paper with a line and a dot. He said the dot is my time on earth and the line is eternity. If I looked at my problems from an eternal perspective, they wouldn't be a big deal. I didn't want to take drugs or bow down to religious idols from other remedies. Those options led me back to the universal call for divine help. "I will give you hidden treasures, riches stored in secret places, so that you may know that I am the Lord, the God of Israel, who summons you by name" (Isaiah 45:3).

Jesus showed me hidden things stored within; the wisdom came with peace. I didn't care if it was a rebuke, a sin conviction, or a vision of a blind spot. I understood from a deep place in my soul that I had met my Creator and He loved me unconditionally. I could handle the truth since Jesus Himself is the truth (John 14:6). I realized that no one on earth, including myself, had access to the center, my soul. The vision came, I saw Jesus, carrying a sharp double-edged sword with accuracy to penetrate my invisible soul. It didn't cut the physical, but His sword cut to my thoughts, memories, intellect, emotions and even the attitudes and groans of my heart. At first, I was terrified, but the love radiating from Jesus moved with unquenchable waves of healing.

I beheld the Wonderful Counselor!

MONTH 1 - Israel Flees Oppression

WINTER SEASON

WILDERNESS MOUNTAIN CLIMB

KINGDUIT | Day 1

"Kind words are like honey, sweet to the soul and healthy for the body."

Proverbs 16:24

The biblical new year is called Rosh Hashanah, which begins in September. Instead of saying "Happy New Year" the Jewish community says "Shana Tova!" This Hebrew phrase means "may you have a good and sweet new year." The full greeting is "L'shanah tovah tikatev v'tailhatem." This translation means "may you be inscribed (in the book of life) and sealed for a good year.[1]" So, grab a Shofar and blow the trumpet of blessing over your life this year! Proclaim KINGDUIT!

The Jewish community celebrates by eating apples, honey for sweetness and pomegranates because the seeds represent being fruitful in many ways. They blow the shofar (ram's horn) hundreds of times which represents a call to battle or community gathering. When they group together, they worship and pray for personal growth in areas like showing grace and being slow to anger. Then they take a personal inventory of how they behaved during the past year to ponder how they can build upon their lives and souls in the coming year.

The exquisite red pomegranate seeds make me think of the precious blood of Jesus Christ of Nazareth reminding Christians of His sweet healing. I can hear Him say to us from Isaiah 1:18 "Come now, let's settle this, though your sins are like scarlet, they shall be as white as snow; though they are red as crimson, they shall be like wool."

1 Thessalonians 5:24 "The One who calls you is faithful, and He will do it."

ART THERAPY DRAW: Draw an image of a shofar horn.

<u>YOUR WILL:</u>

-Say- "Holy Spirit, let me hear your voice this year!"

Day 2 | KINGDUIT

"O Lord, if you heal me, I will be truly healed; if you save me, I will be truly saved."

Jeremiah 17:14

During the ancient time of Jeremiah, things were bad. "King Nebuchadnezzar burned down the Temple of the LORD, the royal palace and all the houses of Jerusalem. Every important building, he burned down." (2 Kings 25:9) If you read this devastating account of Israel's national trauma, you see that Solomon's glorious first stone temple, all the holy furnishings and even the surrounding gates were burned to the ground. The people of God were exiled into slavery, and their hearts were hard like stone, so hard that in Jeremiah 17:1 the prophet described the hearts of God's people like an iron pen with a diamond point. Ouch!

Nonetheless, Jeremiah was God's prophet and the mercy of God that endures forever called for national deliverance in verse 14. He called on the "Lord, the hope of Israel" while he grieved the real reality of the day that God's people simply "abandoned the Lord, the fountain of living water."

If you go to Israel today, some of the surrounding gates from the temple site were destroyed and rebuilt three times and still stand. Yeshua (Jesus) is still longing for His kingdom of righteousness and the deep healing of peace to take place in His Jewish and Gentile children. The world remains in desperate need of mental freedom, and the deep nature of sin is still embedded in the hearts of mankind.

- Think about how your nation and personal life story has elements of devastation and captivity.
- Do you believe Jesus is able to restore and heal the deep-seated sin in your nation, life, and family?
- Have you tried to seek Jesus for deep healing and holy redemption?
- Did that process work and have a lasting effect?

KINGDUIT | Day 3

"He is the Rock; His work is perfect."

Deuteronomy 32:4

An original ancient structure from the temple that was not destroyed was a portion of the west wall. This is referred to as "The Western Wall " and is also known as the "The Wailing Wall" made of ancient limestone in the Old City of Jerusalem. Everyday people from all over the world kneel, gather, stand, sit, and pray at this holy sacred wall.

I had the amazing blessing of praying at this wall in the Old City while I studied Trauma & Resilience at Hebrew University of Jerusalem. I wrote my prayer on a little piece of paper and put it in a crack on that wall. Never would I have imagined when I started my healing journey in 1992 that it would take me all the way to the ancient biblical City of David in 2019.

It could be said that of all the writers of the bible, the psalmist David understood the healing journey better than them all. The book of Psalms is truly the ultimate book of comfort! Interestingly, it is written by a king!

Imagine the biblical story of David from a mental health perspective. Young David had major rejection issues from his brothers that led him to humble beginnings as a shepherd boy on the outskirts of the family farm. That early rejection took root in his young heart and the fruit of it grew into sexual adultery issues, parenting failures and even murder.

Despite his hidden issues, David became king and was entrusted with the master plan of the first Temple of God in Jerusalem. When he died, he was buried in the City of David (1 Kings 2:10).

- Would you be willing to seek the King of Kings and follow Him on a healing journey?
- Can you write down a hidden hurt of your heart on a piece of paper, roll it up, pray over it and give it to the Rock of Ages by faith?

Day 4 | KINGDUIT

"The LORD sought a man after His own heart."

1 Samuel 13:14

"But God removed Saul and replaced him with David, a man about whom God said, 'I have found David, son of Jesse, a man after my own heart. He will do everything I want him to do.' And it is one of King David's descendants, Jesus, who is God's promised Savior of Israel" (Acts 13:22-23).

Why did Father God choose such a broken-hearted boy to be the king that would forever change the course of history for all of time? How could he trust such wonderful things to a man who grew up for greatness, but also failed epically? The LORD sees beyond our brokenness, beyond our family disappointments and is seeking out a man or a woman devoted to Him, no matter what the back story says. Just like the King of the Universe saw a king in David, He also sees greatness, even royalty in you.

We know about David's rejection issues from the bible because the Lord told the prophet Samuel to find a new king from Jesse's sons after King Saul refused to follow the Lord's instructions. Jesse had eight sons but only let seven meet Samuel (1 Samuel 16:10). Imagine how hurtful that was for young David, knowing a national leader came to the house, only to be uninvited to the family meeting. This wasn't the first sibling rejection in David's life.

Know this, wherever you are, whatever has gone down along the line, set your heart on Him and He will set His eyes on you!

"The eyes of the LORD search the whole earth in order to strengthen those whose hearts are fully committed to him" (2 Chronicles 16:9).

ART THERAPY DRAW: Draw the words below - God Sees, God Knows, God Cares.

"Since you have heard about Jesus and have learned the truth that comes from him, throw off your old sinful nature and your former way of life, which is corrupted by lust and deception. Instead, let the Spirit renew your thoughts and attitudes."

Ephesians 4:21-23

You may wonder, how can the Bible be a place to find and help mental health? Honestly, as a believer who has searched for family restoration and then mental health for the last thirty years, this idea that the Bible is the most effective resource for mental healing is a new revelation. I have read these verses for years, but in the last year, I realized the whole book and story of the bible is designed to heal the nations of the world.

The salvation that Christ promises is not just salvation from eternal death, it is an outpouring of divine love that gives an endless supply of relief for the human condition, even though it has become increasingly corrupt and deceived.

This devotional healing theme will be a journey through the land of the bible. God decided to make the geography of Israel the canvas of His masterpiece, so it is fitting that we explore that territory and dip into His "spring of water welling up to eternal life" (John 4:14).

ART THERAPY DRAW: Draw a pyramid, then draw an arrow pointing to the word "promise."

JOURNEY FROM SLAVERY TO PROMISE

Egypt's Slavery > God's Deliverance> Wilderness Healing > Jerusalem's Promise Land

Day 6 | KINGDUIT

"Hagar gave this name to the Lord, who spoke to her: 'You are the God who sees me,' for she said, 'I have now seen the One who sees me."

Genesis 16:13

In the hot, dusty, desert bible sand, family drama unfolded as God was populating the earth with his chosen people. A foreign slave girl who turned mistress got kicked to the dust to die, while pregnant. The wife had fertility issues and didn't trust God, so she found a surrogate at a time without modern technology. The mistress and her husband had to do it the old-fashioned way. Abram's Sarai didn't realize her problem would move from her barren womb to her jealous heart (Genesis 16:3-14).

If this scenario played out in today's time, a wife's ten-year fertility issues could turn from disappointment to depression to anger, then rage and possible double homicide. She would go to a secular counselor and get a DSM-5 diagnosis (Diagnostic and Statistical Manual for Mental Disorders: 5th Edition)[2] for her issues along with additional prescriptions for medication.

The difference between secular therapy and biblical therapy is the name of the healer. Secular counselors are called something like: Dr. So & So/ Counselor Mr. or Ms./Therapist Sir or Madam. Biblical therapy looks to the Lord; Jehovah Rapha, Wonderful Counselor, Prince of Peace, El Roi[3].

A biblical therapy model highlights the role of "the God who sees me - El Roi." El Roi is one of the many names of our biblical King of Heaven who was sent to heal mankind of all infirmities and afflictions of mind, body, soul & spirit. His territory covers the "whole earth," with love/care/concern without shame, condemnation or judgment extending to all the inhabitants of the world

---

ART THERAPY DRAW: Draw God's eyes - El Roi - The God who Sees

KINGDUIT | Day 7

"And as Moses lifted up the bronze snake on a pole in the wilderness, so the Son of Man must be lifted up, so that everyone who believes may have eternal life. For this is how God loved the world: He gave His one and only Son, so that everyone who believes in Him will not perish but have eternal life."

John 3:14-16

The best-selling book of all time according to the Guinness World Records is the Christian Bible with approximately 5-7 billion copies in 1500 years. The most popular verse in the Bible is John 3:16.

Just two verses before in verse 14 we have the image of Moses lifting the bronze snake on a pole. This was a reference to the time in history when God's people were in the wilderness headed to the promise land on the journey out of slavery. The people sinned against God and the price of that sin was death. Snakes showed up in camp and the Israelites started to die. They cried out for help. "Then Lord said to Moses, 'Make a (bronze) snake and put it up on a pole; anyone who is bitten can look at it and live" (Numbers 21:8).

That same snake that tricked the first man/woman in the garden of Eden, who brought sin into the world is the same serpent today that deceives the whole world. Two thousand years later the Son of Man is lifted on the cross as the remedy for life.

ART THERAPY DRAW: Look up the two symbols (USA & International)[4] for medicine and draw them below.

Day 8 | KINGDUIT

"You are receiving the goal of your faith, the salvation of your souls."

1 Peter 1:8-9

When you accept Christ Jesus by faith as Lord of your life for forgiveness of sins and receive the free gift of salvation through the finished work of the cross, you have obtained everything you need for life and godliness inside your relationship with Christ. That means, everything you need to be completely and utterly healed is already inside of you. Basically, Almighty God downloaded it all, even Himself, into you via your believing faith. You were literally yet spiritually born again.

In modern world terms, it's like receiving a Jesus-made computer with every possible capability. In addition, Father God took the only set of keys or passwords from Jesus and gave them to you, so you are the only one with total access to your computer. No one in the universe can access this phenomenal system, not even God. Only you and those you give access to different parts of the system can effect change.

This is the most common reason why the people of the world are not healed, even those who belong to Jesus Christ and possess every possibility and power for every type of change. They are not willing to receive salvation and/or healing.

PREPARE YOUR HEART:

- Find a private place and honestly ask The LORD if you are willing to begin to access the healing power, He died to give you?
- If you wait and listen until you get an answer, write down that information so you can remember the special words.
- ART THERAPY DRAW: Draw the words: "JESUS PAID IT ALL"

"O Jerusalem, Jerusalem, who kills the prophets and stones God's messengers! How often I have longed to gather your children together as a hen protects her chicks beneath her wings, but you wouldn't let me."

Luke 13:34

The Jews eventually made it to the promise land via Joshua's leadership. Many years later Jesus came into the world, grew up and spent three years in the ministry field of Israel. Jesus went to Jerusalem to heal people, and the religious people told him to leave, they didn't want the Healer at church. His response is the verse above.

If you take time to seek God's heart and meditate on this passage, you should sense the deep sorrow of our Great Savior. If your heart is tender enough to allow the Holy Spirit to show you how Jesus felt in His unrequited love and subsequent rejection from His own Jewish people and even the Christians of this day, you should experience a great wave of godly sorrow.

Grieving is a healthy way to release unexpressed feelings out of your soul (mind/intellect/emotions). Some believers call this grieving in the Spirit. If this is happening to you, let it be a beautiful confirmation that you are tapping into the heart of God. Don't stop the holy emotions, let the waves of grace and sensing God's heart wash over you. Stay there, be silent or speak.

"Grieve, mourn and wail. Change your laughter to mourning and your joy to gloom. Humble yourselves before the Lord, and He will lift you up" (James 4:9-10).

Writing feelings down on paper is another way to unload thoughts from the soul. The book of Psalms is a perfect example of King David releasing emotions to the LORD.

"When they came to the oasis of Marah, the water was too bitter to drink. So, they called the place Marah (which means bitter)."

Exodus 15:23

Another reason for the mental health crisis of these times is a lack of understanding about what it takes to accomplish the healing of the mind, brain, emotions, thoughts, intellect, and soul. I believe one reason is a lack of knowledge. "My people are being destroyed because they don't know me" (Hosea 4:6).

Just like the gift of pain is an amazing indicator that something is wrong in our physical body, similarly emotional pain (anger - depression - sorrow - bitterness - anxiety) is indicative of psychological trauma. Often at the top levels of leadership in churches, either the pastors won't share the healing information, they do not understand the process of soul healing, or they aren't willing to open doors of healing at a psychological/soul level. Many believe things will get too messy. On my healing journey when I sought pastoral support, church leaders would not give me wisdom beyond something like, "just pray about it" or "go get counseling."

Fret not, because the Lord your Healer loves all that bitter soul ooze! He longs to fellowship with us all, even in the hard places. That is why He suffered for us on the cross.

Moses led a whole nation (over a million people) out of captivity, it was an enormous task. When they were free from Egyptian slavery, they grumbled against Moses about the bitter water. Moses didn't let them struggle, he cried out to the Lord for wisdom on how to remedy the problems with the people he led. It worked!

ART THERAPY DRAW: Write the words - "THE LORD HAS THE SOLUTION"

"Then Moses cried out to the LORD, and the LORD showed him a piece of wood. He threw it into the water, and the water became fit to drink. There the LORD issued a ruling and instruction for them and put them to the test."

Exodus 15:25

Often people struggling with mental health/trauma issues turn to addictive habits to cope with the pain and then go to rehabilitation to participate in group therapy. This is a great step, participating in group therapy, and will bring much wisdom and support into your life, even if you are not an addict.

The biblical perspective to approach the bitter waters of life is to "cry out to the Lord." Jehovah Rapha (the God who heals) isn't introduced until the bitter water shows up, which is after the Israelites were delivered from Pharaoh's slavery, plaques and even the death angel. God's people just had a major deliverance celebration and straight away, here comes the bitter waters. Their drinking water was bitter, and they complained to Moses, so "the Lord showed him a piece of wood. He threw it into the water, and the water became fit to drink" (Exodus 15:25).

There is much more to healing than problematic behavior, bondage to bad habits and hanging out with godless people. We can be addict-free, relationship liberated, and church going worshippers and yet, still have bitter waters in our mind, our emotions, or our attitudes. The solution is a piece of wood called the cross.

The Lord will pull us out of darkness and into His glorious light and even still, we need the cross to sweeten the bitter waters of what needs to be dealt with in our souls (memory/mind/emotions).

ART THERAPY DRAW: Seek out Jehovah Rapha, draw an image of the God who heals based on Exodus 15:25

Day 12 | KINGDUIT

"If you will listen carefully to the voice of the LORD your God and do what is right in His sight, obeying His commands and keeping all His decrees, I will not bring on you any of the diseases I brought on the Egyptians, for I am the LORD (Jehovah Rapha), who heals you."

Exodus 15:26

The giants that are in the land of America are vile. A long-respected bible preacher has declared that the "West has fallen" because of the perversions of our culture and the indoctrination of sexual immorality to our children.

I learned about this firsthand in 2018 at a National Board of Certified Counselors (NBCC) conference. The established counselors encouraged upcoming therapists to push gender fluidity for children seeking counseling. The Holy Spirit of God inside of me was disturbed. Pushing a perverse agenda on the therapeutic community seeking licensure was appalling. I could not align with that level of immorality and absolute destruction of impressionable children in schools. #DONTMESSWITHOURKIDS

I completed my degree to relentlessly pursue "the Lord who heals you" (Exodus 15:26). [5]I dedicated my counseling education to Jehovah Rapha and joined intercessory prayer groups declaring that "America shall be saved!"

Our faith-based communities and families will be demonically slimed with the perverse mental diseases of this wayward nation if we do not take seriously Exodus 15:26 and pursue Jehovah Rapha via the voice of the Lord (Holy Spirit) with listening, action, obedience, and relentless faithfulness to His word. Our families and marriages depend on it and even more, our future generations need to know how to live for Christ in this dark world.

- LISTEN - Can you hear God's voice via the promised Holy Spirit within?
- ACTION - When Holy Spirit works inside your soul, do you act?
- OBEY - Do you treasure the words and instructions written in the bible?
- BIBLE - When you have increased knowledge of the bible and biblical stories, God can speak to you through His Holy text.

Jesus said, "to open their eyes, so they may turn from darkness to light and from the power of Satan to God, so that they may receive forgiveness of sins and a place among God's people, who are set apart by faith in me."

Acts 16:18

Jesus gave Paul the Apostle of the New Testament the above mission statement, which summarizes the journey from worldliness to godliness. It parallels the journey of the Israelites from Egypt to the Promise Land because Pharaoh represented a type of Satan in the Old Testament.

This verse can summarize the difference between secular and biblical counseling. Just like Pharaoh held God's people in slavery, the power of Satan does the same to New Testament believers. A secular counselor would not say a client needs deliverance from Satan, but God's word speaks and tells the story of how He sets people free from the power of darkness.

- The process for secular counseling is a DSM-5[6] diagnosis or attaching a label to a client, along with therapy and possible prescription for medicine.
- The process for biblical mental healing is natural healing and freedom along with promised forgiveness of sins.

"It is for freedom that Christ has set us free. Stand firm, then, and do not let yourselves be burdened again by a yoke of slavery" (Galatians 5:1).

To make it to the promise land, a believer must fully commit themselves to completing the journey out of darkness and into the glorious light of Christ. No matter how challenging, it is the most rewarding and profitable adventure on the face of the earth.

ART THERAPY DRAW: Illustrate what an Egyptians worldly idol might look like versus an illustration of Jesus.

Day 14 | KINGDUIT

"Then the LORD said to Moses, 'Tell the Israelites to turn back and encamp before Pihahiroth, between Migdol and the sea. You are to encamp by the sea, directly opposite Baal-zephon."

Exodus 14:1-2

In Exodus 14 the Israelites are literally running for their lives. This included 600,000 men plus women and children (Exodus 12:37), who were under the leadership of Moses. Even though Pharaoh released the Israelites from slavery, once they were gone, he changed his mind and gathered 600+ of his chariots along with officers and troops to defiantly pursue and overtake God's people.

When the Israelites saw this, they were terrified and felt utterly betrayed by the Lord & His leader Moses. This made them think they had been set up to die at a dead end by the sea.

Can you remember the time right before your salvation, when you were lost, and your life/soul was empty with worldliness? Some remember the battle that took place prior to turning your life to Christ. This story from the bible is an amazing illustration of what that battle looked like as the biblical type of Satan and his minions unleashed the troops to keep God's future royal priesthood (1 Peter 2:9) in chains.

Thankfully, only seven perfect verses away, the word Moses declares is, "Do not be afraid, stand firm and you will see the Lord's salvation, which He will accomplish for you today; for the Egyptians you see today, you will never see again. The Lord will fight for you; you need only to be still" (Exodus 14:13-14).

A good leader/follower will only follow the voice of the Lord with a determination to obey. When this takes place, extraordinary things will happen! Trust the Lord for healing and deliverance today!

Listen to the voice of the Lord & His faithful leaders!

KINGDUIT | Day 15

"When the people of Israel saw the mighty power that the LORD had unleashed against the Egyptians, they were filled with awe before him. They put their faith in the LORD and in his servant Moses."

Exodus 14:31

The bible says, "Jesus is the same yesterday, today and forever" (Hebrews 13:8). No matter what level of healing you seek to obtain with the Lord, IT IS POSSIBLE. There is always someone on the planet who is equipped to help you cross your ocean of difficulty. The Israelites had to walk across the seabed on dry land to see the Lord save them from their relentless enemy.

God will always be faithful to fulfill His promise, and you must obey by being willing to act. We shall act because He will move on our behalf!

- HIS promise = God displayed mighty power and parted the sea

+

- OUR willingness = Listen to the instruction, walk, and obey

You can read the bible from cover to cover and see these simple patterns played out in story after story. You will read about the mighty acts of God with obedient responses, and you can read about the horrible outcomes and loss of those who refuse to obey with faith and action. Even if there are fearful emotions in play, one can still step out and obey.

This biblical concept is the key to healing, a promise for the willing follower. God is Jehovah Rapha, the God who heals and He always has the power to move. God is also El Roi, the God who sees, and He always knows exactly what is going on in our lives, hearts, and minds.

In the first two weeks of this new journey, we have covered amazing biblical concepts needed to experience the power of healing. From this point, salvation is certain, and a WILLING SPIRIT is necessary to partner with Holy Spirit by faith to receive power from our King and receive mental health and soul healing.

Day 16 | KINGDUIT

"Jesus said, 'Let's go off by ourselves to a quiet place and rest awhile."

Mark 6:31

"Before daybreak the next morning, Jesus got up and went out to an isolated place to pray."

Mark 1:35

Just as Jesus ran to solitude, we must also learn to activate this daily practice of silence, rest, solitude and seeking. It is the only way to cultivate ears that hear what Holy Spirit is saying to the soul.

Think of how you can expand your devotional time to experience more meaningful times of solitude. Ask Holy Spirit what a practice of listening to God and resting might look like. Are you willing to give many long hours to Jesus this year?

WRITE THOUGHTS ON PAPER: "Will you spend extra time talking and listening to me? I am waiting for you." Holy Spirit Helper

KINGDUIT | Day 17

"It was the Lord's Day, and I was worshiping in the Spirit. Suddenly, I heard behind me a loud voice like a trumpet blast. It said, 'Write in a book everything you see..."

Revelation 1:10-11

A common practice of successful people is writing down their ideas on paper. Many people have built buildings from a restaurant napkin. How many more promises from the Lord do believers have to write things down from a quiet place with God, words flowing from Holy Spirit within to help us along our healing journey. Think about it, even now, the King is enthroned in heaven, reading scrolls of remembrance (Malachi 3:16). Could the King be reading your scroll/letter?

It might be a still small voice or a loud glorious trumpet, it doesn't matter, any word from the Lord is a treasure. I hope these past few days you found a notepad or bought a special notebook for this year. If not, do so and dedicate it to the Lord for breakthrough and revelation beyond your wildest imagination.

"For the Lord is the Spirit, and where the Spirit of the Lord is, there is freedom" (2 Corinthians 3:7).

WRITE THOUGHTS ON PAPER: Find a tablet (notebook) and dedicate it to a year of biblical mental health!

Day 18 | KINGDUIT

"I will climb up to my watchtower and stand at my guard post. There I will wait to see what the LORD says and how he will answer my complaint."

Habakkuk 2:1

Then the LORD said to me. "Write my answer plainly on tablets, so that a runner can carry the correct message to others."

Habakkuk 2:2

Even great men of God, His prophets, complain. They go to "wonderful counselor" (Isaiah 9:6) and find answers.

In Mark 6:29, news of John the Baptist's death reached the disciples, and two verses later Jesus wants to be alone. He often went into the wilderness to withdraw, talk to the Father, and pray.

No doubt, in the case of John the Baptist being beheaded, Jesus was deeply grief stricken, probably traumatized. John was his friend from the womb (Luke 1:41). Jesus said in Matthew 11:11, "I tell you the truth, of all who ever lived, none is greater than John the Baptist."

Jesus sought Divine comfort straight away. We must also learn from His example to activate this daily practice of silence, rest, solitude, releasing trauma and seeking. It is the only way to cultivate ears that hear what Holy Spirit is saying to the soul.

The Lord is leading us to observe the biblical narrative of fleeing bondage and trekking through the wilderness with time set apart to seek Him. By believing faith, we can approach God's throne of grace to receive mercy. The New Testament book of Hebrews Chapter 3 & 4 illustrates this concept precisely. Note the key points.

ART THERAPY DRAW: Ponder, then illustrate concepts from Hebrews Chapters 3 & 4

KINGDUIT | Day 19

"Then Jesus said, 'Come to me, all of you who are weary and carry heavy burdens, and I will give you rest."

Matthew 11:28

If you want to read about what the ancient people did to seek the Lord, there are dramatic expressions in the Psalms. David was traumatized over his intense season of fleeing a murderous spirit working through King Saul, which he inscribed on paper. He sought to run to refuge before the Lord and pour out the brutal reality of his situation. He cried to God for mercy by saying "Have mercy on me, O God, have mercy, for in You my soul takes refuge. In the shadow of Your wings, I will take shelter until the danger has passed. I cry out to God who fulfills His purpose for me. He reaches down from heaven and saves me. He rebukes those who trample me. Selah (means rest) God sends forth His loving devotion and His truth. My soul is among the lions; I lie down with ravenous beasts – with men whose teeth are spears and arrows, whose tongues are sharp swords" (Psalm 57:1-4).

This is faith in action, faith that reaches out with real emotional words to an invisible God, with cries filled with hope that God sees, and God hears. Our God is the same God of the Israelites, and He has never changed. "Yesterday, today and forever" (Hebrews 13:8).

ART THERAPY DRAW: Draw a cloud. What would you say to Jesus regarding your lost dreams? Start with this:

"Lord, I give you ____."

Day 20 | KINGDUIT

"When Jesus saw Nathanael approaching, He said of him, 'Here is a true Israelite, in whom there is no deceit.'

'How do You know me?' Nathanael asked.

Jesus replied, 'Before Philip called you, I saw you under the fig tree.'

'Rabbi,' Nathanael answered, 'You are the Son of God! You are the King of Israel!"

John 1:47-49

You may wonder if there is an example from the Bible of Jesus answering a direct prayer? Yes, right here in John 1:47-49. In Nathanael we find one of many people directly praying to Jehovah Rapha for help.

Did the Lord hear you yesterday? Did He speak to you? I hope you wrote it down!

My personal journals document my direct communion with Holy Spirit. Reading those moments of divine fellowship again is a tremendous comfort to my soul. God does see, He knows, He listens, and He speaks. It's true and the Bible is real. You can ask the Lord about any event or moment in your life and receive an answer.

In this devotional, many verses will be highlighted that promise Divine relationship and unending love. It takes a little faith reaching out to wait on the Divine response. Be patient along the journey, it does take time and practice to experience the presence of the Lord. It is always worth every effort!

"This is what the Lord says, he who made the earth, the Lord who formed it and established it - the Lord is his name. Call to me and I will answer you and tell you great and unsearchable things you do not know" (Jeremiah 33:2-3).

ART THERAPY DRAW: Draw a picture of a man sitting under a fig tree alone.

"Why, my soul, are you downcast? Why so disturbed within me? Put your hope in God, for I will yet praise Him, my Savior and my God."

Psalm 42:5

The above verse can be summarized by:

- 1-Soul feeling
- 2-Negative emotion
- 3-Replacement emotion
- 4-Spiritual action

All we know about Nathanael is what Jesus said to him and his call to be a disciple. He could have had an attitude when he told his friend Philip in John 1:46, "Can anything good come from Nazareth?"

If Nathanael lived in modern western society, instead of going to sit under a fig tree all day, he might have gone for a few drinks to ease the tension. He might have gone to a counselor with his possible depression, anger, stress, or disappointment problems.

There, his secular therapist might have diagnosed him with generalized anxiety disorder because he might have had three or more symptoms in a period of less than six months. This coding is found in the ICD-10 (International Classification of Diseases) or the DSM-5 (Diagnostic Statistical Manual of Mental Disorders). Treatment could have been Cognitive Behavior Therapy (CBT) and/or medication.

But Nathanael was not modern, he was ancient Jewish, and his faith and upbringing led him to a fig tree where he cried out to the Lord! His faith taught him to recite passages of holy text from memory.

ART THERAPY DRAW: Can you find a biblical passage that addresses emotions and gives you a natural remedy to overcome those heavy or hurtful feelings?

Day 22 | KINGDUIT

"Moses and the people sang this song to the LORD.

And Miriam sang this song: 'Sing to the LORD, for He has triumphed gloriously; He has hurled both the horse and rider into the sea. Then Moses led the people of Israel, and they moved out into the desert of Shur."

Exodus 15:1, 21-22

There is a wonderful principle in the study of Biblical text called the law of first mention. To fully understand a foundational biblical truth, go to the first place of that subject in the ancient text and find out how that concept was revealed.

Exodus 15 (the second book in the Bible) documents the first song in the Bible, a deliverance song. It is a sacrifice of thanksgiving. How fitting, Almighty God performs the greatest salvation miracle via Pharaoh (Satanic) deliverance and Moses then leads the people in a song of praise. Moses knew the people had not only an incredibly intense day, but a traumatic 400 years of Egyptian homesteading. Moses set this leadership standard: offer the Lord a sacrifice of thanksgiving through worship and praise. This practice of worship to the Lord has never and will never stop for all eternity! Hallelujah!

Singing praises to the Lord is the greatest way to release trauma and solidify your faith. Trust God and experience the joy of salvation!

ART THERAPY DRAW & WRITE: Draw musical notes and your favorite words from Exodus 15. The song lyrics are about the epic Egyptian deliverance.

Worship Listen/YouTube: We the Kingdom - Dancing on The Waves

"And He (Jesus) will be called: Wonderful Counselor, Mighty God, Everlasting Father, Prince of Peace."

Isaiah 9:6

Isaiah wrote the above text about Jesus about 700 years before Jesus was born. This is the most amazing news for 21st century believers, as it relates to mental healing. This prophecy has already come to pass, and New Testament believers have the indwelling Holy Spirit, the Helper, that will forever teach them how to access the Counselor, Comforter, Advocate, Intercessor and Strengthener.

We can seek Divine help, strength, and peace if secular counseling treatment is not liberating. Here is a sample of an anxiety treatment called Cognitive Behavior Therapy (CBT):

Cognitive Behavior Therapy (CBT) involves:

- talking about, describing, or identifying emotions
- owning up to or accepting present emotions
- figuring out how to get rid of existing emotions
- discussing a plan to change thoughts or modify behavior to redirect emotions

---

WRITE A LETTER: Perhaps you have had an experience with a counselor. Can you write a letter to Jesus the "Wonderful Counselor" and review your case with Him?

Day 24 | KINGDUIT

"If we confess our sins to Him, He is faithful and just to forgive us our sins and purify us from all unrighteousness."

1 John 1:9

Secular counseling is participating in a therapeutic environment that has no spiritual or religious foundation. It is based mostly on treatment derived from educated psychologists who formulate different approaches to human behavior. This collective wisdom is derived from a century of modern psychoanalysts who have studied humans enough to understand that through education and learning, a person increases the ability to change behavior.

This concept is highlighted in the Bible from the book of Hosea 4:6 by claiming "people are destroyed from a lack of knowledge." The real difference between the two is summed up in the above verse. Therapy will seek to give people a (hopefully) safe place to unload emotions through talk therapy with the goal of finding a solution for change. This is a great beginning, but secular therapy has no power source to activate change or remove problematic emotions/feelings. All one must do is look at the individuals in Hollywood who have unlimited resources to hire therapists. Then realize that many of those individuals did not find soul-level healing. How is this possible? What is lacking?

Jesus is the only one who can forgive sins and purify all the wrongs connected to that sin.

ART THERAPY DRAW: Draw a sponge with a cross on it. Write down a memory or sin you wish God would wash clean from your soul.

KINGDUIT | Day 25

Forgiveness & cleansing via prayer is at the foundation of healing! Are you willing to release your inventory of wrongs to the only One who makes things right?

PRAYER: Dear Lord, thank you that you have the power to forgive sins and cleanse me from all unrighteousness. I am ready to begin laying down a foundation of confession, repentance, and healing today. Thank you for being the God of love and grace. Thank you for promising me that You will not condemn or shame me when I present my wrongs to you. Thank you for being trustworthy regarding the issues of my heart and the details of my story (Romans 8:1).

I know that I am a sinner, but sometimes I don't understand exactly what I am doing wrong or even when my wrong behavior started. Please help me to understand the cleansing process and give me the courage to bring the hidden things to Your light.

To start, forgive me of my own pride and the ways I think that it is everyone else's fault. This is the unrighteousness that needs your grace and purity. I don't know how you can forgive me for ALL my wicked ways. Today I present to you my willingness to open my heart to the specific things from my life's story that I should confess. I am willing to be forgiven for ways I have participated in this dark world along with the broken parts of my family.

When I hear your voice, help me to acknowledge You with faith. When You show me something out of order, help me to remember to quickly agree and confess that sin in that moment, knowing you desire to cleanse me right away (John 10:27).

Thank you for being my Father in heaven, for loving me and seeing who I really am on the inside. You are God Almighty, the Maker of heaven and earth! Thank you for dying on the cross and shedding your blood so that I can be forgiven and washed as white as snow. Thank you for never leaving or forsaking me. Most of all, thank you for never giving up on me with endless love. I believe you will make me healthy inside and out. Heal me O Lord, and I WILL be healed: body, soul, mind, and spirit. Save me and I WILL be saved. You are the GOD that I praise, I bless and thank you. I love you Lord Jesus (Jeremiah 17:14)!

Day 26 | KINGDUIT

"Then Moses led the people of Israel away from the Red Sea, and they moved out into the desert of Shur."

Exodus 15:22

As we wrap up the end of the 1st month of biblical mental healing, let's reflect. We have secured our salvation and deliverance out of darkness to the light of Christ. We also sang praises of thanksgiving and began to process forgiveness. The journey now moves to find promises the Lord has for us.

No matter where you are in faith, taking a survey of your life before the Almighty is critical these days for many reasons. Many Bible scholars believe we are in the "last days." The Bible talks about a time called the last days, which will be treacherous. They are difficult days, like these days, when many need mental stability and strength. Understanding how to protect yourself and your family without seeking mental healing will be challenging.

Just like the body doesn't work well if you are sick or injured, the mind doesn't work well if there are unresolved issues or emotional wounds that are hidden. It will be difficult to process intellectual challenges in life, family, or business if a believer doesn't possess the skills to be as "wise as a serpent" (Matthew 10:16).

In the case of the ancient Jewish community, the wilderness journey was an opportunity for the people to learn what it would take to be successful enough to get to the Promise Land. As a result, there was testing involved. The standard the Lord set out centered around listening to His voice and obeying His instructions. This was life or death for the people of God because the Egyptian diseases could easily resurface again within their community.

The same is true for us now, the literal physical diseases in the world are numerous and so is the dis-ease of psychological problems.

WRITE THOUGHTS ON PAPER: Find a page in your notebook to list the physical and emotional issues that you would like to find complete liberty.

KINGDUIT | Day 27

"So, God set another time for entering His rest, and that time is today."

Hebrews 4:7

It was 1996, I had been a Christian for a few years while attending church and the Lord was starting to work on my broken heart. I had spent my whole unsaved life seeking approval from my father, without success. Somehow, I got a copy of a book called "Feast of Fire, the Father's Day Outpouring" and I consumed it like a match to flame. The message hit such a nerve inside my heart that after I finished it, I turned back the pages to find the setting of the book. The story was only a year old, and the literal location of the church was a day's drive from my house.

I felt utterly compelled to chase God and found a handful of sisters from my local prayer group ready for a spur-of-the-moment road trip. As soon as we stepped into that house of God, we were served up the same feast of fire I read about. It was a remarkable outpouring beyond my wildest imagination, and we stayed for days.

While there, I talked to believers from around the world and one conversation has never left my understanding. A lady shared with me the importance of entering the "rest of God," much like laying in a river of divine love and putting on a blanket of Holy Spirit, then staying in that space for a long time. It didn't involve any screen, just the Lord. I couldn't wait to go home and try it out.

Thankfully in 1996 television was boring, I did not have a computer and knew nothing about the internet. I was hungry for Jesus, found a blanket, and started marinating on the Bible while seeking the Lord. Since then, I have never heard someone describe a relationship with the Lord quite like the lady from the Father's Day revival.

ART THERAPY DRAW: Draw a picture of what rest means to you?

Day 28 | KINGDUIT

"Yes, my soul, find rest in God; my hope comes from Him."

Psalm 62:5

PRAYER FOR REST: Yes Lord, let me find rest during this life season, a rest that will forever create a new path of blessing over my being. Let me find rest in my mind, body, soul, and spirit because Jesus promised to give me rest (Matthew 11:28).

To start, help me prepare a space for seeking You in such a way that my whole being can let go. Lord, show me how to create the most restful place in my home and/or bedroom. Bless my neighborhood, home, rooms, walls, and bedding to be a holy refuge of your unending love.

I give you the anxiety in my life and cast these cares upon You because you care for me. Right now, I give you these thoughts in my mind. I will write them down in detail on a piece of paper to release them via prayer to you:

____

____

____

As an act of my will, I hand these issues over to you now. You can carry these things. I am literally coming to You today with my weariness and burdened heart because You promise to carry my cares and in return give me a promise of rest. Help me to learn how to release these things to you, to trust you with all my heart and stop trying to understand it all (Proverbs 3:5).

Sometimes it is hard to believe that I can acknowledge you in "ALL my ways," but today, give me the faith to believe that I can let these things go. Show me how to have hope in you Almighty God.

If rest and sleep are at the foundation of feeling better in my mind, then I speak rest and deep, refreshing sleep over myself. Deliver me from nightmares, disturbances, discomfort, and sleep distractions. Help me to turn off my devices at the right time so my mind can slow down. Thank you, Lord, in advance for Divine help (Proverbs 3:6)!

ART THERAPY DRAW: Draw the number of hours of uninterrupted sleep you wish for. Pray and ask the Lord to give you wisdom to improve your sleep time.

KINGDUIT | Day 29

"You can go to bed without fear; you will lie down and sleep soundly."

Proverbs 3:24

If you are resting better, you are on the right track because a big component of excellent mental health is sleep.

Many mental health diseases like anxiety and depression have symptoms that have sleep difficulties, fatigue, and restlessness. In fact, the primary reason for clients in the mental health space being wrongly diagnosed is because of sleep or somatic issues.

My clinical work led me into the public school system as a therapist to children from ages Pre-K through Grade 12. My supervisory social work team gave me the stand-out cases in a special needs school. I was sent to the Pre-K room to help a little boy who constantly disrupted the learning environment by acting out with the other children. The team and teachers labeled him with learning, behavioral and emotional difficulties.

I knocked on the Pre-K door to easily locate the young fellow. Even though he was disruptive and acting out, I knew he was smart. Months passed and play therapy created a trust bond, then the moment happened. The class had outside playground time, so I asked the lead teacher if I could work alone with the little fellow. We sat next to the "feeling buddies" stuffed toys called angry, sad, scared & happy. The little fellow grabbed the scared toy and told me his big brother and sister scared him at night with talk of werewolves and clowns. At that moment, I knew he wasn't sleeping safely and soundly.

Talk therapy helped him release that trauma and within minutes he grabbed the happy "feeling buddy." Things changed for him going forward and I praised the Lord for showing me how to listen to the heart of one of His little children.

ART THERAPY DRAW: Draw circles and Emotional Buddy faces under each emotion. Put a check on the emotional face that you wish was healed in your heart.

ANGRY SCARED SAD HAPPY

Day 30 | KINGDUIT

"The Israelites traveled to Beer, which is the well where the Lord said to Moses, 'Assemble the people, and I will give them water.' There the Israelites sang this song, 'Spring up, O well! Yes, sing its praises!"

Numbers 21:16-17

No, the Lord wasn't serving Beer in "Beer!" It does sound like it though because the people were high. There is a saying that goes, "There ain't no high like the MOST HIGH!" That's what I believe was happening. The Lord was refreshing the people so much that they sang praises and still sing that song today!

The term Biblical Mental Healing came to me a few weeks after I attended a national prayer gathering. We were calling on heavenly assistance to save the soul of America. The man of God leading the service looked at me and told me that God was giving me a ladle to draw water from a deep well of wisdom.

"There is so much in the well, draw it!" he said. "Draw water for the nations, pull water out of the well for generational wisdom to overcome."

I sat there trying to take it in, while at the same time I had no idea what the man of God was talking about. It happened so fast and unexpectedly. I had a paper and pen close by and wrote the words down.

Thankfully, seeking Holy Spirit is my daily routine, so later I wrote on paper from my journal this question. "How can I pull water out of a well for the healing of nations?" I drew a picture of a big ladle with water splashing in and out of the scoop of the ladle and meditated on John 4.

ART THERAPY DRAW: Can you find water in the wilderness? Write your faith answer out?

"I will lead the blind by ways they have not known, along unfamiliar paths I will guide them; I will turn the darkness into light before them and make the rough places smooth. These are the things I will do; I will not forsake them."

Numbers 21:16-17

The best part of being a believer is having the Holy Spirit dwelling inside us at any moment, at any time. When we set our feet on the path of healing, the only one that can stop us is ourselves. We hold the keys to liberty because of our freewill and the Lord promises us that He will guide us along a path of light without forsaking us.

Making excuses for our troubles or blaming other people is never a reason for our inability to experience hope and joy in our souls. For that shift of understanding to happen, we must believe that the Lord can do absolutely anything. Not only can the Lord heal us, but He knows exactly what we need to keep moving forward to change to be the person we always dreamed of being.

The movie, "The Hurricane,"[7] is based on a true story and demonstrates how someone can live in extreme injustice and yet still find a way in their mind, will and emotions to be free on the inside. The movie, starring Denzel Washington, was based on a boxer named Rubin Carter. He was scapegoated, unjustly accused, and condemned to three life sentences in prison. He found inner peace and wrote his autobiography inside his jail cell, which became a story that liberated others. Rubin Carter's testimony was so impactful that Bob Dylan wrote a song about him.

My favorite quote from the movie is when Rubin says with a broken heart, "Hate put me in prison. Love's gonna bust me out."

CONSIDER THIS QUESTION & WRITE: Will you let God's love bust you out of your darkness and suffering? Write your answer here.

MONTH 2 - Jesus the Hebrew

Day 32 | KINGDUIT

"Normally it takes only eleven days to travel from Mount Sinai to Kadesh-barnea, going by way of Mount Seir. But forty years after the Israelites left Egypt, on the first day of the eleventh month, Moses addressed the people of Israel."

Deuteronomy 1:2-3

Wait, what? The journey was only eleven days? But Moses is talking to them forty years later? What happened?

It shouldn't be a surprise to us. How many people do we know, including ourselves, who refuse to change and remain set in their old ways or even die refusing to obey God's word?

That's what happened to the Hebrews, post deliverance (salvation). They settled in the desert, set up tents and expanded their families. When they were challenged as to why they didn't move out with God, they gave excuses like blaming Him and the people occupying the neighboring lands. Basically, they were afraid, but why?

Theologians say they answer questions of the bible, by searching the scripture. So, if you look at the people of God through the lens of a counselor trying to understand why the nation refused to go to the Promise Land., you will find the reason in Exodus Chapter 1. They were afraid.

Just like the Hebrews, God's followers today still deal with fear over issues they are not willing to address. The cultural power structures (government's & national rulers) continue to pursue the oppression of mankind via fear tactics, silencing them from speaking or even preventing them from seeking the truth.

Open the page in the Bible or screen shot Exodus Chapter 1. Get a highlighter and mark the reasons that could have made the Jews afraid. Number and list those reasons. How many did you find?

ART THERAPY DRAW: Illustrate the national problem the Jews had with Pharoah from Exodus Chapter 1.

KINGDUIT | Day 33

"God has not given us a spirit of fear, but of power and of love and of a sound mind."

2 Timothy 1:7

Since I wasn't raised Christian, I didn't know how to live the biblical life. Post salvation, I listened to as much church encouragement as possible to get my life on track, but there came a point where I needed more than bible studies and meetings. I was ready to apply the promises I read in the bible.

I went to church leadership for counsel and asked for help addressing some of the deeper issues that no one was talking about from the pulpit. Their response was, "No."

"No?" I repeated with shock. "God talks about this stuff in the Bible."

Leadership replied "We are not going to open up that can of worms in the church. Just seek God, He will help you."

Looking back, I know that even church leaders were afraid of healing for some reason and now I know why.

God was and is faithful. He provided the most amazing help for the precise issues I wanted to address. I was on my own, so I sought the Lord for understanding. I applied the wisdom I received from the Holy Spirit by faith and got results. The more healing I received, the more freedom became a normal part of my daily life.

From that point on, I promised God I would help others find freedom, especially those who struggled to find answers at church.

When people confess things to me that are difficult, embarrassing, or shameful, my heart swells with compassion. I tell them how much the Lord loves them and longs to help, no matter what the issue is. Then I promise them, whatever it is, if they are willing to seek God out, He will freely give an abundance of supernatural provision, along with power, to overcome anything via Holy Spirit.

The Spirit of wisdom and revelation is alive and well today (Ephesians 1:17).

Day 34 | KINGDUIT

"When we were at Mount Sinai, the Lord our God said to us, 'You have stayed at this mountain long enough. It is time to break camp and move on."

Deuteronomy 1:6-7

What are the mountains in your life, the issues that haven't budged since for as long as you remember? Ma, Pa, and everybody in your family just does and says the same thing. Maybe it is something you picked up as a child, it got lodged in your psyche when your precious mind was innocent and then it hardened into your thoughts as you grew and now, it's stuck like rock.

Sometimes these mountains form on our mental processing systems and memory, then we just accept them as a part of who we are or who we've become.

There was an Italian man who constantly talked with his hands. Somehow his words and hands were linked. His wife asked him to talk only with his mouth for one day. He couldn't do it!

I think God's people were so traumatized from the whole 400-year Egyptian captivity and prayed so long for Divine help that they got stuck out in the desert. It's almost like they shrugged their shoulders, built a tent, had babies, and got comfortable. Promise land, what?

Even though it was forty years later, the Lord never abandoned the Jewish population of millions, "as numerous as the stars in the sky" (Duet. 28:62). Under the leadership of Moses and the elders of Israel, He was waiting for that generation to pass. Then a new generation of warriors could follow the next leader in line, Joshua.

No matter where anyone is, the Lord still looks from heaven watching humanity. He knows exactly who is stuck and what needs to happen next. The Lord said, "Enough...break camp and move on" (Deuteronomy 1:7).

CONSIDER: The Lord saying to you: "ENOUGH . . . BREAK CAMP . . . MOVE ON!"

"You don't have enough faith," Jesus told them, 'I tell you the truth, if you had faith even as small as a mustard seed, you could say to this mountain, 'Move from here to there; and it would move. Nothing would be impossible."

Matthew 7:20

We left the Old Testament book of Hebrews at Mt. Sinai when they got the mountain speech to move on. Now we have Jesus in the New Testament saying to speak to the mountain in your life and tell it to move. All that's needed to accomplish this is small faith.

Wait, what? All we need is a little faith. Then why do some of the issues in our lives seem like huge mountains? Why Jesus, do you make things seem so simple yet all they feel like is impossible? Why Jesus, do you even go on to say, "Nothing would be impossible," when you know how stuck people get in their struggles and issues, especially with family generational habits?

Truth is, King Jesus (KINGDUIT) has the power and authority to deal with anything and everything in heaven and on earth, the entire universe. The King says, a small amount of faith will do it, and He never lies. Jesus is Lord over ALL! His part is the promise; our part is the willingness to act out in faith.

I can testify that the first step of real deep-down healing does feel terrifying, but it's not, it's mostly emotions and feelings. The Almighty's power to heal at once is terrifying to any dark spirit blocking freedom's progress.

CONSIDER & WRITE: Take time to write out your thoughts about the mountains in your life and why faith seems difficult.

Day 36 | KINGDUIT

"See, The Lord your God has given you the land. Go up and take possession of it as the Lord, the God of your ancestors, told you. Do not be afraid; do not be discouraged."

Deuteronomy 1:21

This phrase, "God/gods of your ancestors" or "God/gods of your fathers" is important to understand when it comes to mental health. I was blessed to study trauma and resilience under a seasoned traumatologist. This Jewish professor hosted our class to travel to Israel to practice clinical work in trauma therapy, at Hebrew University of Jerusalem.

I had been praying for years about an area in my life I couldn't understand, yet felt it somehow connected to the "gods of my ancestors." Research finds that trauma from one generation can be passed on to another generation via a chemical mark in our genetics. It's not a gene alteration, but a mark. I believe this is a psychological wound in the mind that hinders people from changing from generation to generation.

It is like a person who goes to the doctor for a check-up and the practitioner asks the patient if there is a history of heart disease in the patient's family, implying that the next generation might have a heart weakness because of a hereditary connection.

When the Lord mentions the phrase, "God of your ancestors," His desire is for the faith of our fathers to be carried on from generation to generation. One generation might pray and work hard to accomplish great things for the Lord and then pass away, but their prayers still live on, and the Lord doesn't forget what He had promised people, even when they die. That's why the bible says, "God's love endures forever, from generation to generation" (Lamentations 5:19).

On the other hand, our "adversary, the Devil" (1 Peter 5:8), doesn't want us to remember the prayers of our ancestors. He likes the focus to remain on failures, which can breed bitterness. When family members repeatedly note the negatives, it results in the offspring living in fear and struggling to believe anything can change for the good. I believe fear is the devil's top weapon of choice and he assigns a "spirit of fear" to keep on with the mental torment, showing up as discouragement.

KINGDUIT | Day 37

"The gods of other nations are mere idols, but the LORD made the heavens."

Psalm 96:5

"Great is the LORD! He is most worthy of praise! He is to be feared above all gods."

1 Chronicles 16:25

The Lord knew the Israelites were scared, that's why He was always saying, "Don't be afraid, don't be discouraged!" They had difficult territory to cross in the wilderness and challenges to overcome to receive the promise land victory. Fear paralyzed them and they just wanted to stay at the community base camp.

God's people depended on God's messengers for wisdom. Clearly, they experienced miracles every day (via a cloud pillar by day and fire pillar by night) that confirmed the Lord was with them, but still they were stuck in fear. They had to fully trust Moses for leadership because they did not have the promised Holy Spirit inside their hearts.

The history recorded in the Bible exposes how God's people followed and bowed down to the mere idols of fear. They had the opportunity and encouragement to fear the Lord above the gods of their time, but they didn't. Moses couldn't get them to change.

This lesson is so clear in my internal God-knower, telling me fear removal is a great place to start for those who desire to live in freedom.

One day I realized I had been afraid for years. It was long ago, but I remember a season of oppression. It was almost like the enemy knew I was going to break-free, so he sent a firestorm in my home. I can't judge the Hebrews for being stuck because I certainly was paralyzed with fear. I can thank God that the Bible uses even difficult stories to bring a reality check along with hope for change.

CONSIDER: What does fear mean to you?

Day 38 | KINGDUIT

"But our fathers refused to obey him. Instead, they rejected him and, in their hearts, turned back to Egypt. They said to Aaron, 'Make us gods who will go before us! As for this Moses who led us out of the land of Egypt, we do not know what has happened to him.' At that time, they made a calf and offered a sacrifice to the idol, rejoicing in the works of their hands. But God turned away from them and gave them over to worship the host of heaven."

Acts 7:39-42

Here is where the Bible uses itself to give insight to other passages in the Bible. The verse above is from the New Testament book of Acts when a man named Stephen gave an amazing summary about his ancestors, the Israelites. It was a speech about God's people in front of the Jewish religious leaders. Stephen obviously carefully studied his generational story in detail, trying to understand his ancestors. That took a lot of effort; going to the temple, reading the ancient scrolls so much that he spoke a fifty-two (52) verse speech from memory. Stephen was a true lover of the Lord! Sadly, he figured out the "fathers refused to obey."

There in the ancient desert, with the miraculous cloud covering by day and fire pillar by night to warm them, the people demanded a golden calf idol. They got tired of waiting for Moses to come from the mountain, so they did their own thing.

Notice in the text, the Jewish people asked for gods with a little "g." They wanted to go back to Egypt. Wait, what? They wanted to go back to slavery under Pharaoh (type of Satan)? Egyptian bondage? Back to the land of gods and idols? Mere idols made by human hands? Backwards to relentless brick making, back-breaking labor? The land of crazy plaques like blood water, frogs, locusts, and death? Yes, it's true, another biblical reality check regarding human nature.

We have the most awesome God, the Lord Jesus Christ! He is worthy to be feared; He is worthy of every effort to go the distance for freedom!

WRITE OUT: Write the word "gods" with a lowercase g. Write the word "Lord" with an uppercase L.

"We have not received the spirit of the world, but the Spirit who is from God, so that we may understand what God has freely given us."

1 Corinthians 2:12

"For God has not given us a spirit of fear and timidity, but of power, love and of a sound mind."

2 Timothy 2:7

When I prayed for healing, the Lord would often give me only one verse of scripture, or only one or two words. I was confused and didn't realize the way the Lord worked. I started to slow down, rest and meditate on that one verse, word, or concept.

With the word fear as a focus, I began to understand how a simple biblical understanding of one word kept me away from tremendous healing.

The above verses are typed out exactly from scripture. Notice the uppercase S in Spirit in the first verse, then the lowercase s for spirit in the second verse. Look again, you will also find uppercase G for God and lowercase g for gods in the Bible. Observing and understanding this is the beginning of "the ability to discern whether a message is from the Spirit of God or from another spirit" (1 Corinthians 12:10).

All the little gods in this world are spirit beings that are constantly drawing humanity into dark places. "God is light, and there is no darkness in Him at all" (1 John 1:5). We must discern or understand when the messages around us or in our heads are light or dark, good, or evil.

The verse above clearly states that fear is a spirit that is NOT from God. God gives us power, love, and a sound mind. The dark evil spirits (or idols) are many, and they delight in using the fear spirit to shut down God's people from moving towards freedom and blessing.

WRITE OUT: Write the word "spirits" with a lowercase s. Write the word "Spirit" with an uppercase S. Ask Holy Spirit for the ability to discern between the two.

INVENTORY EXERCISE

(This listing will help increase discernment. Make a chart like below on paper, then list out different gods/idols. They can be from the bible, from old times, or from modern times. Then write across the names of God and attributes of Holy Spirit that are opposite little gods/spirits).

	little gods/spirits	Holy Spirit
•	materialism	Provider
•	fear of man	Prince of Peace
•	alcoholism	Healer
•	mean-spirit	Loving
•	____________________	____________________
•	____________________	____________________
•	____________________	____________________
•	____________________	____________________
•	____________________	____________________
•	____________________	____________________
•	____________________	____________________
•	____________________	____________________
•	____________________	____________________
•	____________________	____________________

Grace to Leave the Barren Places

PRAYER: Lord, enlighten my heart and mind to understand Your ways. There are many stones to trip on in this modern world, but You promise to guide me along safe paths. Take me from the place I am to a place of greater knowledge of You and Your Holy word.

If I'm not seeing something that is important to my health, open my spiritual eyes. If You, Lord, are trying to talk to me and I don't listen, open my ears. If there is danger in my home or around my family, help me to make things better instead of complaining and arguing with those I love. I need Your promise of protection and deliverance, especially for the innocent ones in my life.

I know there are little gods/idols in my life/home. Give me courage to demolish and overcome each one with relentless effort.

Will you reveal to me the information You believe I am ready to handle today? I am ready to listen to Holy Spirit in my heart.

(Write down the wisdom you receive, even if it seems unexpected)

____

____

____

____

____

____

As an act of my will, I will keep seeking You until I find the solution, Your solution. If I am not willing, forgive me. Grant me a willing spirit that is willing to align my will to Your ways. Thank you for healing my heart! Thank you, Lord, for Your unconditional love!

Day 42 | KINGDUIT

"When Jesus saw him lying there and knew that he had already been there a long time, he said to him, "Do you want to be healed?"

John 5:6

After thirty-eight years, the man in John 5:6 still had a condition without healing. Take note of the pattern of time, close to forty (40) years of struggle, but this time it's Jesus in the New Testament.

When Jesus offered him wellness, he didn't say yes. He told Jesus his condition still existed because of other people, they didn't help him, or they got in the way. If you read/meditate on the text dialogue, you will see that Jesus did not respond to the man's excuses at all. He just said, "Get up, take up your bed, and walk" (John 5:8).

From my experience seeking the Lord, this is exactly how the Lord works with healing, fast! The moment your will and obedient actions align with the Bible or Holy Spirit's revealed wisdom, boom, things happen!

I was young but fed up with an issue that brought much shame and frustration into my life. I knew if I told someone, they would mentally label me and possibly gossip, so I kept quiet. Finally, I went to a wise counselor, but still, I hid my issue.

She said, based on my story, that it seemed like I had the exact issue I was hiding. She heard my excuses and then she saw MY problem. I truly had no idea what the name of my problem was, but God showed it to her. At that moment, she called me out! I was in such denial that I was shocked and trying to grasp the truth, but my heart and Spirit immediately knew she had hit the nail on the head.

As soon as I got home alone, I dropped to my knees, agreed with the actual words she said, confessed my involvement in that behavior and repented. In a moment, it was gone, and I never behaved in that manner again.

By the grace of God, instead of getting a diagnosis, I got a healing!

KINGDUIT | Day 43

"At once the man was healed, and he took up his bed and walked. Now that day was the Sabbath."

John 5:9

Here is scriptural proof that God works fast, "at once." The forty-year Israelite story or modern believing Christians who are not healed, these are examples of mankind issues that are often passed from generation to generation. "Jesus Christ is the same yesterday, today and forever" (Hebrews 13:8). The bible says the Jews could have made it out of the desert in eleven days instead of forty years.

Can you see a picture of God waiting on us to believe, or align our wills to His ways? It is not His fault if healing doesn't happen, especially in mental health.

Mental health trauma or long-standing family issues passed down are not physical inflictions, they are psychological wounds. Therefore, the physical body is not broken, the soul (intellect/will/emotions) has brain impulses/neurons that are blocked. The longer the wounds fester in the mind, it can eventually create a neuron spark pattern in the brain (which looks like a ditch in an MRI). Because the neurons are information messengers, they can easily heal, but it is dependent upon the human will to change in the mind. The work must be done to break free and heal each informational piece in the brain circuitry. The individual must make up their mind, seek to understand each situation and apply new thoughts. Christians apply God's truth.

A former addict told me he got a revelation that his mind could heal just like body parts heal. His counselor informed him it would take 12-24 months of time to heal the physical parts, based on the severity of his addiction. Once he got that information, he set the goal for restoration because he was willing to do the mental parts. It worked!

Jesus said, "I am the truth" (John 14:6). Jesus embodies truth. If you want to know the truth about yourself, ASK JESUS! Jesus will reveal the hidden issues in your life, but you MUST get up and act!

ART THERAPY DRAW: Ask the Lord for a quick healing. Draw the result.

Day 44 | KINGDUIT

"The LORD gives righteousness and justice for all who are oppressed. He revealed his character to Moses and his deeds to the people of Israel. The LORD is compassionate and merciful, slow to anger and abounding in steadfast love."

Psalm 103:6-8

Why does the Lord offer healing to ALL mankind? Because it's His very nature, His existence.

You may say, "But the story of how God used the Passover Lamb for the death angel deliverance, wilderness escape, and promise was for the Israelites, how can that be for me too?"

"As Scripture says, 'Anyone who believes in Him will never be put to shame.' For there is no difference between Jew and Gentile - the same Lord is Lord of all and richly blesses all who call on Him, for "Everyone who calls on the name of the Lord will be saved" (Romans 10:11-13).

The whole counsel of God from the Bible was given to all mankind! The very scripture itself proves this, in other words, when you doubt you can be a part of God's magnificent plan, the perfect answer for you is in the Bible. Everyone means you! Whoever calls on the name of the Lord will be saved and receive the manifold blessings of God.

God's promises do require a response to believe, receive and repent. They require a working out of salvation and deliverance. There is a labor to praying, seeking, listening to Holy Spirit's wisdom about our lives and the lives of the ones embedded in our hearts. That is a work that requires a desire to act upon. It is co-laboring with Divine perfect love. This remarkable partnership is worthy of every effort because as we heal, that healing flows to multiply righteousness.

ART THERAPY DRAW: Draw a globe. Draw the shape of your nation on the globe. Put a heart where you are.

"The blind men went right into the house where he was staying, and Jesus asked them, 'Do you believe I can make you see?'

'Yes Lord,' they told him, 'We do.'

Then he touched their eyes, saying 'Because of your faith, it will happen."

Matthew 9:28-29

"Heal the sick who are there and tell them, 'The kingdom of God has come near to you" (Luke 10:9). God so loved the world that he gave Jesus as a gift, sent from the kingdom of God to man. As a result, a fountain of healing was opened through His sacrifice on the cross. This fountain covers all health issues: body, mind, soul, spirit.

As for the mental health issues, the Lord gently heals the trauma, emotional challenges, and psychological abuse. Holy Spirit brings to our mind one issue at a time. As we respond in obedience, the process is called *sanctification* or being purified or freed from sin (1 Corinthians 1:2).

Jesus is tender and gentle in heart, so he doesn't give us more than we can handle. He knows our brain is like a maze, a field of neuron sparks of informational energy impulses moving through our central nervous system. A controlling person will shock your mentality. Not Jesus, He reveals softly, with love and compassion.

Spend time seeking Him, reading the Bible, writing memories, and listening to Holy Spirit regarding the concerns lodged in your mind. Soon you will understand and start to see with spiritual eyes.

RESPOND IN PRAYER: If the Lord told you He can make you "see" in a new way, how would you respond?

Day 46 | KINGDUIT

"O Lord, you have searched me and know me! You know when I sit down and when I rise, you discern my thoughts from afar. You search out my path and my lying down and are acquainted with all my ways. Even before a word is on my tongue, behold, O Lord, you know it altogether."

Psalm 139:1-4

Your brain is faster than a cell phone message, but the Lord is even faster and discerns your thoughts from a distance. This is because He is omniscient, all knowing.

The question might be, what does a mental health wound look like biologically and naturally? That is a great question!

The central nervous system contains the spinal cord, which is connected to the brain. The soul's storage system is in the brain, which controls thinking, feeling and memory. The spinal cord is the highway that connects the brain and the nerves that run through the whole body. This nervous system has a network called neurons made of electrical impulses and chemical signals that fire messages.

If one gets a cut in their little toe, the mouth says "ouch" right away. The message gets to the brain fast, faster than a text.

The Lord knows every bit of information in each person's life span. He knows each thought, and He understands the way people think. Often mental wounds manifest in bodily issues, which can be indicators as to how mental issues can move to inflict physical issues. The Lord often withholds revealing and healing those details until we ask and position ourselves to listen, believe and receive. Like many Bible stories, His Divine support is connected to forgiveness.

ART THERAPY DRAW: Draw a brain with a brain stem, then roots underneath and hanging down from the brain stem. Label the brain and the roots of the nervous system.

KINGDUIT | Day 47

Jesus said, "I tell you, on the day of judgment people will give an account for every careless word they speak, for by your words you will be justified, and by your words you will be condemned."

Matthew 12:36-37

A great lie the enemy tells people is that no one cares, no one remembers what happened or what was said.

The famous American saying "What Happens in Vegas, stays in Vegas"[2] is a huge lie. Whoever, back in 2003 at the Las Vegas Convention and Visitors Authority, came up with that statement might be in big trouble on the day of judgment. We will as well if we don't start seeking repentance for careless/ damaging words with the help of the Holy Spirit. Jesus said, 'I tell you' for a reason; life, death, cursing, gossip, slander, and criticism come from words. Even words in a text message can be just as damaging. For one lady sent a text message saying, "I hope your family burns." A few months later a home did burn and was lost.

If someone told a child, "You will never amount to anything," those word wounds stay inside the memory part of the child's brain. It's like a verbal power surge, that chars a part of the memory or subconscious and sticks. There's more to it, that pain is only a piece.

Something you said or something that was said, posted or written that matters to you, matters to God. His sacrifice will heal and cleanse us from ALL unrighteousness. If the blood of Jesus is applied by faith, followed by actions to cleanse then remove that wound or offense, that means it will NOT come up on the day of judgment.

The good news is that The Lord is Jehovah Rapha, the God who Heals. He is El Roi, the God who Sees and He is the Omniscient God, all knowing. There is absolutely nothing that He cannot handle and "He cares for you" (1 Peter 5:7)!

WRITE OUT: Write out the verse above from Matthew 12:36-37

Prayer for Judgment Day

PRAY: Like the people of God traveled through a great and terrifying wilderness, the thought of mankind facing Almighty God at the day of judgment is also terrifying. Lord, to think that every word I have spoken, written or texted will be accounted for is overwhelming (Matthew 12:36).

I am a person of unclean lips and unclean thoughts. I'm not holy, far from it. My heart is broken in places, my mind is undisciplined, and my motives are corrupt. I often think the worst of people when I should be forgiving and merciful. I have gossiped and found fault. I often judge when You are the Judge and Lawgiver (Isaiah 6:5).

Forgive me, I am guilty. Show me the right path to find victory in my life on the inside. I believe, help me where I refuse to change and where I don't believe change can happen. Help me to have hope where I have given up. Reveal the wounds hidden away in my subconscious (Proverbs 12:28).

I understand why the Beatles cried, "Help, I just need somebody, Help not just anybody, Help!" Thank you, Lord, that you found me and showed me You. I truly can cry out for help in my times of trouble, my times of need and this time of heart, soul, and personal word examination.

I repent by faith over careless words. I have spoken careless words, curse words, negative words, hurtful words, distrusting words, words that are not encouraging, words that are dishonest and even mean. I give You the cowardly words I've confessed, words that reveal that I fear man more than I fear Almighty God.

I don't know how a lifetime of faithless words can be cleaned up before the judgment, but You are God and there is no other. You promise to carry me through this journey, and You are the faithful One, you are the good One, you are the great One, You are the Holy One (Exodus 19:4)!

Lord, for all your promises to me, I give You willingness to partner with Holy Spirit, to repent and obey for the words you highlight in my mind. I will respond with confession and apology for what is revealed. I believe You will cleanse me from the unrighteous words spoken and wash them by the power of Your blood. You will make them white like snow, that you will remove them. (Isaiah 51:12)!

KINGDUIT | Day 49

"Every careless word"

Matthew 12:36

<u>Careless Word/Text Cleansing List</u>

(On a separate piece of paper: pray, write each word/phrase down, ask forgiveness, burn the list).

"Therefore, brothers and sisters, since we have confidence to enter the Most Holy Place by the blood of Jesus. . ."

Hebrews 10:19

What is the Most Holy Place? Why are we told in the New Testament of the Bible to confidently enter this place?

In the Jewish wilderness, it was a literal place, a space at the back of the tabernacle or tent. It was designed by The Lord to provide mercy and make amends for the people of God. A specific instruction about this one-of-a-kind tabernacle was given to Moses during the wilderness journey. The desert tent had an area named "Most Holy Place." A curtain separated the room from the main area of the space and inside was a special furnishing called a "mercy seat."

Moses's job leading millions of people on a desert escape created natural human conflict. The Jews needed a way to make things right. God provided an extraordinary square room at the end of the tent where the priests made amends with sacrificial animal blood on behalf of the people.

In the New Testament, Jesus Himself is available so mankind can find merciful relief to make amends with God. When Jesus was crucified, body torn and blood spilled, a supernatural door of access was opened. Hebrews 10:19 above is the invitation from Almighty God to confidently enter this sacred space by the "blood of Jesus." Jesus says, "go into your inner room, shut your door, and pray" (Matthew 6:6).

ART THERAPY DRAW: Draw a rectangle. Draw a line in red to make a square at the back of the rectangle (the Most Holy Place). Put a cross in the room. Confidently enter in by faith!

"O God, be not far from me; O my God, make haste to help me!"

Psalm 71:12

One day I was sharing my faith with an unsaved police officer to lead him to Jesus. He said to me, "I know God is real because whenever people are in crisis, they scream; 'Oh My God! Oh My God!' repeatedly."

Truly God is only a call away! When there is an accident and then comes the divine call, "Oh My God!" I heard it being shouted and repeated. It was the cry released from the heart of man. How is this possible and why does this happen so consistently? God did it, "He planted eternity in the human heart..." (Ecclesiastes 3:11).

God is so merciful, that even if we choose to reject Him, He does not reject us. He set Himself in our hearts, in every heart, like an anchor. "This hope is a strong and trustworthy anchor for our souls. It leads us through the curtain into God's inner sanctuary" (Hebrews 6:19). That location is in the heart of mankind (the eternal soul).

The Greek word for soul in Hebrews 6:19 is psyches; it means our spirit, our breath either abstractly or concretely (5590[10]). Therefore, our spirit is abstract, and our breath is concrete Even though our psychological center is in our being, it is not a physical part, it is a spiritual part that God alone can see.

By the grace of God, we were given a physical "picture" of this in the back room of the Old Testament desert tent tabernacle. Later, King David built the space into a glorious architectural masterpiece that was a stone temple. These physical temples that God designed, with an eternal meeting room in the back, kept getting destroyed by world conquerors. Later God switched it up and translated those temples into an eternal meeting place inside the soul of human beings. God said we are like living stones.

ART THERAPY DRAW: Draw the four biblical tents: a desert tent, a stone temple, Jesus body, human body.

Day 52 | KINGDUIT

"As you come to Him, the living Stone - rejected by humans but chosen by God and precious to Him -you also, like living stones, are being built into a spiritual house to be a holy priesthood, offering spiritual sacrifices acceptable to God through Jesus Christ."

1 Peter 2:4-5

Fill in the blanks below:

- Desert Tent - Write below the name of who got the instructions:

  ____

- Temple - Write below the name of who got the plans:

  ____

- Jesus - Write what the verse above says His name is:

  ____

- Body - Write your name: ______________________________
- Your Body - Write what the verse above says your name is:

  ____

ART THERAPY DRAW: Draw a simple picture of each biblical representation below:

<u>Tent</u> <u>Temple</u> <u>Jesus</u> <u>Body</u>

"... Jesus, by a new and living way opened for us through the curtain, that is his body, and since we have a great priest over the house of God, let us draw near to God with a sincere heart and with the full assurance that faith brings, having our hearts sprinkled to cleanse us from a guilty conscience and having our bodies washed with pure water. Let us hold unswervingly to the hope we profess, for he who promised is faithful."

Hebrews 10:19-23

The Bible is divided into two sections, the Old Testament, and the New Testament. Some would say it is a love story about God's heart for humans.

It seemed like the Lord struggled to reach the heart of people during a lot of the Old Testament. He used a few human leaders (prophets, priests, kings, and judges) to govern people. He needed a "new and living way opened" up so people could have direct access to God. Jesus was the New Testament answer, God in the flesh!

There is only one period in world history when the living Jehovah Rapha, Jesus, showed up to walk the face of the earth. It is recorded in the New Testament; Israel was the geographical place Jesus lived. The passion of the Christ is a reference used to explain how deeply Jesus felt about humanity. It references that his tears and blood landed in Israel's sand. His Divine mission was to save sinners and heal people for the blessings of eternity in the Kingdom of God.

The priests and kings did not want people to be healed. Why? They would lose their ability to control and dominate. So, God let them plot to kill Jesus the Healer.

ART THERAPY DRAW: Draw a picture of an open book. Label one side OLD TESTAMENT and the other side NEW TESTAMENT.

"In the beginning was the Word, and the Word was with God, and the Word was God. He was with God in the beginning. Through Him all things were made; without Him nothing was made that has been made. In Him was life, and that life was the light of all mankind."

John 1:1-4

Seek the Word!

ART THERAPY DRAW: Draw a picture of the Bible. Draw a picture of Jesus on the cover of the Bible. Make the Bible look special.

KINGDUIT | Day 55

"For the cloud of the Lord hovered over the tabernacle by day, and fire was in the cloud by night, in the sight of all the Israelites during all their travels."

Exodus 40:38

Above is the last verse in the book of Exodus. It is a most beautiful picture of Almighty God looking after his beloved people in a dramatic way the whole time they were walking out of slavery and towards the Promise Land. The cloud and fire the Lord provided were clear markers for the people to find the path to freedom. "The Lord went ahead of them in a pillar of cloud to guide them on the way" (Exodus 13:21).

He even provided angelic assistance, "and the angel of God, who had been leading the people of Israel, moved to the rear of the camp. The pillar of cloud also moved from in front and stood behind them coming between the armies of Egypt and Israel. Throughout the night the cloud brought darkness to the one side and light to the other side; so, neither went near the other all night long" (Exodus 14:19-20).

This is not only a provision of guidance, but also of protection and companionship. No matter where you are on your healing journey, be assured that The Lord is with you and His angels are protecting you. Just look up!

One day a prayer partner and I were outside encouraging one another. She was praising God for His goodness. She looked at me, then looked up into the sky and said, "Whenever you are struggling in your faith, look up at the sky and the clouds, and you will feel better."

That day her words filled my heart with peace. She was speaking the truth! In Revelation 14:14 John "saw a white cloud, and seated on the cloud was someone like the Son of Man."

ART THERAPY DRAW: Draw the Son of Man seated on the cloud.

Day 56 | KINGDUIT

Divine Presence and Protection

PRAYER: Thank you, LORD, for Your goodness and unfailing love. Thank You for always being there for me and my family. Pursue my loved ones ___________________________________ (name each one) and show them how much you care about them while You watch over them.

Just as You LORD guided the nation of Israel, I claim your promise to Shepherd my journey. It is amazing that I can live in Your house forever, thank You for the promise of eternal life. I praise You now, as an act of my will, and I choose to praise You along the way, no matter what happens. Thank You, Lord, for never leaving me and my loved ones as I call out their names ____, for never forsaking us. Help us to be faithful to You Lord (Psalm 117:2)!

Just like the blood of the Passover Lamb protected the Israelites escaping the darkness of Egyptian slavery, I apply by faith that same wonder-working power in the blood of Jesus today over my life, over my family's lives. I claim it for healing and deliverance from all darkness. I claim it for the healing of our souls, deliverance from accidents, injury, sickness, witchcraft, perversion, financial oppression and any attack on our homes, marriages, and children (1 John 1:7).

We hide in the secret place of the Most High and rest in the shadow of the Almighty. Help us to be faithful to You so that we can receive Your promise of shelter, to deliver us from any plague and give angelic guardianship in all our ways. Just as You gave the Jewish people divine protection in traveling out of Egypt and through the wilderness of healing, I receive divine protection in this modern world's highways and airways.

Thank You, Lord, for Your great love, Your great salvation, and for having ears to hear my prayers. Help me to walk in a manner worthy of this great love, honor, and amazing protection. (From Psalm 91).

"For He will command His angels concerning you to guard you in all your ways."

Psalm 91:11

KINGDUIT | Day 57

"This is the way; walk in it."

Isaiah 30:21

Whenever embarking on a mission, it is important to look for signs that you are headed in the right direction. If one were to climb Mount Everest, it would be smart to check the weather for heavy snow and wind. Likewise, when embarking on a journey with the Lord, He knows we need encouragement along the way, and it can be fun to look for signs of His grace.

I was looking for a mental health counseling internship, so I reached out to a Christian practice. I found a godly man, former military, who gave me clinical advice about the counseling profession. He told me most of his counseling sessions with Christians involved listening to the clients' issues and pointing them to the Word of God. He then covered them in prayer. It was such a confirmation of my own mental health journey.

Another sign of hope regarding the Israeli perspective for mental health was a random gift that was sent my way during the writing process of this devotional. It was a large illustrative book titled "Promise Land" with the forward penned by a Jerusalemite! Wow, I told only three friends to pray over this devotional and three family members. God is so good. He knows exactly what we need to continue seeking healing, hope and His will in these times!

- Write encouragements that found you during these two months of Biblical Mental Healing.
- How has understanding mental health from a biblical point of view revealed God's will for your life?

Wisdom for Mental Healing

PRAYER: Thank you, Lord, for showing me that You are the God who heals. I give you this time of rest, help me to stay here with you and meditate in your great love. Help me to have the grace to keep praying for my healing. Thank you for helping me understand that you care for me in every detail of my life, and that you are willing to redeem my life. I receive the grace to race, race away from the barren places and on to new paths of righteousness (Exodus 15:26).

There are many long-standing memories that seem impossible to remove yet help me to believe you can truly renew my mind, body, soul, and spirit. Just as you forgive me for careless words, Lord, show me how to find you in the mistakes of the past.

Where were you when this happened: ______________________________
____
____?

(Begin to expose hurtful memories that you remember to the Lord)

Lord, I've always wished some things would have turned out better. I don't know how to heal the broken places. If I knew you back then, perhaps I would have made a better choice. Lord, I didn't know you then. Heal my broken places. Show me how to stop circling around the deserts in my life, in my mind. Show me the way to resolve the past so that I can heal, be at peace and live in the present.

I desire to live more in Your presence every day. Show me how to live in the fruit of your Spirit, to live in love, joy, peace, patience, goodness, kindness, faithfulness, gentleness, and self-control. Show me how to have courage even when others don't (Galatians 5:22).

Thank you for being gentle and kind with me on this wonderful adventure. I love you Lord.

Girl Hears God Movie: Look up *YouTube* Trailer - *Joan of Arc* (1999) Leelee Sobieski as Joan[11] A historical testimony of faith. Watch and witness a nation saved by a girl who listened to God.

"Whether you turn to the right or to the left, your ears will hear a voice behind you saying,

'This is the way; walk in it."

Isaiah 30:21

The prophecy above was directed to the "People of Zion who lived in Jerusalem" (Isaiah 30:19). It was another promise for divine help. They had previously cried for 400 years in Egyptian slavery, but the promise above states "as soon as He hears, He will answer you" (Isaiah 30:19).

That scripture aligns with the New Testament promise from Jesus which states; "My sheep listen to my voice; I know them, and they follow me" (John 10:27). Experiencing a dynamic relationship with the living God is a real thing. He sees, He hears and communicates with His children. The question is: are we looking, listening, and acknowledging Jesus via Holy Spirit? If not, why not?

The absence of addressing Almighty God in our lives is one of the pitfalls of the modern psychology movement. Psychology might diagnose the one seeking and hearing God's voice as religious cognitions, even though studies acknowledge the lack of clinical research validating the effectiveness of faith. Instead, hearing voices can be interpreted by a counselor as auditory hallucinations which can point to signs of different psychotic disorders.[12]

Remember the national heroine Joan of Arc[13], she was the young girl who saved France from English conquest in the 1400's? She loved God so much that she trusted in the Lord for divine help. She carried a victory banner with a message of wisdom to lead a campaign to save a nation. Joan was willing to do her part and even risk her life. Surely, the "Lord's eyes found her heart fully committed to him" (2 Chronicles 16:9), so He strengthened her to do the impossible and France was saved! Some say the USA wouldn't exist without Joan's epic conquest.

Religious leaders called her a witch for claiming she heard God's voice. Today, the psychiatrists might have wrongly diagnosed her with a psychotic disorder. Joan heard the Lord and got the battle plan despite heavy religious persecution, leading to death by fire. Joan found incredible courage and obeyed the Lord's voice. Vindication came from the Pope years later when a statue beautified her at Notre Dame cathedral.

MONTH 3 - Joshua the Victor

Day 60 | KINGDUIT

"God chose things the world considers foolish in order to shame those who think they are wise. And he chose things that are powerless to shame those who are powerful."

1 Corinthians 1:27

History proves the above verse time and time again. Truly world history is HIS-story. God chose Joan of Arc (a powerless young girl) to save France to shame England and even France. The English thought they had the power to dominate French territory, oh no! The religious leaders thought they could extinguish faith by fire, oh no! Joan's story will never die, and we will see her in heaven!

Pharaoh thought the Jews were powerless slaves, oh no! "For the foolishness of God is wiser than human wisdom, and the weakness of God is stronger than human strength" (1 Corinthians 1:25).

God's wisdom stood against the ancient Pharaoh in Egypt all the way through world conquerors, even great philosophers of the ages. The message of the Bible is crystal clear, clearer than the miracles of Jewish history and the wisdom of Greek scholars. Even today, following great minds will not compare to seeking Holy Spirit for wisdom to overcome.

The evil army spiritual forces that deceive the world cannot stand against the righteousness, holiness and redemption promised to those who are in Christ Jesus!

Even if you feel weak, small, or unimportant, take heart! Seeking Holy Spirit inside of you by a faith that stands on the finished work of the cross of Jesus Christ of Nazareth will give you everything needed to find total liberty and healing!

TALK TO THE LORD: Thank Him for the cross.

"No eye has seen, no ear has heard, no heart has imagined, what God has prepared for those who love Him. But God has revealed it to us by the Spirit."

1 Corinthians 2:9-10

Imagine living in the times of Jesus. Imagine sitting near a pool where Jesus visited the sick who waited for a healing miracle and hearing Him say, "Do you want to be healed?" Imagine witnessing a negative response to that offer.

You might have wanted to yell out, "Say YES!" But instead, you hear only a bitter excuse of blaming others for the issue. And then you can't believe they had Jesus the one and only right there, in the flesh.

I feel certain those words would have stuck with the hearers around that pool their whole life, yet with an added dimension of the utter beauty of the moment. Imagine being where Jesus came to heal. To listen to the richness of the sound of HIS voice, the smell (good or bad), the feeling of water while present with Jesus (the spring of living water), the surrounding atmosphere, and the amazing gaze of HIS love. That phrase, coming from the son of God, is so deep! How could one deny such a glorious invitation to the super-abundant life?

Greater still, how has humanity overlooked such great healing derived from perfect love? Has it been the resistance of Satan, the greed/deception of the medical/mental health community, the duplicity of the religious spirit, the "deceitfulness of wealth" (Mark 4:19)?

There is more! The promise above is the gift of something so outstanding that our senses can't even imagine it. What is it? What has the Almighty prepared for those who truly love God? The only way to find out, according to the Bible, is via revelation "by the Spirit!"

ASK THE LORD: Ask Holy Spirit for a revelation of His vision for your life.

Day 62 | KINGDUIT

"The Spirit searches all things, even the deep things of God. For whom among men knows the thoughts of man except his own spirit within him? So too, no one knows the thoughts of God except the Spirit of God. We have not received the spirit of the world, but the Spirit who is from God, that we may understand what God has freely given us."

1 Corinthians 2:10-12

The best counselor in the universe doesn't know the possibilities inside each client. We hope the good counselors sincerely try to lead people to the truth. But honestly, even good counselors don't know if the client even wants to get better, especially in the world of rehabilitation and addiction. Those clients are often forced into counseling due to the consequences of their actions.

The bible says no one knows "the thoughts of man except his own spirit within him." One day at work I met a sister in Christ, and we talked about loving God. She told me she was in a season of seeking the Lord, telling Him how much she loved Him, or so she thought. Immediately Holy Spirit spoke these words to her spirit: "No, you don't love me!" She was deeply convicted in her "own spirit" and knew it was true based on her lifestyle. "God revealed it to her by the Spirit" (1 Corinthians 2:10). The revelation she received from the Spirit, expressing spiritual truths, in spiritual words wrenched her heart and she responded in true faith by mourning over her inward condition. She spent weeks sitting before the Lord, crying out in honest communication to Jesus. It was her step toward biblical healing!

I met her a year later. Since she had a foundation of Holy Spirit wisdom and honesty, I asked her if she ever formally asked the Lord to bless her with soul-level healing? "No," she replied.

I responded with the biblical question right from the words of Jesus, "Do you want to be healed?" I wasn't hoping for a response, I asked so she could experience Jesus the Healer. . . and she was silent.

The effect is like a holy knock on the door of the human heart. It's "the deep things of God." Jesus waits for you to desire healing. It seems simple, but it is profound and at first hear, it elicits silence.

"And this is what we speak, not in words taught us by human wisdom, but in words taught by the Spirit, expressing spiritual truths in spiritual words."

1 Corinthians 2:13

Like the lady from yesterday, one can say they love God, but they don't. The words that came to her "by the Spirit, expressing spiritual truths" were undeniable in her mind, so she opened the door of her heart (or she was willing to listen to Holy Spirit's voice) and decided to allow herself to be "taught by the Spirit."

Jesus knows if someone doesn't want to be healed, they won't be healed, even if they say they do. God himself waits. "Here I am! I stand at the door and knock. If anyone hears my voice and opens the door. I will come in and eat with that person, and they with me" (Revelation 3:20). Therefore, a willing heart is a dynamic movement toward supernatural healing via "Wonderful Counselor" (Isaiah 9:6). That decision should lead to a willing arm that opens their personal internal door of access, thus allowing Jesus to walk right on in by faith.

And guess what, Jesus does more than walk in! He reveals the deep things a person needs to be satiated (like a good meal) with hope. Someone can have a new realization of self along with receiving rich wisdom the Lord will reveal to each seeking individual. This type of understanding is found in Divine communion.

ART THERAPY DRAW: Draw the Son of Man knocking on your door.

ASK THE LORD: Say out loud to Jesus: "Do I truly love you?"

Day 64 | KINGDUIT

"The natural man does not accept the things that come from the Spirit of God. For they are foolishness to him, and he cannot understand them, because they are spiritually discerned. The spiritual man judges all things, but he himself is not subject to anyone's judgment. For who has known the mind of the Lord, so as to instruct Him? But we have the mind of Christ."

1 Corinthians 2:14-16

Diagnosis[14] is a foundation in all fields of health, as well as the practice of USA/ International counseling. Diagnosis is "the art or act of identifying a disease from its signs and symptoms via investigation of the cause or nature of a condition, situation or problem. It involves making a decision by diagnosis in the form of a statement or conclusion." In counseling, classifying mental disorders started in 1893 with the International Classification of Diseases (ICD)[15]. The Diagnostic and Statistical Manual of Mental Disorders (DSM)[16] was first published in 1952 in America adding behavior disorders to mental disorders to diagnose individuals.

Diagnosis comes from the Greek word "gnosis," to know. Interestingly, the original text of the New Testament is in Greek. The word gnosis is coded 1108[17] in Strong's Greek Concordance[18], an index used to develop multiple language translations of the bible, first published in 1890. Consider the historical timing when medical diagnosis started. First, in 1890, the bible translation from Greek to English was published. One could access the Bible in English finding the Greek translation to "know/ gnosis" God. A few years later in 1893 the International Classification of Diseases published a diagnostic manual, turning attention away from Healer God and towards diagnosing practitioners. Knowledge is foundational to the whole basis of a Christian's life. The prefix "dia" means through, throughout or completely. God's manual, the Bible, is about diagnosis or complete knowledge of Him. He wants us to know ourselves in His light. Above is a verse to help understand how the Lord feels about gnosis/knowledge. "For God, who said, 'Let there be light in the darkness,' has made this light shine in our hearts so we could know (1108 gnosis) the glory of God that is seen in the face of Jesus Christ" (2 Corinthians 4:6). The Bible is quoting Genesis 1:3 from the beginning of human existence. You can't get more original than Creator in the beginning of time. The Trinity (Father, Son, Holy Spirit) always had us in mind and intended that there would be light shining in our hearts just like the glorious light of His physical world. Without a doubt, God doesn't want us to be in the dark about our mental health! In fact, Jesus was angry at the leaders of his day because they hinder people from accessing the gnosis of God. Jesus said, "Woe to you experts in the law, because you have taken away the key to knowledge (1108). You yourselves have not entered, and you have hindered those who were entering" (Luke 11:52). A spiritual man seeks gnosis over a natural man's diagnosis. Think about DIAGNOSIS vs. GNOSIS.

GNOSIS PRAYER

PRAY: Dear Lord, it is amazing that the light You turned on during the first day of creation is the same light You made to shine in my heart, so I can know You. This is so deep, and yet You are helping me understand your vast love (Ephesians 1:18).

I pray that the eyes of my heart may be enlightened in order that I may know the hope to which God has called me. Thank you for wanting the light of life to shine on me (Revelation 3:20). Make me a spiritual man/woman that truly knows You. Help me to break out of the natural man's earthly perspective.

Thank you, King Jesus, that You care so much about me that You will even visit me and knock on the door of my heart! I am in awe that You long to have a meal with me to help me understand how to live life with divine illumination.

Lord, give me ears to hear. I am listening for Your voice in the form of a knock. I am ready to open the door of my heart to You now. Show me how to dine with You, even though I don't quite understand this concept. Show me how to sit with You, how to listen to You, how to talk to You and how to gnosis (know) You!

Lord, this process of healing is so different. You convict me of my sin and offer cleansing forgiveness right away. The world tells me everything that is wrong with me, so I identify with my personal wrongs for a lifetime. Lord have mercy!

You want me to know the glory of God, seen in the face of Christ in such a way that I will have light shining in and from my heart. You want me to have the mind of Christ. You give me shalom, peace (2 Corinthians 4:6) (1 Corinthians 2:16).

Open my eyes to see, know and understand. Grant me a spirit of repentance. Thank you for Your unconditional love, acceptance, correction, discipline, and help. Forgive me for all my wrongs! I believe and receive your healing in my life! Thank you (Psalm 119:18)!

Day 66 | KINGDUIT

"This Festival of Purim would never cease to be celebrated among the Jews, nor would the memory of what happened ever die out among their descendants."

Esther 9:28

In late winter/early spring, Israel has a special celebration called Purim. This is an ancient holiday that is still celebrated to this day, to remember the Divine deliverance of the Jews during the time of Queen Esther of Persia. A wicked leader named Haman plotted to annihilate the entire nation of Israelites, but God positioned Esther and her cousin Mordecai to act and turn the tables on Haman's evil plans. The whole story is documented in the Book of Esther to testify of the Lord's protection over His people.

The Jews still celebrate this biblical holiday every year with special food, gifts to the poor, and dressing up. They remember and retell the stories about how The Lord continues to protect their nation, even in the face of utter destruction. This is one way the Jews remain strong.

This holiday exemplifies the resiliency of the nation Israel. Jewish people remember that national protection is never to be taken for granted. "Blessed is the nation whose God is the Lord" (Psalm 33:12).

Have you ever felt like there was some type of evil plot against your life, family, or nation? I have! During the time of the year when Purim was celebrated, I went to a vegetable market frequented by Jews. I would hear them delightfully preparing for The Festival of Purim. The joy got my attention and made me curious about the special story of deliverance and fueled my quest for victory.

If your nation is under attack in any way, pray Psalm 33 over your people, that the Lord would be your help and shield!

ASK THE LORD: Pray out loud Psalm 33 as your declaration of divine mental deliverance.

"But Mordecai found out about the plot and told Queen Esther, who in turn reported it to the king, giving credit to Mordecai."

Esther 2:22

On your journey for biblical mental healing, consider that our big God likes to use ordinary people. No matter what you are standing against in your life, a divine turn-around is possible. Will you be the change agent in your nation? Start to look for something special to remember your quest this year to inspire you to go the distance.

Every nation has special days of remembrance that are often traced back to small groups of people. Think about your nation. What have your people done to survive and sustain peace and prosperity?

In America, as I write from a hotel overlooking the Hudson River and the Freedom Tower in New York City, only two miles away is Liberty State Park. This is the home of Ellis Island and caretaker of the Statue of Liberty. Lady Liberty holds out the light of enlightenment with her message of welcome and freedom. "She cries with silent lips. 'Give me your tired, your poor, your huddled masses yearning to breathe free" (The New Colossus)[12].

The sunlight is still faithfully shining on those American monuments, proclaiming liberty for all! Why, because the founding fathers came to the USA seeking religious freedom for their families. They turned in their hearts from a kingdom of men wanting control to the Kingdom of God that proclaims liberty. They even printed currency with the words, "In God we Trust!" Though challenged, the American message endures by the mercy of God.

ART THERAPY DRAW: Can you attach a symbol or memento to remember this journey of epic mental healing? Draw it below.

"The Lord has driven out great and powerful nations before you, and to this day no one can stand against you. One of you can put a thousand to flight, because the Lord your God fights for you, just as He promised."

Joshua 23:9-10

Joshua was like a superhero with an invincible blessing. He is first introduced in the bible in Exodus 17. The Amalekites attacked Israel early along their desert journey. "Joshua did as Moses had instructed him and fought. So, Joshua overwhelmed Amalek and his army with the sword" (Exodus 17:10, 13).

Note case study (in-depth look at an individual's background) summary:

- He paid attention to Moses's mistakes and took mental notes
- He was an excellent assistant and carefully listened.
- He followed instructions, which prepared him to lead later in life
- He willed courage by overcoming traumatic life events
- He trusted Moses to watch/pray over him and his men during dangerous assignments
- His obedience inspired the Lord to give/proclaim a scroll as a reminder (Exodus 17:14)
- He received the victory blessing from the Lord - Jehovah Nissi - The Lord is my Banner

---

DELARE OUT LOUD: The LORD is my banner! Read Exodus 17:8-16

ART THERAPY DRAW: So far, we have read about Joan of Arc's and Joshua's banner of victory. Draw a banner of victory for yourself.

PRAY: The Bible says in 1 Timothy 3:16 that "all scripture is God-breathed and useful for teaching, rebuking, correcting and training in righteousness." I thank you that the life/story of Joshua is useful to me! I pray his life will impact me in a way that I will be marked with abounding hope. Awaken a new level of healing in my mind, body, soul, and spirit for the rest of my life. Thank you for the grace of God inside the biblical narrative!

On our wilderness journey towards Biblical Mental Healing, we virtually walk out of the desert towards the well. Therefore, a review or case study of the life of Joshua will give examples of extraordinary mental fortitude in the face of extreme difficulty and challenge. Where Moses failed to get to the Promise Land, Joshua prevailed.

Yesterday's leading verse was Joshua's case summary of his view of the LORD. He took no credit for leading millions of Israelites to the Promise Land. Furthermore, Joshua spoke of the power of each individual Israeli citizen to accomplish great conquests. But the truth is, like Moses, Joshua was the leader and got every instruction from The Lord. He then obeyed to accomplish a monumental task: leading the most resilient nation of all time. He did the work, relentlessly served, became strong, and showed courage during his entire lifetime. He made mistakes along the way but was quick to acknowledge his faults and make things right with God and man.

My heart remained in a state of awe as I meditated on the life of Joshua. No doubt, he carried the banner of Jehovah Nissi (physical and spiritual victory) from day one until his death. He did this despite his childhood slavery trauma in Egypt, forty years of wandering/waiting in the desert, and then conquering barbarians to get into the Promise Land. This vast plot of land is still the most sacred and sought-after land in the world. Joshua did it! Joshua found mental fortitude and healing, Joshua spent decades in the shadows of greatness, and he refused fear!

Counselors often write an in-depth analysis of groups or individuals to understand behavior. The Lord provided a whole book in the bible called Joshua so we can observe victory!

READ AND GAIN UNDERSTANDING: Book of Joshua

Day 70 | KINGDUIT

Ancient Desert Counseling (Session 1)

Let's pretend Joshua sought biblical mental health counseling before making it to the Promise Land. He might have said something like: "I've been helping Moses since I was forty. I promised him I would be faithful to God and support him along the desert journey. I remember when the journey was supposed to be only eleven (11) days. I figured, no problem, I will help Moses and then I can find my place in the Promise Land and start my own family. But that was forty (40) years ago and I'm tired of this circling! I know that Moses is a great leader, I mean, you should see the miracles and the glory of God that surrounds him every single day! But the people don't respect him, and they are so rebellious, it's no wonder I'm still here. I get angry sometimes, but I'm not letting go of God's promises. I just know God is faithful and able to do it!"

The counselor says, "Joshua, thank you for sharing today. You said it was a problem with the people, right? Are you willing to obey?"

Joshua replied, "Yes!"

The counselor asks; "Aren't the Israelites divided up into families?"

He answered, "Yes, they are in family tribes. Between all their issues with their family members and all the trauma that is still in the camp from the slavery days, they are so fearful. In addition, when Moses sent us to spy out the Promise Land, most of our guys were terrified and reported bad news media about the giants in the land. Consequently, the people are stuck. I don't think they will ever get out of this wilderness. But I am not afraid, I've seen the Lord do amazing things and I believe we can do anything with the Lord Almighty on our side. It's the people!"

The counselor replies to Joshua, "What I'm hearing you say is that there are two types of challenges that Moses can't fix even despite his great leadership team and his connection to God. The one issue is family centered, and the other issue is a fear of the giants in the Promise Land."

"That's exactly it!" says Joshua. The counselor replied, "Perfect, I'm listening correctly! In our next session I'm going to give you an assignment and we will discuss the tools you'll need to solve this problem!"

KINGDUIT | Day 71

Ancient Desert Counseling (Session 2)

Joshua showed up for session two ready to listen to the counselor's assignment. He says, 'Thank you for helping me see my two challenges. I've been thinking and praying about family issues and fear blockers all week. I've decided that I am ready to do whatever it takes to make a change on my own, even if Moses is not with me. God has shown me that this assignment is going to be my breakthrough tool.'

The Counselor replies, "Awesome Joshua, it will be an honor for me to watch you carry the baton of God's glory into the Promise Land! God had a good reason for letting you shadow Moses all these years, but I believe you are ready."

"I want you to make two lists on two different pieces of paper. Be as brutally honest as you can because no one, not even me, will see these lists. On the first paper, give the title on the top 'Family Issues.' On the second paper, title it 'Community Fears.' Try to summarize each item into one or two words per listed issue or fear. Here is a sample below."

"If you have a brain freeze, ask Holy Spirit to remind you of items to fill in. Take as much time as needed because you don't want to miss one thing! Begin to pray over each issue. Jehovah Rapha will give you wisdom and revelation about how to solve these long-standing issues with your willing spirit."

Family Issues	Community Fears
• Rebellious	Giant Killers
• Corrupt	Crossing Failure
• Stiff-necked	Government Terror
• Unbelieving	False gods
• Terrified	Trauma Triggers
• ____________	____________
• ____________	____________
• ____________	____________
• ____________	____________
• ____________	____________

Day 72 | KINGDUIT

"I cry aloud to the Lord; I lift my voice to the Lord for mercy. I pour out my complaint before Him; I reveal my trouble to Him. . . I look to my right and see; no one attends to me. There is no refuge for me; no one cares for my soul. I cry to You, O Lord: 'You are my refuge."

Psalm 142:1-2, 4-5

Biblical Healing Assignment

In your notebook, take time to fill in your issues. Check the small circle after you have prayed over each item. Right down any insight you have because of your prayers.

Family Issues	Community Fears
• ________________	________________
• ________________	________________
• ________________	________________
• ________________	________________
• ________________	________________
• ________________	________________
• ________________	________________
• ________________	________________
• ________________	________________

"But if you refuse to serve the LORD, then choose today whom you will serve. Would you prefer the gods your ancestors beyond the Euphrates? Or will it be the gods of the Amorites in whose land you now live? But as for me and my family, we will serve the LORD."

Joshua 24:15

This is Joshua's famous victory speech and summary of his life. Joshua is one of the few men who personally experienced the entire Israelite story from slavery all the way to the Promise Land. He was Moses's faithful and relentless assistant on the long journey. Sadly, Moses made a mistake and didn't get to the Promise Land, but Joshua did.

Joshua totally understood the little god versus big GOD concept. He saw the Hebrew people live as slaves under Pharaoh, he witnessed the incredible leadership of Moses, saw the miracles, and heard all the fearful complaining that kept the people stuck. I believe he realized that the issues of family and community were spiritual in nature because he labeled them "gods" of ancestors and "gods" of certain lands.

Somewhere on the journey, Joshua determined that nothing, not giants or battles, not fears or suffering, would keep him from generational blessing. He remembered the Bible stories and prayers of his ancestors: Abraham, Isaac, and Jacob. Joshua also understood that his adversaries worshiped false gods in the land and taunted the people with past failure so they would be afraid and never believe anything good could happen.

I believe Joshua had forty years to ruminate on the problems in the camp and he discerned that a spirit of fear was the devil's top weapon of choice. The enemy used the fear emotion to keep the community away from God's promises.

- Are there faithful prayer warriors in your past generations that asked God to do something special with future offspring?
- Are there gods in your ancestry line that you can name?

Day 74 | KINGDUIT

"All scripture is God-breathed and is useful for teaching, rebuking, correcting and training in righteousness."

2 Timothy 3:16

How can you enjoy healing from the life of a biblical testimony? The answer is, by utilizing God's power scriptures. First read, then let the truth shock and correct, then align and train the mind to change. The change brings right living. Joshua's testimony is marked by obedience and victory. He obtained freedom for the nation of Israel because he told his mind to align with The Lord.

We must understand the difference between Old Testament freedom versus New Testament freedom for the end-time Christian. Freedom in the Old Testament meant owning land, family, and agriculture (business), living in peace from natural enemies, and experiencing fellowship at the Tabernacle. Joshua had to overcome natural enemies that occupied the land of promise. This included thirty-one kings covering a massive plot of land in Israel. This location marked the site of the Tabernacle which is now called the Temple Mount in Jerusalem. It is the most sacred and holy location to God. The Bible calls the temple site the "apple of his eye" (Zechariah 2:8).

As we continue to live in the New Testament now, we don't conquer land, we purchase it. The Lord doesn't ask us to battle flesh and blood, in other words, we don't fight natural enemies. Our battles are against spiritual enemies and our flesh. Our promise of freedom is within our "whole spirit, soul and body" (1 Thessalonians 5:23). This is also a sacred and holy location to God because He deposited Holy Spirit in the heart of born-again believers.

Joshua destroyed territorial enemies, one by one. Like Joshua sought the Lord for every battle strategy and directive for every plot of land, we must seek the Lord for every issue in our personal case study. We master our mind and flesh by addressing concerns one by one. We ask the Lord to forgive and heal. In other words, we conquer ourselves. As the Lord leads, we will conquer them one by one. What makes the Lord a "wonderful counselor" (Isaiah 9:6) is that He is all-knowing and has the perfect case plan to provide complete healing which leads us to further usefulness and victory at a personal, generational, community level and beyond.

"The people replied, 'We would never abandon the Lord and serve other gods. For the LORD our God is the one who rescued us and our ancestors from slavery in the land of Egypt. He performed mighty miracles before our very eyes. As we traveled through the wilderness among our enemies, he preserved us."

Joshua 24:16-17

This is how the people answered Joshua when he asked them to choose which god/God to serve. They clearly witnessed the difference between the slavery of idol worship and the glory of the Lord!

You see, the gods of the ancient world were visible statues or people that they literally bowed down to as an act of worship or bondage as slaves.

Unless you go to a foreign temple and bow to statues or images, it looks different today. Most modern people in the west bow down to things in their heart or in their bodies via physical acts.

For example, if you gave into a spirit of fear, it would happen in your mind where others couldn't see. You could demonstrate it by crying with signs of insecurity like a child, but most adults don't do that unless they are in an emergency. Perhaps if one bowed down to a spirit of alcoholism, someone might witness one relentlessly drinking, smelling like a brewery, or hearing one say, "I need cocktails!"

One day I saw a man drinking and he kept staring at a bar cart full of alcohol. I thought to myself, he has a drink in hand, why is he looking at more drinks. At that moment Holy Spirit spoke one word to me, "alcoholism." That man was under the influence of an alcoholic god/idol/spirit.

Since God gave me a spirit of power and love, I prayed for the spirit of alcoholism to leave that man. Immediately he stopped staring at the bar and was done drinking at that event.

ASK THE LORD: Pray for discernment with a sincere heart, you will notice new things inside yourself and with other people.

Old Testament JOSHUA - IS A TYPE OF - New Testament JESUS

(Type of Christ) (foreshadow of Jesus)	(Who is, Who was, Who is to come)
Name: Hebrew Yeshua (Joshua)	**Name**: Greek Jesus
Meaning: Lord is Salvation	**Meaning**: He will save
Law: Moses got the law but couldn't get the Jews to the Promise Land	**Law:** Religious leaders kept the law, Jews were forbidden receive healing
Fear: Jewish spies emotional fear kept people from going into the Promise land of freedom, inheritance and and tabernacle worship.	Fear: Believers go into a fear spirit will stop them from receiving the blessing promise of love, power & a sound mind.
Victory: Joshua achieved victory to lead a nation to Promise Land.	**Victory:** Jesus always leads in triumphal victory.
Put to Death: Joshua put to death the natural enemies blocking victory.	**Put to Death:** Jesus asks us put to death sinful, earthly things within.
Abundant Life: Jew's land of Israel, family, peace, sacred temple site.	**Abundant Life:** Jesus give abundant deliverance from evil & bondage.
Scarlet Thread: Joshua the liberator of Jericho sent spies who saved prostitute Rahab and family from city destruction via scarlet rope.	**Blood of Jesus:** Power to stop evil and wicked ways. Blood of Jesus cleanses sin whiter snow & frees prostitute Mary.
Jehovah Nissi: The Lord is my Banner of Victory - Joshua's scroll	**Banner**: Jesus the lover, His banner over believers is love.

[20]The biblical type is a symbol or shadow representative of things to come. Bible scholars find the Old Testament is a "type" or foreshadow of the New Testament. This gives the believer a rich feast of symbolism to help know (Gnosis) God.

OLD TESTAMENT

Moses > Joshua > David >Solomon

Written Law > Conqueror/Victor > Stone Temple Plans >Built Temple

---

NEW TESTAMENT

Bible > Jesus > Holy Spirit >Priests

Word of God >Disarmed Powers >Sword of Spirit >Spiritual House

---

ART THERAPY DRAW: Identify and draw symbols that represent each Old Testament leader's contribution. Then identify and draw New Testament symbols.

Day 78 | KINGDUIT

"Our ancestors had the tabernacle of the covenant law with them in the wilderness. It had been made as God directed Moses, according to the pattern he had seen. After receiving the tabernacle, our ancestors under Joshua brought it with them when they took the land from the nations God drove out before them. It remained in the land until the time of David, who enjoyed God's favor and asked that he might provide a dwelling place for the God of Jacob. But it was Solomon who built a house for him."

Acts 7:44-47

God had a very specific plan to redeem humanity in the Old Testament. The Jews had their backs against the wall during the captivity of Pharaoh (Satan). The Jews were stuck for 400 hundred years. They cried out to God for deliverance from bondage. Since God has ears to hear and eyes to see, He took notice.

Consider how humanity hasn't changed much since the beginning of time. People get in trouble, so they get emotional, cry, and look for ways to find relief. I'm pretty sure the Jews looked for help on their own, but after hundreds of years and their cruel labor getting worse instead of better, all they had was God.

It's interesting that in these modern times, it has only been a few years that the idea of "mental health" has surfaced to the forefront of mankind's mindset on a global level. During my days as a young Christian, mental healing was not a topic at church, even though the faith community has the solution for every possible psychological issue through the healing and cleansing power of the blood of Jesus Christ. Not only can the Lord heal mental problems and the sin bound up inside those issues, but he also cleanses, washes, and removes all the mental type of infirmities down to the root level. That means He can break the generational sin that remains while taking care of each concern without diagnostic labels, gossip, shame, judgment, or a spirit of condemnation, which can often exacerbate mental issues.

Just like God directed Moses, Joshua, David, and Solomon with a pattern for success, be assured, He most certainly has an end game victory strategy for us today!

"Now, therefore,' Joshua said, 'Get rid of the foreign gods among you and incline your hearts to the LORD, the God of Israel.'

So, the people said to Joshua, 'We will serve the LORD our God and obey His voice."

Joshua 24:23-24

In the early 90's I was a new Christian. I dedicated my life to Christ, got baptized, served at church, studied the bible, and joined a prayer group. I was young in my faith and tried to grab hold of the One who held me. I remember trying to read the bible for myself, the text was so deep and mysterious. I was never much of a reader growing up, which made it challenging, but I was captivated by the power of the Holy scriptures. At the time, I didn't understand the person and work of Holy Spirit, even though He was really rocking my world.

I attended a prayer meeting at church and for several weeks there was an Australian man visiting to pray. His accent was memorable, and he spoke these special words during his visit: "Those who cling to worthless idols forfeit the grace due them." I had absolutely no idea what that phrase meant, but somehow it got sealed in my soul. I did nothing with the mysterious words.

Years later I started my healing journey with a slow start. I still didn't understand Holy Spirit, so I struggled to find a way to deal with my memories. I prayed, only to hear one word – "SUGAR." I shrugged my shoulders. Nothing changed, so I prayed again and heard – "SUGAR!" Sugar? I was like young Samuel who heard his name called (1 Samuel 3:5) and thought it was his mentor Eli, but it was God's voice calling his name. Again, I would hear "Sugar" in my spirit. It was perplexing. I didn't know about God's voice or Holy Spirit. I kept praying about my issues and got the word again. Finally, I said, "God if this is You, I will give up sugar and stop eating it for a year." Then boom! That phrase from the Aussie popped into my head, "Those who cling to worthless idols forfeit the grace due them" (Jonah 2:8).

I realized I had made an idol out of my sugar habit. I stopped the grace of God from flowing to me. Boom! That moment Jehovah Rapha opened an unstoppable healing river in me that became the most wonderful remedy for my soul! Thank you, JESUS!

Day 80 | KINGDUIT

"On that day Joshua made a covenant for the people, and there at Shechem he established for them a statute and ordinance. Joshua recorded these things in the Book of the Law of God. Then he took a large stone and set it up there under the oak that was near the sanctuary of the LORD. And Joshua said to all the people, 'You see this stone. It will be a witness against us, for it has heard all the words the LORD has spoken to us, and it will be a witness against you if you ever deny your God."

Joshua 24:25-27

ART THERAPY ACTIVITY: Draw a picture of the oak tree and large stone from the verse above, then draw ears on the stone. Plan to take a walk outside or find a trail hike and look for a large stone to be a witness for your faith. Stop to say a prayer near the stone and tell the Lord that you "will serve the Lord your God and obey His voice" (Joshua 24:24).

"For the law was given through Moses; grace and truth came through Jesus Christ."

John 1:17

The Jewish community of the Old Testament relied on leadership from Moses to get them to the Promise Land. Moses was the undeniable answer to their cries for deliverance. No one stood up to Pharaoh except Moses. He came out of the desert on a divine mission with the voice of God giving him every single directive to accomplish a national deliverance from 400 years of captivity.

For that generation of Israelites, the only form of worship they witnessed was idolatry. The nation of Egypt was full of monuments that were an architectural display of idolatry. Funny enough, guess who made the bricks that built those monuments, the Jews! I'm sure Satan hiding inside of Pharaoh laughed and mocked the Lord. Pharaoh said, "Come, let us deal shrewdly with them, or they will increase even more; and if a war breaks out, they may join our enemies, fight against us, and leave the country" (Exodus 1:10).

Moses received the law from God on the mountain and believed the law (or religious system) would get the Israelites on the path to promise, but it didn't work. The people were stuck in the idolatry trap. They needed a victorious warrior with a new plan, so Joshua got the job done by following the voice of God.

To this day, if Satan is in the world hiding behind people and godless institutions, he will never let go of his control and/or hold on humans. He knows the idolatry bondage locks people up very well. He must be commanded to leave by a power system/authority figure bigger than himself.

Almighty God looked down from His heavenly throne and saw the problem. When Joshua (a type of Christ Jesus) led the Jews to the Promise Land, God set in motion the final solution when "grace and truth came through Christ Jesus" (John 1:17).

Joshua's story ends with three burials. Joshua, Eleazar the priest and the bones of Joseph that were laid in the plot near Jacob's well. Consider why the law or religion didn't work to free the Jews? Write out your response:

Day 82 | KINGDUIT

"I will lead the blind by ways they have not known, along unfamiliar paths I will guide them; I will turn the darkness into light before them and make the rough places smooth. These are the things I will do; I will not forsake them."

Isaiah 42:16

Decades ago, as I prayed for healing, I felt like I was in a desert because people weren't talking about mental health. I didn't know what to look for. I was on an unfamiliar path. But God fulfilled His promise to guide me along a new path.

I was attending a vegetable class while trying to stay away from sugar. At the vegetable class, I met a precious Jewish lady, and we had a great conversation. We talked about eating out of the garden and being healthy in body and spirit. She kept sharing with me, then grabbed a tiny Jewish book from her purse. It was a Hebrew/English prayer booklet full of scriptures. She told me to read/recite it every day, out loud for forty days.

Hebrew people often read the Psalms aloud to gain the favor of God. They intentionally celebrate life by practicing/praying for happiness with intention. Daily events that are common to most are celebrated with prayers of gratitude. For example: enjoying the fruit of the garden, kindness of others, hospitality, supporting others, seeking forgiveness, good body functioning, growing, and learning.

At that time, I did not understand the cultural ideology of reciting prayers out loud. The Holy Spirit was making me aware that this lady was sent from Him and that I should treat her with respect and gratitude. I graciously received her sacred booklet of Psalms and asked Holy Spirit what to do with it. Immediately I was drawn to follow the forty-day encouragement, but Holy Spirit added that I should get up every night from midnight till three a.m. to decree scriptures over my life.

I knew that "life and death are in the power of the tongue" (Proverbs 18:12) and "the unfolding of His words gives light; it gives understanding to the simple" (Psalm 119:130). I had children in my home, so I knew that I would have privacy and freedom after midnight to pray out loud without anyone hearing but the Lord. Those 40 evenings with Holy Spirit were wonderful!

PROMISE LAND DECREE

SPEAK OUT LOUD & DECLARE

- I declare, I am born of God, I love God, I will carry out His commands and love others. In this way I overcome the world. It is not a burden, but a blessing to seek the Lord and listen to His voice (1 John 5:4).
- Like Jesus, I surrender my will to the greater purpose of my Father in heaven. His name is holy, and I proclaim His will be done in my life (Matthew 26:42).
- Even if I don't understand how to find total mental freedom, I will never give up because God is faithful to complete the work, He started in me. I have liberty in Christ. I won't let myself be burdened by the yoke of slavery from this world and its evil ways (Philippians 1:6) (Galatians 5:1).
- I thank God for giving me victory through my Lord Jesus Christ! I have victory over sin and death through Jesus Christ. I won't let anything move me. I give myself to the work of the Lord, every day, inside my own mind, soul, emotions, thoughts, and spirit (1 Cor. 15:57).
- I have control over my will; therefore, I will live in love and grace. I overcome all darkness by the blood of the Lamb of God who will wash away all confessed sin, rebellion, and transgressions (Revelation 12:11).
- Every time I come near the Lord, He rescues me, delivers me, is merciful to me, then He covers me, protects me, and gives me refuge (Psalm 91).
- Jesus will send me the Advocate, the Spirit of Truth to guide me into all truth. I receive the promises of what He will make known to me (John 15:26).
- Like Joshua and Jesus, I will not only leave the deserts of my life, but I walk out full of the Holy Spirit. This will be evident in my emotional life with attitudes of love, joy, peace, patience, goodness, faithfulness, gentleness, self-control. When I fall short, I'll ask for forgiveness, make things right and keep walking by faith (Galatians 5:22). In Jesus's powerful name I pray!

Day 84 | KINGDUIT

"Jesus came to a town of Samaria called Sychar, near the plot of ground that Jacob had given to his son Joseph. Since Jacob's well was there, Jesus, weary from His journey, sat down by the well."

John 4:5-6

The bible is spectacular for a multitude of reasons; here is one of them. The last verses in the book of Joshua mentions Jacob's land as the physical location to bury Joseph's bones. The verse above in the New Testament is where Jesus introduces himself hundreds of years later near Jacob's burial plot as the giver of water which "becomes a fresh, bubbling spring within them, giving them eternal life" (John 4:14).

Can you see it? Jesus positions Himself by a well offering a drink to a woman from eternal springs of living water. He knows she has issues and needs a drink for her soul. Can you see it? The first biblical spring in Genesis 16:14, where God reveals Himself to a distressed woman as El Roi, the One who sees, sees her. God even set up an angel at that first spring to help the woman. Here, with perfect foreshadowing from the Old Testament, there is King Jesus sitting by a well offering the gift of God. Praise the Lord by faith for the eternal fresh, bubbling, life water in your soul for healing!

ART THERAPY DRAW: Illustrate a desert well. Sing old Hymns like "Spring Up Oh Well" and "What A Mighty God We Serve."

"For the Lamb at the center of the throne will be their shepherd; 'He will lead them to springs of living water. And God will wipe away every tear from the eyes."

Revelation 7:17

Here we read another Old Testament to New Testament to the New Jerusalem in heaven comparison with the lamb. The Lord told Moses to command the Israelites to present to the Lord lambs without defect as burnt offerings. This was the Hebrew's recipe for divine communion.

Years later, John the Baptist showed up and understood the bigger picture. John knew exactly who Jesus was. "John saw Jesus coming toward him and said, 'Look, the Lamb of God, who takes away the sin of the world" (John 1:29)!

Later when Jesus walked around Israel in the New Testament, knowing He would be the sacrificial Lamb of God who takes away the sin of the world, he sat down near Jacob's land, by a well, ready to listen to the cares of a woman's heart. Jesus was resting, tired from his journey, yet ready to demonstrate divine care and love. Soon a woman with issues with her husband arrived to draw water.

He listens, even though he knows her story and says, "whoever drinks from the water I give them will never thirst. Indeed, the water I give them will become in them a spring of water welling up to eternal life" (John 4:14).

Jesus spoke to her in the present, but He was also speaking of the future for all believers in heaven. He will be in heaven, at the center of the throne ready to Shepherd us by the spring. There Jesus will be wiping tears!

MEDITATE: Imagine God wiping every tear from your eyes.

Day 86 | KINGDUIT

Jesus said to her, "Everyone who drinks this water will be thirsty again. But whoever drinks the water I give him will become in him a fountain of water springing up to eternal life."

John 4:13-14

Jesus is talking about the difference between natural water that sustains physical life for drinking and the water that gives spiritual life for all eternity.

Even though Jesus was sitting at the well of the Old Testament patriarch Jacob, a covenant father of Israel, he understood that the Jewish community had yet to acknowledge the Messiah. They still had Jerusalem, the law, the land, and even Jacob's well. They still had religion, yet they lacked eternal life. When the woman heard Jesus talk about eternal life, she responded by talking of worship in Jerusalem. Yet again, Jesus kept mentioning the type of water he was interested in, the spiritual everlasting water.

Jesus said . . . "The true worshipers will worship the Father in spirit and in truth, for the Father is seeking such as these to worship Him" (John 4:23).

ART THERAPY DRAW: Illustrate the difference between a natural spring in nature and a spring welling up to eternal life inside your life in Christ.

KINGDUIT | Day 87

"The woman said, 'I know that the Messiah (called Christ) is coming. When He comes, He will explain everything to us.'

Jesus answered, 'who speak to you am He."

John 4:25-26

The woman at the well is finally understanding the point Jesus is trying to make about eternal life, so she mentions Messiah's return.

Jesus basically says, "I'm here!" He most certainly was the fountain of living water that was present at Jacobs well to explain everything and reveal himself as the Messiah.

Jesus showed up on site two thousand years ago at Jacob's well with refreshment and He still is the source of endless refreshing for our souls. Just like He knew every detail of that Samaritan woman's life, He also knows every detail of your life. He truly can speak to you about everything from any perspective.

He came as the Lamb of God to provide the perfect blood that delivers humanity from the death angel and washes all things clean, whiter than snow. He came to explain to anyone who calls on His name everything they need to tap into the eternal well of healing.

Even though your issues might be deep, the gift of God can still access every part of you in need of help. He understands the days are evil and the time is near. We don't have to be perplexed, lack hope, confused about the world or our past, or unsure on how to be ready for our eternal future. Jesus is the One for you!

Day 88 | KINGDUIT

"Then the woman left her water jar, went back into the town, and said to the people, 'Come, see a man who told me everything I ever did. Could this be the Christ? So, they left the town and made their way towards Jesus."

John 4:28-29

During this encounter in John 4:4-42 when Jesus speaks to the woman, the information shocks her into belief. In describing Jesus, she said He was "a man who told me everything I ever did" (John 4:29). God will have to explain his divine omniscient ability (the state of knowing everything) one day in heaven. What is clear is that our lives are an open book before Christ Jesus. That means Jesus not only delivers us from death, he also completely redeems EVERY aspect of our lives if we draw near him.

I believe the Lord has His servants on the earth to assist us in seeking divine help. Books are already written and being written with all the information you need to be totally healed.

Nonetheless, her statement is stunning. How did Jesus tell the woman at the well EVERYTHING she ever did? It was like her life story flooded out of the mouth of Jesus to her ears and into her heart. She had to stay in his presence long enough to listen to his voice and receive her own testimony about herself. There she believed so much that she ran home to tell the whole town her experience. When she told this testimony to her neighbors, many believed that Jesus was the Savior of the world.

Indeed, he is "the King eternal, immortal, invisible, the only God be honor and glory for ever and ever" (1 Timothy 1:17).

KINGDUIT | Day 89

"Many of the Samaritans from that town believed in him because of the woman's testimony, 'He told me everything I ever did.' So, when the Samaritans came to him, they urged him to stay with them, and he stayed two days."

John 4:39-40

It all started with a simple woman on a regular day. The Lord knew she needed to talk, so He sat down in a place where He knew she would visit. There He helped her unravel her story.

That's how biblical mental healing came to me. I went to be refreshed by fellowship, and I met a girl who said Jesus explained many complex situations about her life through journaling. Journaling? I didn't get it. Later she brought her notebooks to the group to prove her testimony. I looked, and in my spirit, I knew it was her heart poured out upon the pages of simple lined paper. She wouldn't stop talking about the Lord and what He did for her. Then she asked me if she could teach me how to write down my worries, then listen to the Lord and write again things I heard in my spirit.

Her testimony influenced me, and I found a notebook and started writing. Then I told my best friend and even showed my husband. Within the next year we all had a regular practice of journaling with Holy Spirit. We tapped into the well of living water and our lives changed.

Jesus's words were alive and active, flowing into our lives with healing. We kept drinking, which became a "fountain of water springing up to eternal life" (John 4:14) in our souls. In the beginning it wasn't easy, in fact, it was extremely difficult. When that pure, holy water of fellowship with Jesus and Holy Spirit started to flow, it unclogged a lot of sin, bitterness, transgressions, and ugly long-standing pain. That stuff started to wash up on the pages of our notebooks. Conviction was a regular part of our lives.

Jesus, bit by bit, started to reveal things we didn't even understand. We kept writing and seeking and soon the wisdom flowed. With each truth, we repented. Sometimes we shared with one another what God was showing us. One sin was so embedded, my friend and I agreed to pray about it together until that issue was no longer a part of our lives. That prayer lasted years, but the Lord broke the chains, and we were free!

Day 90 | KINGDUIT

"Because Jesus lives forever, he has a permanent priesthood. Consequently, he is able to save to the uttermost those who draw near to God through him, since he always lives to make intercession for them."

Hebrews 7:24-25

The story from the last days visiting Jesus by the well of eternal life proves why Jesus is called "Wonderful Counselor" (Isaiah 9:6). He knows everything, every word, every story, and every back-story about our lives. Then He not only prays for us, but He also "always lives" to make intercession for us. If we choose to draw near Him, He will reveal the information about our lives that has gotten us to our current state of mind. Then He gives more, promising to save us to the uttermost (entire, complete, perfect, through all time) no matter what the issue, He will do it! He will be your Prince of Peace! Shalom Shalom!

Jesus truly is the only wonderful counselor. Yeshua is the Messiah, anointed one to be the King, Savior of the world! He is worthy of all glory, all honor, and all praises. Blessed be the Lord our God. King of the Universe!

ART THERAPY DRAW: Illustrate what being saved to the uttermost looks like for your story.

MONTH 4 - Living Water

SPRING SEASON

WELL AND BE WELL

Day 91 | KINGDUIT

"Lord, you are the hope of Israel; all who forsake you will be put to shame. Those who turn away from you will be written in the dust because they have forsaken the Lord, the spring of living water."

Jeremiah 17:13

PRAYER FOR SPRINGS

PRAY: Dear Lord, it's true, I have forsaken Your water spring, and I can get dusty. Forgive me! I don't want to forsake you. I turn to you, Spring of living water. Thank you for loving me with an everlasting love, for leading me with Your cords of kindness, with ties of love. Give me the enduring prayer that leads to freedom. Send me a friend that I can trust and pray with regularly, show us so we can encourage one another and increase our power to heal (Hosea 11:4).

Thank you for your love for Jerusalem! Truly you have been faithful to bless and keep that nation to this day. Bless the Holy City, I pray for peace in Jerusalem. May all who love that city prosper. May there be peace within those walls and towers (Jeremiah 4:10).

Had it not been for the Jews and the Holy Scriptures, I would have never been found by you. Even in the barren places of my life, you promise to open rivers. Even in my sad valleys, you have divine springs. There is so much healing to be found in You, help me to receive Your abundance. Thank you for shining Your love and light in my life without fear, shame, or condemnation. Thank you for having the power to completely save my soul (Psalm 103:7).

I want to be well. Thank you for always praying for me like you said in Hebrews 7:25!

"My people have committed two sins. They have forsaken me, the spring of living water, and have dug their own cisterns, broken cisterns that cannot hold water."

Jeremiah 2:13

Jeremiah was a prophet of the Lord at a time when the people of Jerusalem went into exile. The nation lost everything in the desert sand and were forced to leave their homeland.

History is a brutal story of wars where kings destroyed buildings and displaced people. The power structures that are opposing today have existed from generation to generation. During a national crisis are people/families. When they are displaced, traumatized, weak, sick, in some type of captivity to something or someone, mental health often gets lost in the desert sand. They are like broken vessels that lack refreshment.

Often, one of the first activities a counselor will ask a client to do is write down on a paper a list of existing major life crisis. It is a written form to list disruptive life events with columns that indicate whether the person witnessed it, experienced it, heard about it, or the bad event was a part of their job. Basically, when someone has layers of stressful things happening in their life at the same time, it is normal to be distressed. The counselor can help them process those events.

This list has stayed in my memory from Psychology 101 during my bachelor's studies. It has often reminded me that whenever I go through major changes in my life, it's okay to feel weird, sad, or even sick because I'm dealing with several difficult events.

The bible describes this on a national level as a war season or a peace season. When people go into idolatry, the nation falls apart. When a righteous God-fearing leader is in place, there is peace and prosperity.

The Lord gives a water analogy about the state of the nation. Either their well is full because they honor "the spring of living water" or the nation's well is broken, empty and holds no water. Think about your life as a vessel, it's condition.

ART THERAPY DRAW: Draw a cracked clay pot with a broken piece of pot next to it.

Day 93 | KINGDUIT

"Then the LORD God formed man from the dust of the ground and breathed the breath of life into his nostrils, and the man became a living being."

Genesis 2:8

The clay/water/life analogy started with God the Creator at the beginning of the natural world in Genesis 1 & 2. God made us from the "dust and breathed the breath of life" into man. This verse proves our creation along with our connection to the natural world. "Yet you, LORD, are our Father. We are the clay; you are the potter; we are the work of your hands" (Isaiah 64:8).

When you mix dust and water, you get clay. Then clay can be used to build a well to hold water, called a cistern. Our bodies, which are kept alive by water and breath, are originally made from dust. Similarly, original wells that are not broken or cracked hold water to sustain agriculture and food supply. Clay can also be formed to build homes. Clearly, God speaks of the significance of dust/clay/cistern in the Bible to help us understand His view of abundance like a spring.

Clay Cisterns	We are the clay
well-Leviticus 11:36	like treasure - 2 Cor. 4:7
marriage - Proverbs 5:15	we are dust - Job 10:9
faith-Jeremiah 2:15	lump of clay - Romans 9:21
sin/broken pots - Isaiah 30:14	clay say potter - Isaiah 45:9
cleanliness - Leviticus 11:36	lifted out of clay - Psalm 40
offspring - Genesis 3:20	we are dust - Psalm 103:14
Water hold- Jeremiah 2-13	like clay/people - Dan 2:43

"But we have this treasure in jars of clay to show that this all-surpassing power is from God and not from us. We are hard pressed on every side but not crushed; perplexed, but not in despair; persecuted but not abandoned; struck down but not destroyed."

2 Corinthians 4:7-9

Even though we are dust and clay, so are the nations and people. Like a potter, God has his hand on the whole world. Each life, each person's group and nation can be the recipient of His love and divine shaping. Each life can choose to let His hands use divine tools to carve a vessel with honorable purpose. Yes, God has tools!

During my most overwhelming trial I asked the Lord to show me something to help me get through my hard place. An unexpected gift came to me from a dear friend visiting from another country. She gave me a net bag full of tiny clay pots. I opened the bag and grabbed a precious pot and as I did, it fell out of my hand and onto my concrete driveway. My heart fluttered; did it break? No, there was just a chip on the lip of the small vessel.

In the moment that I looked upon the chip, Holy Spirit spoke to my heart. "This trial is but a chip, I am your spring of living water (Jeremiah 2:13) and I will remain securely held in your clay jar."

"As a father has compassion on his children, so the Lord has compassion on those who fear Him; For He knows our frame; He is mindful that we are dust" (Psalm 103:13-14). No matter what is going on in world history or our lives, Almighty God is Lord of All. He has the power to rebuild anything, especially fully surrendered Christians (little-Christ followers).

ART THERAPY DRAW: Draw a clay pot on a potter's wheel. Write your name on the clay pot. Draw a pair of big hands labeled "the Lord."

Happy Passover

As the first day of Passover celebrations start on a Friday evening, the Jewish community prepares a special Passover dinner called Seder. They light candles and eat a symbolic meal representing the Passover story so they can remember and retell the story of their freedom.

This holiday has taken place since the first Passover in Egypt when the blood of the lamb kept the death angel from killing the firstborn males. Later a man named Jesus showed up who is "the Lamb who was slain from the creation of the world" (Revelation 13:8).

When Jesus was on earth, he prepared for Passover by willingly going to the cross as the Lamb slain for mankind's sins. "It was just before the Passover Festival. Jesus knew that the hour had come for him to leave the world and go to the Father. Having loved his own who were in the world, he loved them to the end" (John 13:1).

You might ask, what does this story and the Jewish community have to do with my mental health? We all need a counselor with a means to wash and clean our souls, leaving us with Shalom (peace). This story embodies why and how Jesus is the "Wonderful Counselor, Mighty God, Everlasting Father, Prince of Peace" (Isaiah 9:6).

Night One: Passover Seder

KINGDUIT | Day 96

Step-by-step Seder Meal/Jesus Passover Lamb fulfillment

The Seder meal has 15 steps to remember God's deliverance of the Jewish people. Each step symbolizes the biblical story of Jesus as the Lamb of God.

Passover	Spring of living water
1. Sanctify	Sanctify by the truth
2. Wash Hands	Give me a clean heart
3. Appetizer	Appetizer
4. Break middle of the Matzah body	Matzah = Jesus broken
5. Tell Exodus story	Exodus - Christ deliverer
6. Wash hands again	Word of God washes
7. Blessing over bread	Communion bread
8. Matzah, pierced, no yeast	Pierced by sword, no sin
9. Bitter herbs	Bitter herb drink refused
10. Hillel Sandwich, bitter and sweet	Suffering is bitter and then sweet redemption
11. Festive Meal, About overcoming/freedom	Festive meal Jesus invites us to dinner
12. Eat Afikomen - soul level nourishment.	Satisfied taking communion
13. Grace after meals = trust God is over you	Grace gift, not works
14. Psalms of Praise – sing	Psalms of Praise - sing
15. Accepted-Transform dark world to light	Accepted - Jesus leads from darkness to light

Day 97 | KINGDUIT

"The evening meal was in progress, and the devil had already prompted Judas, the son of Simon Iscariot, to betray Jesus."

John 13:2

"The devil has been sinning from the beginning. The reason the Son of God appeared was to destroy the devil's work" (1 John 4:8). Finally, Jesus is the One who showed up to do something about it!

The devil, your enemy, has been hiding for a long time. He likes to disguise behind normal, good, and bad people. In the above verse he is hiding behind Judas. In Egypt, he hid behind Pharoah. Add Hitler or only evil leaders in history. Satan even hides behind good people like priests, for example, those trusted with the secrets of church going souls. He hides behind cultural influencers whose artistic expression leads people off the righteous path.

The secular mental health community does not talk about the presence of evil, even though humanity knows that evil/devil does exist in this world. Not only does Jesus talk about the devil, but He also destroys the devil's work and empowers His followers to do the same.

The devil really thought he destroyed Jesus by using Judas to get him arrested pre-crucifixion, but it didn't work. The crucifixion provided a holy sacrifice the religious system couldn't give. "Jesus sacrificed for their sins once for all when he offered himself" (Hebrews 7:27). "Through Jesus, everyone who believes is set free from every sin, a justification you were not able to obtain under the law of Moses" (Acts 13:39). All sins confessed and forgiven; past, present, and future are covered by Christ's blood just as if they never happened.

ART THERAPY DRAW: Draw a stick figure of a person with the devil hiding behind their shoulder. Label who that person is and write down how the devil influenced their actions in a negative way.

"You were dead because of your sins and because your sinful nature was not yet cut away. Then God made you alive with Christ, for he forgave all our sins having canceled the record of the charges against us and took it away by nailing it to the cross. And having disarmed the powers and authorities, he made a public spectacle of them, triumphing over them by the cross."

Colossians 2:13-15

The cross gives you the cleansing that comes from forgiveness along with the ability to forgive those who have sinned against you, but it also gives you incredible power to triumph over evil.

Just like God demonstrated mighty power to destroy Pharaoh (Satan) through the parting of the Red Sea for the Jews, in the same way Jesus's sacrifice "disarmed the powers and authorities" or evil forces in the world.

There are MANY wonderful people in the world who try to do good, who try to change, who put forth much effort to be different from their troubles, but they just can't get free, even with a great counselor. Or they get free but refuse to forgive and lose their family.

This struggle can breed hopelessness, especially people who honestly share their story with a counselor, just to be stuck with a diagnosis that makes them feel worse. Then their family or community labels them for the diagnosis, and an identity can form. Now there is a new problem.

Here is one difference between Biblical Mental Healing and Secular Counseling. Not only does Christ forgive sins, offenses, transgressions, and human errors, but He "canceled the record of charges against us and took it away." Jesus removes the burdens of the human soul while also disarming the (evil) powers hiding behind those burdens.

PROCLAIM & PRAY: Put your name in the above verse anywhere you see the words your or you and pray it out loud several times!

Day 99 | KINGDUIT

"Just as Moses lifted up the snake in the wilderness, so the Son of Man must be lifted up that everyone who believes may have eternal life in him."

John 3:14-15

During this season of Passover and Easter celebrations, we can contemplate how history has held on to the two most celebrated biblical holidays which are centered around healing and deliverance. The battle of good versus evil has been going on for a long time, but the Lord has always taken the final win for victory.

The healing of the Israelites from the bronze snake (Numbers 21:8) in the Old Testament wilderness was a foreshadow of the serpent's crafty move to crucify Jesus on a cross. He ended up being outwitted by God, since the sacrifice of Jesus redeemed and empowered mankind to take back authority to destroy the works of the devil. God used Jesus to turn the tables on the snake!

The ultimate healing doesn't take place on earth. It takes place in heaven, but it doesn't start there. The healing started working when Jesus was the Passover lamb who provided salvation for the soul of humanity.

ART THERAPY DRAW: Read Numbers 21:4-8. Draw a snake on a pole next to a cross.

The Jewish Passover Festival is an 8-day Celebration of Freedom. On this day the Jews enjoy time with family.

Holidays have a purpose to celebrate the memory of valuable historical days. They also serve as a time to rest from work and enjoy times of refreshment. Having a good day with friends and family can be a nice break from the hard work of pursuing personal mental health.

Make time to enjoy fellowship & joy!

Day 101 | KINGDUIT

"Jesus stood and said in a loud voice, 'Let anyone who is thirsty come to me and drink. Whoever believes in me, as Scripture has said, rivers of living water will flow from within them."

John 7:37-38

The Jews had been celebrating the Passover for two-thousand years by resting from skilled work and enjoying family time. They did not understand that only eight months prior to that 2,000th Celebration of Freedom, Isaiah's prophecy of Wonderful Counselor and Prince of Peace was literally standing in the sand proclaiming the above!

"He was speaking about the Spirit, whom those who believed in Him were later to receive. For the Spirit had not yet been given, because Jesus had not yet been glorified" (John 7:39).

You may have been wondering all this time, what does the bible have to do with mental health? Jesus "stood up and called out with a loud voice" to answer that question with crystal clarity.

A perfect picture of excellent mental health is having a soul (mind, will, intellect, emotions) like a clear spring of pure water. All the bitterness, selfishness, pain, trauma, greed and perversion would be gone, and the life flow would be joy, peace, endurance, and a love that refuses to give up. Since humans came from dust mixed with water, we are clay vessels. If one has never pursued mental healing, they are probably clogged up with guck. A careful and consistent internal washing could clean up troubles to make us a glorious bodily vessel of refreshment. Then with cleansed words spoken, each person would be so down to earth and honest, yet captivating and kind. Even if they were aged or beaten down, their faces would glow with joy and sincere love, eyes bright with hope.

ART THERAPY DRAW: Draw Jesus standing on top of a gushing water source of your choice. Give him a talk bubble that says the words from the verse above.

"By faith Moses, when he had grown up, refused to be known as the son of Pharaoh's daughter. He chose to be mistreated along with the people of God rather than to enjoy the fleeting pleasures of sin. He regarded disgrace for the sake of Christ as of greater value than the treasures of Egypt because he was looking ahead to his reward. By faith he left Egypt, not fearing the king's anger; he persevered because he saw him who is invisible. By faith he kept the Passover and the application of blood, so that the destroyer of the firstborn would not touch the firstborn of Israel. By faith the people passed through the Red Sea as on dry land; but when the Egyptians tried to do so, they were drowned."

Hebrews 11:25-29

This day of the Festival of Freedom is when the Jews celebrate the miracle parting of the Red Sea. God's national rescue via deliverance from Pharaoh is stunning. Starting with Moses's birth during the genocide of male babies, then the oppressive labor, the plaques, the death angel, the high-speed chariot chase, the sea parting, the sea swallowing the enemy, and the first worship song. The details foreshadow Christ the Messiah, and yet the Jews still don't acknowledge Jesus as Messiah.

Based on the text above, Moses saw Christ! By faith he saw the big picture. By faith Moses was also willing to suffer, forsake worldly treasure, endure anger, listen, carefully, carry out divine instructions, obey an invisible Christ and save a nation! Moses's leadership paved the way for global salvation, including your healing today!

Understanding the Old Testament stories will give you a graphic, visual picture of how Christ is going to deliver you from satanic oppression, just like He did for the Israelites. Art therapy drawing will help your mind visualize a real historical event that can be like the struggle you may be facing. Even though our historical time has different challenges, our battles are real.

ART THERAPY DRAW: Draw a door with blood on top. Then draw Moses standing with arms raised in a path between two oceans.

Day 103 | KINGDUIT

"By this Jesus meant the Spirit, whom those who believed in him were later to receive. Up to that time the Spirit had not been given since Jesus had not yet been glorified.

On hearing his words, some of the people said, 'Surely this man is the Prophet,'

Others said, 'He is the Messiah.' Still others asked, 'How can the Messiah come from Galilee?"

John 7:39-41

To this day, the Passover remains, and God has been faithful to the nation of Israel. Yet, on this final day of celebrating, the Jews are still looking for the Messiah and the redemption God promised.

Jesus taught the disciples how-to walk-in victory when He "healed the sick, raised the dead, cleansed those who had leprosy, and drove out demons" (Matthew 10:8). When Jesus, God in the flesh, showed up some of the Jews said, 'He is the Messiah.'

Nonetheless, they rejected and demanded Jesus be crucified. The religious leaders hated when Jesus started to heal people! Jesus knew those Jewish leaders were going to let the Romans brutally crush his body and send him to a merciless cross. He didn't want to go through with it, but those rivers of living water rushed through and gave him a vision of joy for the suffering he would endure. This event is heart-breaking to think about, and extremely humbling if you know Him, believe Him and have been forgiven by Him.

Despite the national betrayal by His own people, even still, His heart was for them when Jesus sent out his disciples with instructions to "Go rather to the lost sheep of Israel" (Matthew 10:6).

WRITE IT DOWN: Write a sentence down that describes your thoughts about Jesus before you were saved.

KINGDUIT | Day 104

"Having loved His own who were in the world, He loved them to the very end."

John 13:1

If the goal of our faith is the salvation of our souls (1 Peter 1:9), then what was Jesus's goal, since He always has a perfect soul?

Just like Joshua's banner was victory, Christ's fulfillment of that victorious banner came in the form of complete love . . . till the end! Meditate on Christ's love today. Ask the Lord to give you a huge download of divine LOVE!

ART THERAPY DRAW: Draw a man running towards a big heart with the word "GOD'S LOVE" written inside.

Day 105 | KINGDUIT

"If you love Me, you will keep My commandments. And I will ask the Father and He will give you another Advocate to be with you forever-the Spirit of truth. The world cannot receive Him because it neither sees Him nor knows Him. But you do know Him, for He abides with you and will be in you."

John 14:15-17

The love gauge is a great way to track your healing progress. When your body is hurting, the no-pain gauge will let you know healing has happened, but it's different for the soul. If the waters of your life are bitter, that's an indication that there is more healing work to seek. Look for sweet, refreshing water that feels like love splashing around your life. A loving soul sings, smiles, forgives, is overflowing with peace, and has hope even when there are sad tears.

Jesus says love is tied to keeping the 10 Commandments, so you must read the bible to understand what the commandments look like in real life.

We've already established that Jesus lives to intercede/pray for us in Hebrews 7:25, so you are covered. So, what is Jesus praying for? He is praying for a helper called the Advocate. The advocate is: freely given, free of charge, from the Father. The Holy Spirit's help is the highest form of help in the universe: it lasts forever, stays close on the inside, is a capital Spirit of Truth, and a divine legal entity that defends the believer against the "accuser of the brethren" (Revelation 12:10)! Revelation 12:9 will let you know who has a case against you, accusing you before the Lord.

On top of all that, the Advocate is invisible and unknown by the world, so one must activate faith to tap into this incredibly amazing supernatural healing resource.

Interestingly, on a secular mental health platform, if you were to go see a therapist, they would start a file on you called a case study. These documents on file would be an in-depth study of your life, your history, your family tree, your behavior patterns, and different aspects of your story. The therapist would review your case to find the best treatment plan to assist in your mental health journey.

ASK JESUS: Do I have the "Advocate"?

KINGDUIT | Day 106

"And again, Jesus said, 'Peace be with you! As the Father has sent me, I am sending you.' And with that He breathed on them and said, 'Receive the Holy Spirit. If you forgive anyone's sins, their sins are forgiven; if you do not forgive them, they are not forgiven."

John 20:21-23

The disciples had just lost Jesus to death on a cross. They gathered at home, devastated with grief. On the third day Jesus was raised from the dead, so he showed up at the disciple's home to offer them peace along with the promised Holy Spirit.

Jesus offered the gift of Holy Spirit, but the disciples had to receive the gift. This pattern is: Jesus gives, you receive. Then "freely you have received, freely give" (Matthew 10:8). This is how spiritual fruit is multiplied to make Christians (little-Christ's).

Give > Receive

Forgiven > Forgive

Receive > Give

Forgive Again > Forgiven.

ART THERAPY DRAW: Write the word RECEIVE many times. Then draw hands open and lifted to heaven. The Lord has so much to give, will you receive?

Day 107 | KINGDUIT

"And you also were included in Christ when you heard the message of truth, the gospel of your salvation. When you believed, you were marked in Him with a seal, the promised Holy Spirit, who is a deposit guaranteeing our inheritance until the redemption of those who are God's possession - to the praise of His glory."

Ephesians 1:13-14

The gift of Holy Spirit wasn't just for the disciples; it is for all those who believe in the gospel and are saved. At that point, a secret seal marks believers and the bible says the seal is Holy Spirit. Holy Spirit is the Advocate, Spirit of truth, and Helper that we need to build ourselves up in faith leading to redemption.

Many people describe Holy Spirit living inside in different ways. Some call Holy Spirit the internal knower, inward witness, discerner of spirits, and holy helper. It takes time seeking the Lord and the Word to develop a relationship with Holy Spirit, but one way you know if it is Holy Spirit is from a manifestation of emotional fruit in your soul. "But the fruit of the Spirit is love, joy, peace, patience, kindness, goodness, faithfulness, gentleness and self-control" (Galatians 5:22-23).

Many mental health treatments and therapies center around behavior modification. Biblical mental healing starts with salvation and immediately includes a gift fruit basket of nine beautiful emotions to lead you on a path of right living, joy and peace.

ART THERAPY DRAW: Draw a basket of nine different fruits. Name and label each of the fruits to match the nine fruits of the Spirit. Write down why each garden fruit has the characteristics of the spiritual fruit and how each fruit will improve your mental health.

"Paul took the road through the interior and arrived at Ephesus. There he found some disciples and asked them, 'Did you receive the Holy Spirit when you believed?'

They answered, 'No, we have not even heard that there is a Holy Spirit.'

So, Paul asked, 'Then what baptism did you receive?'

'John's baptism,' they replied.

Paul said, 'John's baptism was a baptism of repentance. He told the people to believe in the one coming after him, that is, in Jesus.' On hearing this, they were baptized in the name of the Lord Jesus. When Paul placed his hands on them, the Holy Spirit came on them, and they spoke in tongues and prophesied."

Acts 19:1-6

The Lord knew when I was ready to become serious about my mental health. God sent into my life other believers that understood the soul-level healing part of sanctification. Interestingly, they asked me the exact same questions as Paul asked the disciples in Ephesus. When you read the Book of Ephesians, in the first verse Paul addresses the "saints in Ephesus, the faithful in Christ Jesus" (Ephesians 1:1). That people group was ready to receive "every spiritual blessing in the heavenly realms" (Ephesians 1:3) which is the gift in Christ Jesus.

I was baptized and knew about Holy Spirit, but never formally received Holy Spirit. My new friends in faith insisted I received Holy Spirit by faith, stating that the John 14:16 "Helper" is who I needed to find total freedom and mental health.

You will know for yourself if you are serious about your faith when you have obeyed in a baptism of repentance along with receiving Holy Spirit. Remember "the eyes of the Lord range throughout the earth to strengthen those whose hearts are fully committed to him" (2 Chronicles 16:9). Step into His baptism wells by faith! Are you ready?

Day 109 | KINGDUIT

"When the day of Pentecost came, they were all together in one place. Suddenly a sound like a blowing of a violent wind came from heaven and filled the whole house where they were sitting. They saw what seemed to be tongues of fire that separated and came to rest on each of them. All of them were filled with the Holy Spirit and began to speak in other tongues as the Spirit enabled them."

Acts 2:1-4

Jesus promised the disciples that after he was raised from the dead and glorified in heaven, he would send Holy Spirit. They watched Jesus rise into a cloud and disappear from their sight. They were given a new group name, apostles, which means sent out ones.

Surely, they were still adjusting to the loss of Jesus while trying to wait for this promise of Holy Spirit. The Lord initiated the first download of Holy Spirit in a profound way, with a sign that seemed to be fire over their heads. Fire purifies, fire illuminates, but holy fire cleanses the sacrifice of our lives for His purposes in our time and season.

The first visual manifestation clarifies how very critical Holy Spirit is for our mission in our times. We need that same fire light the Hebrews had now! We can be "sent out" as apostles too! We need Holy Spirit! Acknowledge the work of Holy Spirit at work in your life with sincere respect and honor!

ART THERAPY DRAW: Draw group people with each person having flames overhead.

"John answered them all, "I baptize you with water. But one who is more powerful than I will come, the straps of whose sandals I am not worthy to untie. He will baptize you with the Holy Spirit and fire."

Luke 3:16

If you were thinking yesterday, the baptism of fire was just for the Apostles, you'd be mistaken. John the Baptist was the first one to witness or testify to the power and glory of the coming Christ. His job was to prepare the way. "He went into all the country around the Jordan, preaching a baptism of repentance for forgiveness of sins" (Luke 3:3). He spoke before crowds of Jerusalemites looking for the Messiah and described what the salvation of God would do for people. I see it as a beautiful description of mental health:

"Every valley shall be filled in, every mountain and hill made low. The crooked roads shall become straight, the rough ways smooth."

Luke 3:9

- Find a page in your journal and sit with Holy Spirit.
- ART THERAPY DRAW: Draw two simple mountains with a valley in between. Draw a crooked road and a rough way.
- Ask Holy Spirit to help you identify the mountains, valley's, crooked roads, and rough ways in your life. Write this down because whatever Holy Spirit identifies is very important and powerful.
- Then ask how He will lower the mountains, fill in the valleys, straighten out and smooth over the other areas of your life. Write down that wisdom so that you can read it later when you make decisions.

Day 111 | KINGDUIT

"Astounded and perplexed, they asked one another, 'What does this mean?' "But others mocked them and said, "They are drunk on new wine!"

Acts 2:12 -13

Peter wasn't going to let the false accusation of men disrupt the holy moment, so he addressed the crowd. It seemed like Peter was so filled with Holy Spirit that he laughed at the drunk comment saying, "It's only the third hour of the day!"

God sent a violent wind from heaven and filled the gathering place of the apostles with Holy Spirit at a very specific time. They were ready to be filled and sent out. There was a group dwelling in Jerusalem of "God-fearing Jews from every nation under heaven" (Acts 2:5). Those individuals heard the wild sounds ringing out. They heard the words declaring the wonders of God in their native languages and they were astounded and amazed. They came outside and gathered to talk about it and some mocked the disciples.

Only three years prior, crowds had gathered in the desert to hear John the Baptist proclaim these very things would happen, starting with Jesus, along with an explanation of this "Holy Spirit and fire" baptism. John said it was for all the people in those crowds.

When Holy Spirit and fire fell from heaven just like John said, it started with the disciples, the leaders Jesus raised up. But God knew the wind ringing heavenly sounds would get the attention of the locals from every nation under heaven and soon, there was a crowd.

When God starts to move, it draws attention and people start talking and trying to interpret supernatural events. Some seek answers and some start mocking. Keep seeking and trust the Lord, He has all the answers, most of which are in the Bible.

ART THERAPY DRAW: Draw an abstract expression of what a violent wind with wild sounds ringing might look like. Imagine how profound God can move to draw others to His ways.

KINGDUIT | Day 112

"Then Peter stood up with the Eleven, lifted his voice, and addressed the crowd. 'Men of Judea and all who dwell in Jerusalem, let this be known to you, and listen carefully to my words. These men are not drunk, as you suppose. It is only the third hour of the day!"

Acts 2:14-15

I don't know when it started, but it seems like any emotional outburst in American territory is labeled as crazy, unless you are a performing musician. I've been in other countries where it is strangely quiet. Thank God for noisy babies, shouts from the African nations and screams from the Islanders haka dance. They are the sounds of life, expressing deep things of the heart. People were not meant to be silenced, that's control! They are meant to sing praises, shout, exalt, grieve, mourn, wail, and be free to express all those emotions to our loving King Jesus.

God showed up big time in Jerusalem with winds blowing so violently that it made ringing sounds. When Holy Spirit dropped on the disciples/apostles, boom, they were filled, and their tongues couldn't help but be on fire and make sounds and speak out in many languages. Take note that Holy Spirit's power net went out to all nations! It was a foreshadow of heaven.

"Behold, a great multitude that no one could number, from every nation, from all tribes and peoples and languages, standing before the throne and before the Lamb. . ." (Revelation 7:9).

If the physical body bleeds, oozes, pusses, tears up, groans, coughs, and snots, why should the issues that flow from the heart and a troubled mind not express itself in some type of tear, sound, or snot?

Scripture records Jesus' sweat-stressed blood before he was brutally beaten, he made loud noises, he shouted and even cried like a momma bird with a longing to cover Israel. God laughs and thunders. Even the rocks cry out, the earth blows and rains, while the natural world is a symphony of innumerable sounds.

Why can't people, the beloved children of God, express a beautiful mess of expressive noise or a supernatural prayer of fellowship in unified calling out for divine help? It's not weird, it's healthy!

Day 113 | KINGDUIT

Peter said, "No, this is what was spoken by the prophet Joel: 'In the last days, God says, I will pour out My Spirit on all people. Your sons and daughters will prophesy, your young men will see visions, your old men will dream dreams. Even on My menservants and maidservants I will pour out My Spirit in those days, and they will prophesy."

Acts 2:17-18

Peter stood up and boldly defended the faith at a hinge moment in history. The law of Moses turned into a system of performance and control that hardened hearts. People feared religious leaders more than they feared God. Peter urged the crowd to grab the promises of God!

Since that time, God has been faithful to pour out His Spirit on all people, but many have become so dignified they don't seek Holy Spirit, or they don't get the teaching because where leadership is concerned it might look messy. I'm not sure why someone would deny the magnificent blessings of the Lord that come directly from Holy Spirit, other than fear. Those pesky spirits of fear, shame and condemnation try to keep people away from the Lord.

Let it not be so in your life. Now is the time of God's favor. Now is the moment to seek the Lord and receive every gift He has freely given you listed in the Bible. Call on Him, He is close to you!

CALL ON THE LORD: Ask Him for wisdom about your life. Pray that you get a divine vision or dream. Write it all down so that you can meditate, pray, and prepare to fulfill God's purpose for your life.

"Peter replied, 'Repent and be baptized, every one of you, in the name of Jesus Christ for the forgiveness of your sins, and you will receive the gift of the Holy Spirit. This promise belongs to you and your children and to all who are far off-to all whom the Lord our God will call to Himself.'

With many other words he testified, and he urged them, 'Be saved from this corrupt generation."

Acts 2:38-41

Decades ago, I was at college with my young peers, we were seeking the Lord and one girl told us she wanted to get baptized. She felt an urgency to obey in the moment. We reached out to the local church, but they only offered baptism formally, at specific times. The Lord wouldn't let us let go and convicted us that we had the authority of agreement in our small group of believers. We decided to find a pool and baptize our sister in the name of Jesus Christ for forgiveness of sin. It was an awesome blessing!

No matter where you are, God has people all over the world that will obey and serve, whatever the need. Once you pray or hear from Holy Spirit, pay attention, put on your spiritual ears, and start looking for the answer, because it is close.

Back then, my church didn't emphasize the promise of Holy Spirit connected to baptism, so I lacked understanding. One day I was seeking, and Jesus so profoundly impressed me that something was about to happen. I was at my secular job and went to the bathroom before my lunch break. In the stall next to me I heard a lady singing worship. When we washed hands, I told her I liked her singing and she asked me, "Have you received the gift of the Holy Spirit?" She ministered to me in the name of the Lord, and I received!

"A time is coming and has now come when the true worshipers will worship the Father in the Spirit and in truth, for they are the kind of worshipers the Father seeks" (John 4:23). Dearly beloved, the time is now! We are in the last days of grace. You are reading this devotional because the Lord wants you saved, forgiven, and healed in your mind, body, soul, and spirit. Jesus wants His beautiful bride, the church, spotless and dressed in white. Now is the time!

Day 115 | KINGDUIT

A Time to Heal

PRAY: Lord, you say there is a time and season for every activity under heaven, grace my life to align with your heavenly clock. Give me peace when it seems like the nations of the world are not at peace. I speak "Shalom, Shalom, Shalom" over myself, my family, my nation, the world (Ecclesiastes 3:1).

I pray for the leaders of my nation, that they would have divine wisdom along with a desire to lead in righteousness and justice. Give them incredible signs that Almighty God is watching them and expecting them to honor Your ways (1 Timothy 2:1).

Grant me a willing spirit to receive and follow Holy Spirit by faith. Grant me courage to trust you with all my heart. Forgive me for ways I block or guard my heart from You and the ways I don't guard my heart from the things that steal my peace and mental health (Psalm 51:12).

I know the Bible says to forgive, give me a willing spirit to release the pain, frustration, and anger towards individuals and memories that are hard to let go. Lord, if there is a counselor that fears You and serves you that can help me unload and unpack issues in my life, show me. I will start talking about the details of my life. If it is a person, or group of humble people gathered to seek healing, show me your ways Lord. Help me not to judge the outside but trust You (James 4:2).

Lord, if I need to follow You in baptism, help me to obey Your commands. I am willing to receive all your gifts Lord; I will listen and look for your path of righteousness to open before me (Acts 2:38).

Lord Jesus, I claim the power of your blood to wash me and give me clean hands and a pure heart. Only by grace can I be healed and live in your wells and fountains of unending cleansing, refreshment, and renewal. Give me eyes to see and ears to hear what Holy Spirit wants to show me, even if it is difficult. I love you Lord, thank you for forgiving, cleansing, and healing me for Your glory! In Jesus Name (Proverbs 20:12).

Wisdom's Call

"Repent at My rebuke! Then I will pour out my thoughts to you, I will make known to you, my teachings. But since you refuse to listen when I call and no one pays attention when I stretch out my hand, since you disregard all my advice and do not accept my rebuke, I in turn will laugh when disaster strikes you; I will mock when calamity overtakes you."

Proverbs 1:23-26

The above text shows a reason for disaster. Either you or someone from your ancestry has bowed to the gods/idols. It's not a joke, but many mock God and take His name in vain. Many won't seek the Lord for wisdom regarding life's disasters.

God laughs at those who refuse to repent! Sometimes the hard way is the only way to victory. If it takes hardship to wake up and get things right, praise God for your trouble. You might say, "I've honestly lived right!" Joshua would have truly said that too, but his family/fellow Jews were worshiping idols and false gods, and the community was literally stuck in the desert. To break that off his family line, Joshua had to be the one to go to battle to stop the insanity! Look at Paul, he taught New Testament believers to battle in Ephesians 6!

Some of the worst characters in the Bible are murderers, prostitutes, and religious zealots who repented. The Lord loves the outcast and the disregarded! He understands back stories that make people act out. Whoever is willing to repent and receive His love and power will be vessels of honor.

If you are still breathing, there is hope! You still have a chance to repent, turn to the Lord and escape the soon coming judgment. Repentance (180 turn) brings cleansing and forever sin removal.

ART THERAPY DRAW: Draw a triangle road sign with U-turn arrow. "Peter replied, Repent and be baptized, every one of you, in the name of Jesus Christ for the forgiveness of your sins. And you will receive the gift of the Holy Spirit." Acts 2:38

Day 117 | KINGDUIT

"The Lord will guide you always; He will satisfy your needs in a sun-scorched land and will strengthen your frame. You will be like a well-watered garden, like a spring whose waters never fail."

Isaiah 58:11

This book is the fruit of my healing! I hope it's like a spring that nourishes your Jesus vine unto soul fruitfulness!

Thirty years ago, Holy Spirit started walking in the garden of my life, which was a tangled mess. One thing I had was a deep desire for things to be made right. I was ignorant to the ways of God, but He kept drawing me near with cords of kindness while I possessed faith to follow.

The journey is wonderful and treacherous at the same time, but His love is better than life's hardships. I realized, He keeps showing me glorious things, so He is worthy of my quick obedience! My journey started with a strong biblical foundation, then service and prayer training, a season of dietary changes and fasting, major family forgiveness, deep pruning soul work, then the secular mental health counseling master's degree, then National cultural mental health swamp shock, intercession and warrior training, and more supernatural equipping for total victory.

Just like precious Saint Peter got to deal with Satan's sifting as wheat through his life, so did I. The One who lives to intercede for me ensured my faith would not fail. As I turn back to give what was freely given me via this devotional, its intent is to strengthen my brothers and sisters all around the world (from Luke 22:31-32). Jesus, my true vine, appointed me to go and bear lasting fruit from my God Garden, fruit that will remain!

ART THERAPY DRAW: Draw a grape vine filled with fruit.

"This is to my Father's glory, that you bear much fruit, showing yourselves to be my disciples.."

John 15:8

A mother had a psychologically sick child and didn't know what to do. A traumatic accident left the toddler marred on the outside of his body. The doctors cared for the child's wounds, but the event was so shocking that it completely shut down the child's emotional expression. As he grew, his body healed, but his mind was stuck. The boy wore a hoodie to hide his scars and didn't talk, cry, or laugh. When the medical community stopped providing solutions, the mother was beside herself and prayed for a solution. She clung to Psalm 103.

Just like Mary anointed Jesus' feet for His death, resurrection and life, the mother was impressed to put oil on the child's feet by faith and pray for an emotional, psychological resurrection of her son's invisible soul. She sensed the process would take time and would be a difficult because the Lord would let the child's memories surface, causing emotional trauma from recall.

The mother had to be patient and comfort the child when the memories surfaced. She anointed the child's feet and prayed every day. At first the child was traumatized again with memories and started fearful moaning. The mother stayed close and kept praying. Then the child started crying out words, describing the incident. Mom listened and helped the child remember. Soon the child was talking more and elaborated on the visions he saw in his mind from the incident when he was a toddler. The mother filled in the blanks, kept loving gently and tenderly while he retold the story. Because the child was surrounded by his kind mother in a safe place to process emotions, they cried together. The mental pain was leaving day by day, and one day the child said, "It's gone! I'm better!" They shared the story again, and as his mind healed, they soon could make the story funny and laugh about the odd event. The child was emotionally restored because his mother tended to the healing of her son's mind, memory, and emotions.

"Bless the Lord, oh my soul; all that is within me, bless His Holy name. Bless the Lord, O my soul, and forget not all his benefits-who pardons all your iniquities, who heals all your diseases, who redeems your life from the pit, who crowns you with loving kindness and compassion."

Psalm 103:1-4

Day 119 | KINGDUIT

"When Jesus had washed their feet and put on His outer garments, He reclined with them again and asked, 'Do you know what I have done for you? You call me Teacher and Lord, and rightly so, because I am. So, if I, your Lord and Teacher, have washed your feet, you also should wash one another's feet. I have set you an example so that you should do as I have done for you. Truly, truly, I tell you, no servant is greater than his master, nor is a messenger greater than the one who sent him. If you know these things, you will be blessed if you do them."

John 13:12-17

As Jesus washes our feet, we should follow His example and care for others. The story of a mother's faith and love is a real example of how simple, yet profound psychological restoration can be. This is true for adults, young people, or anyone, if they are in a safe counseling/talking space, they heal quickly. The trauma is like a weed sprout that easily pulls out of the dirt and the empty space is filled with loving health, then sealed with divine protection. Still, they must return to a safe living situation.

Most of us reading this devotional are adults with issues that have embedded themselves in our hearts, choking our minds with the enemies lies that, over time, have come to intertwine with our identity. That's why the liar (devil) loves to mess with a young generation's soul, knowing that his wicked plans will mar the mind as he/she grows into adulthood, making it harder to change. The vile attack on children in school and on social media surely is the work of the enemy.

If it's difficult to press into this mental healing relationship with our King Jehovah Rapha, it's normal. Perhaps acquiring and using the encouragement in this devotional will equip you to pass on the healing to the next generation of young ones. They must have a chance at the freedom of mental health so they can carry Christ's light in the days to come. God is a faithful and good God. He will never leave us, He will help us and He will do it! Kingduit!

ART THERAPY DRAW: Draw a picture of a foot washing bin. Get a bin and wash and anoint your own feet. Then ask Jesus to help you walk out your mental healing journey so that your internal soul-strength will grow.

A Prayer for Children

PRAY: "For this reason, since the day we heard about you, we have not stopped praying for you and asking God to fill you with the knowledge of His will in all spiritual wisdom and understanding, so that you may walk in a manner worthy of the Lord and may please Him in every way; bearing fruit in every good work, growing in the knowledge of God" (Colossians 1:9-10).

We bless the children of our nations with a deep awareness of their Abba Father in heaven, that He watches over them and protects them. May they know that Almighty God is only a call away. We pray that every child will be divinely and supernaturally protected, especially with their sexual identity.

"We bless them to be strengthened with all power according to His glorious might so that they may have full endurance and patience" (Colossians 1:11) to endure ridicule, overcome social media pressure, find the Shalom peace of God, and believe God is greater than the darkness of the world. Supernatural protection, in Jesus Name!

We bless them with joy, a child's carefree and wonder-filled joy. We bless them with happy parents, laughing friends and pure companions. We bless them with rich souls, minds, emotions, and intellect that can grasp the goodness of God in the land of the living. We bless them with exposure to the Word of God and the stories of the bible in simplicity and love. At a young age, may they desire to live a life worthy of the Lord, to please Him, no matter what happens.

We bless them with divine vision, to see the Lord and want to serve Him with a good attitude and a hard-working spirit. May they possess a will for goodness and grace, a forgiving spirit and a heart that never gives up. May they have a divine vision that God has angels to care for them and a reward for them in heaven as they run in God's race.

May they receive such amazing blessings in their days that they know beyond a shadow of a doubt this is from GOD! They say in their hearts, "God loves me so much, God always blesses me! I will love and serve Him all my days, even if it's hard or I struggle to find a godly friend, I LOVE JESUS!" As a result, they know the King of Healing and glory - all their days of their lives!

MONTH 5 - Temple Foundation

KINGDUIT | Day 121

"I will make rivers flow on barren heights, and springs within the valleys. I will turn the desert into pools of water, and the parched ground into springs."

Isaiah 41:18

It can be difficult to pursue mental healing. Those I know who found the courage to face themselves struggled with the unpacking of things hidden inside the soul.

One master's class I took was about Family Systems. Therefore, I had to review my family tree with fellow students. I couldn't stop crying, shaking and tears kept flowing as I completed my verbal assignment under the listening ears of my professor and classmates. As we studied, we all experienced some type of brokenness, exposure to our internal denials, trembling, and outbursts of anger. One semester we participated in group therapy. Oh my, Lord have mercy! Then the secular sex therapy class, which was marked by godless perversion. My brain needed divine cleansing along with multiple prayers spoken over me, so that I could persevere and keep my heart pure.

During our studies at Hebrew University of Jerusalem, we did the clinical work of Trauma Counseling. It involved processing personal tragic events amongst us. What a hot mess we were: shaking, crying, pushing back for fear, national debates (the group was from countries around the world), judging classmates' stories, and stopping the process of therapy because it was too hard.

The global leader of that program is the founder of the Israel Center for the Treatment of Psychotrauma. His father was a doctor who survived the Holocaust. We were under the best care in the world as it relates to trauma removal and still, we were shaken. No matter what is inside, know that the God who made the lilies of the valley, a symbol of returning to happiness, is right by your side with a promise to never leave you. His love for you endures forever and ever!

ART THERAPY DRAW: Draw a brain with something stuck inside representing a traumatic event. Show your picture to the Lord. Ask Him to protect your soul, give you the timing and courage to process it one day.

Day 122 | KINGDUIT

"When you pass through the waters, I will be with you; and when you pass through the rivers, they will not sweep over you. When you walk through the fire, you will not be burned; the flames will not set you ablaze."

Isaiah 43:2

What an amazing promise to claim for our biblical mental healing journey as we put our souls before the living God of the Universe, the one whose love endures forever. The Lord is our perfect rose in the garden, and its troubled thorns come from the world. Jesus said, "I have told you these things, so that in me you may have peace. In this world you will have trouble. But take heart! I have overcome the world" (John 16:33).

I cannot urge you enough to diligently and with great consistency, offer your mental health up to the Lord. Jesus will be right there with you every step of the way, even providing helpers on the path. You may go through all types of waters; from tears to swells of tragic memories, to rivers of hardships, yet He will never let go! As the fires of human anger, hurt, anxiety, resentment, stress, strain, betrayal, abuse, lies, and bitter pain surface with great distress in heart, mind and even trembling of body, Jesus will not let you be consumed. He will guard those flames and make sure they produce a refining like gold. The cleansing removes until the ash turns white and blows away.

PRAYER OF THANKS

Thank you, Lord, for being my Maker, forming me in the womb of my mother. Thank you for helping me along this season of healing. Thank you for blotting out my transgressions and cleansing my sin. Thank you for being faithful to complete the healing work that you have started in my heart and soul. Thank you for understanding all my thoughts, all my ways, all my stories and all the events in my life. Thank you that you won't let the waters of those events overwhelm me and you won't let me be torched by the fiery trails that have transpired along the way. Most of all, thank you that your love endures forever and ever. Your love is perfect. Thank you for peace and renewal. Hold me Lord, as I receive lasting blessings!

ART THERAPY

- a creative review of your healing journey -

No one can count the ways people heal, from a whisper to a whirlwind, music, drums, nature, water, history, food, movement, art, relationships, the list goes on. The more knowledge one has about the healing process, the more they can apply the kaleidoscope of resources to lead them to green pastures of peace and rest.

Art museums are an incredible way to see how history and culture utilized creative expression for help and healing. The bible utilizes it all, especially art! The original temple tabernacle tent was designed by the Lord to visually communicate God's presence and involvement in the lives of His people. It was a beautiful and deeply symbolic detailed rendering of the entire history of the world, humanity's relationship to God and even a picture of heaven. Before that, Noah's ark was an enormous active installation, a structure never seen by man's eye. It included the building reveal with an epic animal kingdom grand finale' displayed to highlight the severity of God's divine message to mankind through Noah.

The primary way therapy is done with children is through art and non-verbal creativity/play. That gives us a clue that it doesn't matter what the art looks like, what it is made of, or the value of the components, it's about the desired effect in the human heart and mind. Jesus said, "Let the little children come to me, and do not hinder them, for to such belongs to the kingdom of God" (Mark 10:14). Therefore, if art therapy is good for children, surely it is good for us!

You will be prompted to draw simple things as you read this devotional. Drawing is intended to help your mind grasp biblical and therapeutic concepts so understanding will increase. In addition, your personal drawings will mirror your feelings. The art will help you understand yourself and even serve as another means to communicate with the Lord.

ART THERAPY DRAW: Draw a picture of how the God of the Bible will shower His love on you as it relates to mental healing.

Day 124 | KINGDUIT

"Therefore, come out from them and be separate," says the Lord. "Touch no unclean thing, and I will receive you."

2 Corinthians 6:17

BIBLICAL ACTIONS	COUNSEL INSIGHTS
• Confession	Trauma Removal
• Forgiveness	Releasing Emotions
• Resting in Christ	Unpacking Life Events
• Role of the Will	Behavior Review
• Soul-level Healing	Attaching Meaning
• Role of Prayer	Talk Therapy
• Helper Holy Spirit	Writing Therapy
• Soul Salvation	Role of Pain/Suffering
• Decree Speaking	Rest/Restore Sleep
• Survey Lists Forgiveness	Family Ancestry Insight
• Bible Reading/Gnosis	Diagnosis
• Singing/Worship	ICD-10 & DSM-5
• Holy Spirit vs. spirits	Safe Sharing Space

"And I will be a Father to you, and you will be my sons and daughters, says the Lord Almighty.' Therefore, since we have these promises, dear friends, let us purify ourselves from everything that contaminates body and spirit, perfecting holiness out of reverence for God."

2 Corinthians 6:18

Sit before the Lord & rest in His presence. Write down thoughts and/or wisdom. Freely talk to Him about any subject, then listen.

ART THERAPY DRAW & WRITE: Illustrate a location that you think you would be the most comfortable experiencing the Lord as the Wonderful Counselor. Draw a cloud in the air close by and label a name of God, for example: Father, Abba, Jesus, Healer, Holy Spirit, Prince of Peace, etc. . . . Then write out a mental healing subject that interests you at this point in your journey, for example: fears, stresses, anxiety, deep wounds, personality flaws, etc... Make sure you take time to listen and write or illustrate the wisdom you received.

Day 126 | KINGDUIT

"When Moses went up on the mountain, the cloud covered it, and the glory of the Lord settled on Mount Sinai. For six days the cloud covered the mountain, and on the seventh day the Lord called to Moses from within the cloud. The Lord said to Moses, "Tell the Israelites to bring me an offering. . . Then have them make a sanctuary for me, and I will dwell among them. Make this tabernacle and all its furnishings exactly like the pattern I will show you."

Exodus 24: 15-16 | 25:1-2, 8-9

This month we will use art therapy to review what we learned about Biblical mental health from God's house. We will have many simple assignments to help us understand critical concepts to better relate to our Wonderful Counselor!

Today we are going back to the desert, under the leadership of Moses. The Lord loved Moses and as recorded in Numbers 12:3 & 7, Moses was humbler than anyone on the face of the earth. He got visions, dreams, prophesies, and the Lord said Moses was faithful in all His house. Clearly the Lord trusted Moses to carry out His wishes as found in Exodus 24/25, which was to have a tabernacle tent built to exact specifications, including furnishings.

Can you imagine the God of the Universe showing you a design project, including interiors and lighting with the intent to dwell within your community? It's astounding! Even more amazing, this design is the foreshadowing of a part of your life as a believer.

When I realized the weight of this, I created a simple glass tent about five inches tall and put it on my nightstand. I look at it with the wonder that His great love is inside the tent of my body!

ART THERAPY DRAW OR BUILD: Build a simple tent from scrap or found materials.

"But that night the word of the Lord came to Nathan, saying, 'Go and tell my servant David that this is what the Lord says: Are you the one to build for Me a house to dwell in? For I have not dwelt in a house from the day I brought the Israelites up out of Egypt until this day, but I have moved about with a tent as my dwelling, in all My journeys with all the Israelites, have I ever asked any of the leaders I appointed to shepherd My people Israel, why haven't you built Me a house of cedar?"

2 Samuel 7:4-7

One reason King David was a man with a heart for the Lord was that he cared deeply about the things of God. He loved to praise, worship, love, trust, repent, revere, obey and hold sacred the physical things God designed from Israel's history.

Joshua led the Jews out of the desert and into the Promise Land, but he didn't get instructions to reassemble the tabernacle tent. The first king the nation of Israel had, King Saul, mostly ignored the physical historical artifacts designed by God during his forty-year reign. On the contrary, King David built a special tent to make sure the sacred furnishings endured through the war season.

When King David defeated Israel's war enemies, the Lord gave him rest on every side. That's when King David told the Prophet Nathan, he couldn't rest in his home knowing the Lord's furnishings were in tent storage. King David pulled on God's heart strings because that night the Lord spoke to Nathan from the scripture above.

Straight away God made a covenant with David, that his descendant (King Solomon) would build the house of God. King David was promised a kingdom and a throne that endured forever because Jesus was a direct descendant from the line of King David. To this day, the City of David is just outside the old city of Jerusalem. "This is the genealogy of Jesus the Messiah the son of David" (Matthew 1:1).

WRITE IT OUT FEELINGS TO THE LORD: David wrote how he felt about God: "I love you, Lord; you are my strength" (Psalm 18:1). What would you write?

Day 128 | KINGDUIT

"Now, Lord my God, you have made your servant king in place of my father David. But I am only a little child and do not know how to carry out my duties."

Solomon in 1 Kings 3:7

Solomon's father, King David, passed away and left him with the architectural plans to build the first stone temple patterned after the tabernacle Moses received on Mount Sinai.

What an enormous responsibility for a young man! But, without a doubt, Solomon understood the importance of his assignment. The building design of the first stone temple is in 1 Kings 6, 7, 8, 9, & 10, it's a fascinating read in the Bible. The story is paired with Solomon's enormous wealth and splendor. These scriptures will clarify the rich value, glory, and majesty of God's house.

ART THERAPY DRAW: Draw a picture from Solomon's temple design project or wealth. For example, there were 15-foot carved wooden angels made for the temple and 25 tons of gold given to Solomon each year.

"For we are the temple of the living God. As God has said: 'I will live with them and walk among them, and I will be their God, and they will be my people."

2 Corinthians 6:16

You might be thinking, how did one of the most sacred places on the earth in the most epic geographical center of the world, go from Solomon's Temple on the Temple Mount in Israel to right here and now in the temple of my body?

God did it! The tent design in the wilderness pointed to the Lord in every stunning detail. The power, manifestation and glory of God was present for the people and yet they were still rebellious. Hundreds of years had passed, and God provided Saul as King and the sacred articles were in storage. Only David grasped the grand value, so he honored the Lord with a desire to build the first stone Temple. Years later the Jews still rebelled, and that temple was destroyed.

Years had passed and the second Temple was erected, but religious and governmental systems were so corrupt that the temple grounds became a money exchange marketplace. When Jesus witnessed materialism, he was livid and destroyed things. "The Jews then responded to him, 'What sign can you show us to prove your authority to do all this?'

Jesus answered them, 'Destroy this temple and I will raise it again in three days.'

They replied, 'It has taken forty-six years to build this temple, and you are going to raise it in three days?'

But the temple Jesus had spoken of was his body" (John 2:18-21). Jesus was thirty-three years old, that means the second Temple was built 13 years prior to His birth and only stood for another 40 years after his death.

God was doing something new in world history. Jesus was a new temple that was mobile and was a human tabernacle! The old system didn't work and God so loved humanity that He needed people to have 24-hour access to His mercy seat, to forgiveness, cleansing, equipping and wisdom. That's why Father was seeking worshippers who worship in Spirit and in truth! No more buildings and systems, only love, power, and a sound mind! "Christ in you, the hope of glory" (Colossians 1:27)!

THERAPY EXPLAIN: Summarize how did God moved from invisible to in us?

Day 130 | KINGDUIT

"And they are to construct an ark of acacia wood, two and a half cubits long, a cubit and a half wide, and a cubit and a half high. Overlay it with pure gold both inside and out and make a gold molding around it."

Exodus 25:10-11

The translations of the dimensions above are close to four feet long by two feet two feet wide and high. It is a gold overlaid rectangular box, with two winged angels facing each other on top of the ark lid. Part of the instructions for beginning the work, was that material provisions were to come from a man "whose heart compels him" (Exodus 25:2). The Lord loves a willing heart!

This ancient chest is the holiest artifact of all time. It was designed by God, managed by Moses, and crafted by skilled Israeli workers. It carried the presence and glory of God, and with that holy designation, those who touched it outside the Lord's instructions were killed. The ancient chest, called the ark of the covenant, moved with the Israelites as they possessed the Promise Land. "At that time the Lord set apart the tribe of Levi to carry the ark of the covenant of the Lord, to stand before the Lord to minister and to pronounce blessings in his name" (Deuteronomy 10:8).

If you translate that into our post-Christ understanding of the temple of God, it's another amazing miracle of grace that we carry the presence and glory of God, and yet live. The New Testament describes it this way; "Beyond all question, the mystery from which true godliness springs is great" (1 Timothy 3:16).

ART THERAPY DRAW: Search and look up a picture of the Ark of the Covenant that includes gold inside and out, angels, and carrying poles. Draw a simple replica of a rectangular box with two angels and poles. Think about or ask why God would put His glory in this box?

"And you are to construct the mercy seat of pure gold, two and a half cubits long and a cubit and a half wide. Make two cherubim of hammered gold at the ends of the mercy seat, one cherub on one end and one on the other, all made from one piece of gold."

Exodus 25:17-19

She cried out, "Oh my God!" in devastating emotional pain. "Where is God?" she screamed.

The Christian counselor said, "He's right here, inside you and me." Then quoted Jesus regarding Holy Spirit in John 14:27; "Peace I leave with you; My peace I give you . . . let not your hearts be troubled; nor let them be fearful." In a moment, whoosh, the peace of God filled the small room, and the woman took a breath and got quiet.

What happened? The counselor understood the reality of God at work inside the mind of a human. The only difference between the two was knowledge and application. If the lady was not taught in a faith setting, or did not listen to the teaching, and then did not apply the truth, or did not seek understanding, or did not believe, then she would not understand the reality of Christ, the Prince of Peace inside her being.

The bible is God's expression of Jesus Christ. If you want to find God, Jesus, or the Holy Spirit, look deeply into the Word. In the passage above we have a golden rectangular box with angels on top, similar in dimension to the human torso and head. The soul's mind, intellect and emotion is located in the torso. Those who have received the mercy of God through Jesus have total spiritual access to the throne of God in heaven, a golden city with worshiping angels. Since we have the "mind of Christ'" (1 Corinthians 2:16), we are told to confidently enter the Most Holy Place by the blood of Jesus.

ART THERAPY DRAW/CONSTRUCT: Draw a model of the ark by taping four business cards into a rectangular box, with open ends. Tape two straws on each side for poles. Be creative, make two angels with wings on top.

"The Holy Spirit also testifies to us about this. First, He says: 'This is the covenant I will make with them after that time, says the Lord. I will put my laws in their hearts, and I will write them on their minds'. Then he adds: "Their sins and lawless acts I will remember no more."

Hebrews 10:15-17

"Place the cover on top of the ark and put in the ark of tablets of the covenant law that I will give you" (Exodus 25:21). "I will put my laws in their hearts, and I will write them on their minds" (Hebrews 10:16). "He will command His angels concerning you to guard you in all your ways" (Psalm 91:11).

Your simple mode from yesterday shows how God moved around in the Old Testament Israel.

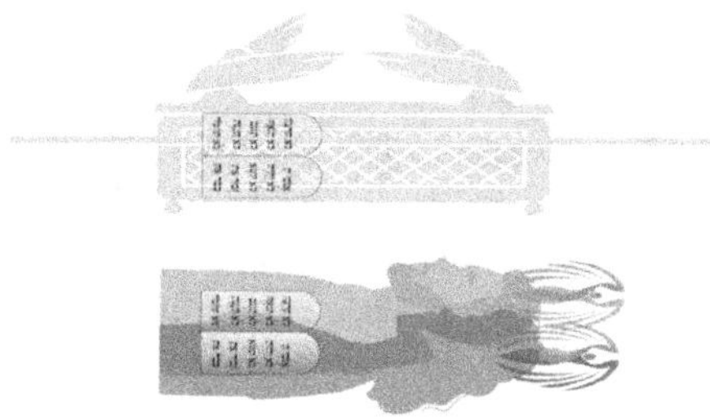

WRITE IN GOD'S INSTRUCTIONS: Where were the tablets of the covenant law placed in the Old Testament? ______________________
Where were the covenant laws placed in the New Testament? ______________________

"Behind the second curtain was a room called the Most Holy Place, which had the golden altar of incense and the gold-covered ark of the covenant. This ark contained the gold jar of manna, Aaron's staff that had budded, and the stone tablets of the covenant."

Hebrews 9:3-4

Constructing simple mock temple furnishings for ourselves like you did in yesterday's study, can help us understand more of what the Lord has put in our hearts and written on our minds. If the kingdom of God belongs to the little children and we are encouraged to humble ourselves so God can lift us up, then these simple exercises will yield fruit in our lives. If you have children or care for children, bring them into this art therapy.

During this review month, let's keep constructing/crafting the holy articles and furnishings so a strong foundation of God's vision over our lives can grow in behavioral and spiritual manifestation. Art therapy exercises will help understand how the presence of God can increase in our lives.

These exercises align with the biblical action of bible reading and specific study along with attaching symbols. On the counseling insights side, it helps with the attaching meaning to healing. The Lord told Moses to put the three items listed below into the Ark of the Covenant (the gold-covered box with angelic lid). Therefore, gather your scale model of the Ark of the Covenant. Then make/collect something symbolic to the three items listed below.

ART THERAPY DRAW: "And you are to construct. . ." Exodus 25:17 Draw the three items below. Think of how Moses literally put these items in the solid gold ark in obedience to God's instructions.

- Gold Jar of Manna
- Aaron's staff that budded flowers
- Stone tablets of the covenant

Day 134 | KINGDUIT

"Jesus said to them, 'Very truly I tell you, it is not Moses who has given you the bread from heaven, but it is my Father who gives you the true bread from heaven. For the bread of God is the bread that comes down from heaven and gives life to the world.'

'Sir,' they said, 'always give us this bread.'

Then Jesus declared, 'I am the bread of life. Whoever comes to me will never go hungry, and whoever believes in me will never be thirsty."

John 6:32-35

God wanted to preserve the miracle of manna (bread-like wafer) in the desert so that the descendants of Israelites would remember the forty years God provided food from heaven for the Jewish people. Moses was commanded to have Aaron put a jar with the manna from the wilderness journey in the Ark of the Covenant before the Lord to be kept for the generations that followed.

When Jesus walked in Israel, people gathered by the thousands to listen to His teachings, they were hungry for God. Just like the Hebrews from the wilderness journey depended on God to rain down bread from heaven, the Jews looked for heavenly signs because they kept retelling the bread story of their ancestors. They told Jesus, "Our fathers ate the manna in the wilderness, as it is written: 'He gave them bread from heaven to eat" (John 6:31). Jesus could and did perform the real bread miracle! When Jesus repeated the truth that He indeed was the bread of life, the source of life and the heaven-sent provision for eternal life sent by God the Father, they grumbled and doubted Him.

Today Jesus is still the bread of life. He is the heavenly gift from the Father. He will provide everything you need for life. What do you need? He is the source, so ask Jesus for your daily bread. He can satisfy you! Believe that He exists and seek Him!

PRAY OUT LOUD: I am blessed in the name of Jesus Christ of Nazareth, the Most High God sent from Heaven. I have supernatural sustenance in all my ways. May heavenly provisions come my way. I will know they are from the hand of the God. My eyes are blessed with enlightened visions of total healing, liberty & peace!

"So, Moses spoke to the Israelites, and each of their leaders gave him a staff-one for each of the leaders of their tribes, twelve staffs in all. And Aaron's staff was among them. Then Moses placed the staffs before the LORD in the Tent of the Testimony. The next day Moses entered the Tent of the Testimony and saw that Aaron's staff, representing the house of Levi, had sprouted, put forth buds, blossomed, and produced almonds. Then Moses brought out all the staffs from the LORD's presence to all the Israelites."

Numbers 17:6-9

The staff represents leadership and authority. When a shepherd leads sheep, the rod or staff is used for protection, discipline, guidance, and power. We find the rod or staff throughout many passages in the bible. It is a tool for parenting, the comfort of God's divine correction and a symbol of God's power.

Aaron and Moses co-led the Israelites, even though Moses was the head leader. Aaron's staff was used in Egypt to demonstrate the power of God over Pharaoh's magicians. Even though they led with excellence, the Jews became embittered and grumbled against Moses's leadership. God told Moses to have all the tribal leaders put their staff before the Lord so God could sort out the leadership conflicts. Aaron's staff was the only one to bud, blossom and produce fruit.

In our times, the end times, the word staff represents church leadership. The bible says to "mark this: There will be terrible times in the last days. People will be lovers of themselves, lovers of money, boastful, proud, abusive, disobedient to their parents, ungrateful, unholy, without love, unforgiving, slanderous, without self-control, brutal, not lovers of the good, treacherous, rash, conceited, lovers of pleasure rather than lovers of God-having a form of godliness but denying its power. Have nothing to do with such people" (2 Timothy 31-5). Even modern leaders need God's help! Look for holy fruit (like Moses did) with leaders and those who influence your life.

ASK THE LORD: Pray for wisdom regarding your church leadership. Are they Holy Spirit led & able to navigate end-time challenges?

Day 136 | KINGDUIT

"The LORD gave me two stone tablets inscribed by the finger of God. One of them were all the commandments the LORD proclaimed to you on the mountain out of the fire, on the day of the assembly. At the end of the forty days and forty nights, the LORD gave me the two stone tablets, the tablets of the covenant."

Deuteronomy 9:10-11

The bible tells us exactly why God gave us the original stone tablets of the covenant or ten commandments. It was to keep His people out of slavery. He spoke the words to the people of God in a dramatic way. "All the people witnessed the thunder and lightning, the sounding of the ram's horn, and the mountain enveloped in smoke, they trembled and stood at a distance" (Exodus 20:18).

Look up the 10 commandments in Exodus 20:3-17, write them on two pieces of paper shaped like tablets while closely paying attention to the things in life that will keep you from being enslaved. These simple commands are like boundary lines that still work to protect your life from oppression. "I am the LORD your God, who brought you out of the land of Egypt, out of the house of slavery" (Exodus 20:2).

ART THERAPY DRAW: Look at your drawings of the commandments and ask the Lord if you have participated in any of the activities listed that would enslave you. Write down how those actions have kept you from experiencing freedom.

KINGDUIT | Day 137

"Then the Lord said to Moses. 'Tell the Israelites to bring Me an offering. You are to receive My offering from every man whose heart compels him. This is the offering you are to accept from them: gold, silver, bronze; blue, purple, and scarlet yarn; fine linen and goat hair; ram skins dyed red and fine leather; acacia wood; olive oil for the light; spices for the anointing oil and for the fragrant incense; and onyx stones and gemstone to be mounted on the ephod and breast piece. And they are to make a sanctuary for Me, so that I may dwell among them. You must make the tabernacle and design all its furnishings according to the pattern I show you."

Exodus 25:1-9

The God-centered construction project for the Israelites was a tent. It was a place of worship, but it was also a place of healing, cleansing, sin removal, sacrifice, protection, and a divine meeting location that included God, men, women, and angels. The Hebrews willingly collected the supplies to build the tabernacle. God's pattern had to be constructed precisely to welcome the manifold glory of God Almighty.

The manifold glory of God is an epic manifestation of God in multi-faceted meanings and implications. It is a glory that covers time, space, dimensions of heaven, earth, sky, holy fire, humanity, history, the angelic and eternal. Getting the build right meant the beginning of global redemption to fix the fall at the Garden of Eden. If the Jews got it right, then the glory of God would fall from heaven, resulting in a cause for high praise and sincere worship!

Since God previously displayed a different ark installation with Noah that ended in global destruction by water, He was doing a new thing in the desert with Israel. Understanding the tabernacle is foundational to our time in history as well as our personal lives. The goal of the Lord's New Testament project will never end and will accomplish everlasting eternal glory! "Then the cloud covered the tent of meeting, and the glory of the LORD filled the tabernacle" (Exodus 40:34).

WORSHIP: YouTube SING - "OUR GOD REIGNS!"

Day 138 | KINGDUIT

"Then the cloud covered the tent of meeting, and the glory of the LORD filled the tabernacle."

Exodus 40:34

Forty days after Easter is Ascension Day, the day Jesus Christ ascended into heaven through the clouds. He then sent the Holy Spirit and gave His authority to the disciples so they could do the greater works.

We have inherited that mandate as the Lord tabernacles amongst us, moving around in the tent of our bodies. Have you considered the tremendous power you possess as a believer? Do you believe the glory of the Lord can fill your bodily tabernacle? Do you know you reign with Christ? Have you ever used your authority to overcome any Pharaoh-like hold in your life to free your mind?

Since the goal of our faith is the salvation of our souls, what happens when our soul gets some cleansing and redemption? We start getting filled with inexpressible and glorious joy because we love God so much and believe He can free our souls. Then get ready, because the glory will happen, not just a little glory, the glory of the Lord that fills the earth and displays the wonders of our great God.

Take time to sing out and fill your heart with the honor, blessings, and high praises of our King. He is worthy of our songs of praise and worship. "Now to the King eternal, immortal, invisible, the only God, be honor and glory for ever and ever. Amen" (1 Timothy 1:17).

MEDITATE ON GLORY: Take time to keep singing and soaking in His presence! If you don't have any worship music that thrills you, ask the Lord to bring it to you. He knows exactly what your soul is longing to sing in this season of your life.

"Make a veil of blue, purple, and scarlet yarn, and finely spun linen, with cherubim skillfully worked into it. Hang it with gold hooks on four posts of acacia wood, overlaid with gold and standing on four silver bases. And hang the veil from the clasps and place the ark of the Testimony behind the veil. So, the veil will separate the Holy Place from the Most Holy Place."

Exodus 26:31-33

We have reviewed several items in the tabernacle: a simple tent, a scale model of the ark of the covenant/testimony with poles, a flowering, budding, almond branch, a golden jar for manna, and two tablets with the ten commandments written upon it. Today we will observe and construct the veil.

You can use string, yarn, paper, fabric, straws, a computer graphic, or whatever you can find to put together a small blue, purple, scarlet curtain with angels in the pattern, a gold pole and four silver bases. The silver bases can be nickels or dimes. Have fun and intentionally use the verse above as a directive. Today we build a mock curtain, tomorrow we tear the mock curtain as an action of faith.

This curtain was placed in the back of the tent to separate the Most Holy Place from the rest of the tent called the Holy Place. There are amazing illustrations online of this God designed structure. Only certain Hebrews could enter the most holy tent with the Lord's special furnishings. Understanding this veil will certainly give you holy confidence to draw near to God to find more and more mental freedom and liberty.

Remember that this curtain was a foreshadow of something in the New Testament that is spectacular.

ART THERAPY CONSTRUCT: Read the verse above and build the veil using simple objects. I used nickels, straws, glue, and paper I colored to match the verse. (HINT: Children love this kingdom stuff!)

Day 140 | KINGDUIT

"And when Jesus had cried out again in a loud voice, he gave up his spirit. At that moment the curtain of the temple was torn in two from top to bottom. The earth shook, the rocks split, and the tombs broke open. The bodies of many holy people who had died were raised to life."

Matthew 27:50-52

For those of you who feel like there is drama in your life or that you are criticized for that drama, God loves you and He can handle it all!

The crucifixion of Christ is often called the passion of Jesus. The final days of His life on earth were very dramatic. God was making a huge statement through the life of Christ. Even the natural world took part in this display of redemption. The earth shook, the rocks split, tombs broke open and a very special thick curtain in the temple, the curtain from Moses's desert design, was invisibly torn. It tore in two from top to bottom, that's approximately a 43-foot-high curtain rip.

The curtain had remained in one piece almost two thousand years since the time it was constructed. Then this moment happened: Jesus cried out in a loud voice, gave up His spirit, died, and the curtain ripped in half! The curtain spontaneously tears open completely from the top to bottom.

It was called a veil, which has many meanings, but primarily a veil is used to conceal something. Whether a bride's beautiful face at a wedding, the truth of the gospel, or in this case the entrance to the most holy place on earth. The thirty-by-thirty-foot square room composed of divine furnishings was now open to all, whosoever believes in the son of God, Jesus Christ of Nazareth! Behind that curtain is the ark of testimony and the mercy seat with angels of protection. "Let us approach God's throne of grace with confidence. . ." (Hebrews 4:16).

- Get curtain craft from yesterday (or a napkin)
- Think about the symbolic colors, metals, angels
- Find the center and top section
- Thank Jesus for opening veil for you to find and have direct access to God
- Tear open the curtain craft (or napkin) from the top to bottom and pray with thanksgiving!

"And place the Bread of the Presence on the table before Me at all times."

Exodus 25:30

The Lord's Presence

PRAYER: Spirit of the living God, fall fresh on me with your presence. Thank you, Jesus, for being the Bread of Life, without sin, without yeast, the perfect sustenance for my life. You are holy and there is none like you. I place the bread of Your presence at the center of my heart (John 6:35).

"You have made known to me the path of life; You will fill me with joy in Your presence, with eternal pleasures at Your right hand" (Psalm 16:11). Like King David Lord, I also say "I saw the Lord always before me. Because He is at my right hand, I will not be shaken. Therefore, my heart is glad, and my tongue rejoices; my body also will rest in hope" (Acts 2:25-26). Let me experience your presence Lord, to see you and sense your nearness, let me have a happy heart, a hope filled soul and a praising mouth. Let my mind and body be healed because I seek you with all my heart and believe!

"Tremble, O earth, at the presence of the Lord, at the presence of the God of Jacob, who turned the rock into a pool, the flint into a fountain of water" (Psalm 114:7-8)! Even in turbulent times, your presence gives me peace. No matter what happens in the nation, city and family, your presence can break through the hard places in my life. You will satisfy my soul with healing and help.

From this day forward, my spirit will run to the table of the Lord, and I will acquaint myself with the bread of the presence of the Lord. Yes Lord, "You prepare a table before me in the presence of my enemies. You anoint my head with oil, my cup overflows. Surely your goodness and love will follow me all the days of my life, and I will dwell in the house of the LORD forever" (Psalm 23:5-6). I desire the good things from God's table. I will hunger for righteousness. I will find great joy in the Lord, I will be protected, I will have peace (Matthew 5:6)!

ART THERAPY DRAW: Draw a simple table with a loaf of bread on top.

Day 142 | KINGDUIT

"Then you are to make a lampstand of pure, hammered gold. It shall be made of one piece, including its base and shaft, its cup, and its buds and petals. Six branches are to extend from the sides of the lampstand - three on one side and three on the other."

Exodus 25:31-32

Do a word study: Search and read the occurrences of the almond tree in the bible. Seek out and understand the symbolism of the almond tree. The lampstand in the holy place of the tabernacle was like an almond tree, or you can say it was a golden almond branch lamp complete with blossoms, buds, and petals. This lampstand has multidimensional meaning, here are a few:

- Stages of growth: almond flower/bud/blossom
- Sevenfold lamp pointing to the sevenfold Spirit of the Lord
- Jesus is the light of the world (John 8:12)
- You are the light of the world (Matthew 5:14)
- Almond tree prophetic/symbolizing watchfulness
- Almond branch (Aaron's staff)
- Oil based light - Holy Spirit

Now it's your turn to search scriptures and learn why this sacred golden oil-based lamp was placed outside the most holy place of the tabernacle tent. Find the hidden meaning and symbolism of the almond tree, especially for these end times.

Every time of study into the Word of God is an investment of healing into our soul and mental health. As we read the Bible, our mind gets renewed and transformed into God's holiness so that we can find God's will. No doubt God wills our minds to be strong, but He can't make that happen, we must be willing to seek out God's will. "Do your best to present yourself to God as one approved, a worker who does not need to be ashamed and who correctly handles the word of truth" (2 Timothy 2:15).

"Command the Israelites to bring you clear oil of pressed olives for the light so that the lamps may be kept burning."

Exodus 27:20

Almost three decades ago, on Christmas, my husband and I were seeking the Lord, looking to find God's purpose for our lives. We had only walked with the Lord for a few years, so no doubt, we were in the bud stage of our spiritual development. Our home was filled with festive holiday decor, and we each bought a special gift for one another. That Christmas morning my gift was a large oddly shaped box lying flat on the floor. I opened it to find a unique bronze metal light fixture in the shape of a branch with leaves and flowers opening in front of white lights. At the time I had no biblical understanding of prophetic symbolism, but the Lord knew I needed a clear picture of His intentions for my biblical journey.

That year I read the bible through and found an inspiring verse that said: "Your wife shall be like a fruitful vine within your house; your children will be like olive shoots around your table" (Psalm 128:3). I didn't realize then how precious fruitfulness and olive oil was to the Lord.

The lampstand in the tabernacle used pure olive oil to keep the lights continually burning before the Lord. God knew I'd quest for mental healing even more when children came along. My hope for them to have a childhood filled with God's light and love was paramount.

What I didn't realize at the time was that pure olive oil can only be produced by a pressing of the olives. If I would seek the Lord during life's hardships, I could produce lasting illuminating Holy Spirit oil in my heart as I parented a new generation. I could shine before the Lord just like my special lamp, and just like God's holy lampstand with an intention to glorify God on the inside.

Even though we can't see the physical light of God in our lives, the Lord can see that light in us every day. He knows how to use the pressure of this world in transforming us into something more illuminating than the best light show, something that will shine for generations, even into eternity.

ASK: Ask the Lord to give you wisdom about your personal lamp with His light inside.

Day 144 | KINGDUIT

"Jesus said, 'At that time the kingdom of heaven will be like ten virgins who took their lamps and went out to meet the bridegroom. Five of them were foolish, and five were wise. The foolish ones took their lamps but did not take any oil with them. The wise ones, however, took oil in jars with their lamps. The bridegroom was a long time in coming, and they all became drowsy and fell asleep."

Matthew 25:1-5

At the almost midway point of this devotional, you may be thinking, "I thought this was going to be a therapeutic manual, not a bible study. There are so many scriptures!" Or perhaps a religious spirit speaking through a local church goer is saying, "You can't take the bible literally, just pray to Jesus!" Maybe your mother is saying, "Whatever you do, just keep taking your prescriptions (pharmakeia in the Greek Bible/Strongs 5331)[21] and you will be fine."

Don't take my word for it, listen to what Jesus is saying about this time in history from Matthew 25:14-15. "Because of the multiplication of wickedness, the love of most will grow cold. But the one who perseveres to the end will be saved." Jesus also said to "be as shrewd as snakes and as innocent as doves" (Matthew 10:16).

The only way to outwit a serpent is to be wise like the serpent. Jesus modeled this for us when He was tempted by the lies of the enemy in the desert. Jesus used the sword of the Spirit, the Word of God to get the devil to leave Him alone. Jesus is the Word and Jesus is perfect, so it was easy for Him to come up with the proper scripture at the right time to defeat the lies. On the contrary, we must study the Word to get strong. Jesus humbled himself as a human being and suffered with that forty day fast, but Jesus also went to rabbinical school to study the scriptures as a young man.

Jesus knows a wicked culture does many things to humans, quenching divine love. Mental health problems can surely bring even a good man or woman down. Jesus is urging us to be wise and fill the lamp of God inside our spirit with fresh, pure Holy Spirit oil, enough to keep our lamps burning all the way until His surprise return. He doesn't want us drowsy with depression and sleepy because we are world-weary, Jesus wants us illuminated with holy fire and glory!

"The bridegroom was a long time in coming, and they all became drowsy and fell asleep."

Matthew 25:5

Seeking the Lord takes energy and mental determination. If it was easy, everyone would pursue God. It's exhausting and the stress of dealing with hard times, oppression, or deep-seated issues makes us want to just go to sleep and nap. You might see a counselor for this type of sleep issue and there might be a depression diagnosis, but the bible will point to something different.

Pursuing the Lord for mental health has greater challenges because the Lord will certainly lead the willing spirit of a man or woman straight to the root issues of the problems, they seek deliverance from. Root-level healing often brings opposition because when we get to the root, freedom rings in the soul. The enemy hates freedom!

Before I was liberated in Christ, I went through a season of intense spiritual warfare where sleep was my only relief. A blessed friend called to strengthen me with prayer until I found a way out of the darkness. Now I enter rest to seek Him instead of escape sleeping.

"Wait for the LORD, be strong and take heart and wait for the LORD" (Psalm 27:14). God knows waiting is difficult, especially in these times of immediate gratification. Jesus warns that the kind of sleep that prevents us from seeking Him will leave us without the oil needed to enlighten our hearts to overcome darkness.

Even the disciples couldn't stay awake when Jesus was sorrowful and deeply distressed prior to His crucifixion. "Then Jesus returned to His disciples and found them sleeping. "Couldn't you men keep watch with me for one hour?" he asked Peter. Watch and pray so that you will not fall into temptation. The spirit is willing, but the flesh is weak" (Matthew 26:40-41). Interestingly, the words of Jesus connect sleep with temptation.

If you stay up late to spend time with the Lord or get up early to seek His face, you will bring JESUS JOY which in turn will bless you beyond your wildest imagination. Your need for rest will come. "Behold, He who watches over Israel will neither sleep nor slumber" (Psalm 121:4).

"At midnight the cry rang out: But while they were on their way to buy the oil, the bridegroom arrived. The virgins who were ready went in with him to the wedding banquet. And the door was shut."

Matthew 25:6, 10

Oil Gathering Prayer

PRAYER: Wonderful Counselor, you were a man of sorrows, you were acquainted with grief, You were also despised and rejected, You were disregarded by people and yet You remained faithful. You are the Light of the world! Just like the golden lampstand was made of hammered gold and the oil was made from pressed olives, I praise you for staying faithful to the end, even when you had nails hammered in your body and thorns pressed into your head. Your mission of love as a human on the earth was executed with perfection. Now you truly understand the human condition, you understand me! Thank you that you never sleep or slumber, thank you that you live to pray for me!

When my hope seems lost, I can only think of suffering and bitter memories and my soul is downcast within me, I will remember Your great faithfulness, love, and endless compassion. Help me to endure the challenges of this world in faith (Isaiah 5:27) (Lamentations 3).

The Bible says depression is not always about me, depression is also rooted in oppression. Teach me Your way, O LORD, and lead me on a level path, because of my oppressors. Deliver me from foes, false witnesses, and the enemy of my soul. When I feel hard pressed on every side, let me know I don't have to be crushed, perplexed, or in despair. When I am persecuted for seeking You, let me know I will not be abandoned, struck down or destroyed. Let Your life be revealed in my spirit, soul and body every day (Psalm 121) (Isaiah 53) (2 Corinthians 4).

Your goodness is greater than anything happening around me. Help me to wait patiently for You, to be strong and courageous. Let my life bring you joy at the wedding feast in heaven. Give me oil for my inward lamp via Holy Spirit so that I will be prepared for your return. Lead me to the perfume and incense that brings joy to my heart so I will have the joy of the Lord as my strength (Proverbs 27:9).

"At midnight the cry rang out: 'Here's the bridegroom! Come out to meet him! Then all the virgins woke up and trimmed their lamps. The foolish ones said to the wise, 'Give us some of your oil; our lamps are going out.'

'No,' they replied, 'there may not be enough for both of us and you. Instead, go to those who sell oil and buy some for yourselves.'

But while they were on their way to buy the oil, the bridegroom arrived. The virgins who were ready went in with him to the wedding banquet. And the door was shut. Later the others also came. 'Lord, Lord,' they said, 'open the door for us!'

But he replied, 'Truly I tell you; I don't know you. 'Therefore, keep watch, because you do not know the day or the hour."

Matthew 25:6-13

Jesus's parable continues with lamp oil urgency as another Old Testament pattern shines into our moving and breathing lives today. Keep praying and seeking Jesus.

The Lord was also serious about the oil for the desert tabernacle. It had to be in the lampstand, and it had to be on everything. "Take the anointing oil and anoint the tabernacle and everything in it; consecrate it and all its furnishings, and it will be holy" (Exodus 40:9). Even Aaron and his sons were to be anointed.

When Jesus sent the disciples out for their healing ministry, He said the sick were to be anointed with oil. One recipient of healing, Mary Magdalene, experienced so much healing that seven demons came out of her. She got the oil blessing so much that she invested in expensive fragrant oil, saved it up in a special jar and paid her healing forward right to the feet of the King of Kings and Lord of Lords! Guess who Jesus visited first after His resurrection? Mary Magdalene!

Often, we obey Bible promises by faith, not knowing exactly how our blessing of obedience paid off. But this Holy Spirit oil promise paid off for Mary very well. Jesus made sure she was the first to smell the divine fragrance post-cross. Then, her story was placed in the Holy scriptures for all time.

Day 148 | KINGDUIT

"The LORD said to Moses, 'Take the following fine spices; 500 shekels of liquid myrrh, half as much of fragrant cinnamon, 250 shekels of fragrant calamus, 500 shekels of cassia - all according to the sanctuary shekel - and a hin of olive oil. Make these into a sacred anointing oil, a fragrant blend, the work of a perfumer. It will be the sacred anointing oil."

Exodus 30:22-26

"Then Mary took about a pint of pure nard, an expensive perfume; she poured it on Jesus' feet and wiped his feet with her hair. And the house was filled with the fragrance of the perfume" (John 12:3). Proverbs 27:9 says perfume and incense bring joy to the heart. Imagine being the one who anointed Jesus to give Him joy of heart before His brutal sacrifice. Imagine the comfort Mary brought to Jesus in His hour of need. The oil didn't come from religious service; it came from a heart of love and devotion from seeking the heart of her Savior.

I've never heard of a counselor anointing their clients with oil. When I attended secular counseling and/or Christian counseling, I was never anointed for mental healing. Yet when I joined sisters in the faith during a small group, we anointed each other. We gathered specifically for mental healing. That meeting began with a dab of oil on the forehead and a prayer of faith asking Holy Spirit to make us holy and set apart our time for soul-level healing. It worked!

When we gathered to seek Jehovah-Rapha, His presence and divine intervention worked among us! Amid tears from releasing trauma or shame, were the tears of unity, sisterly love, and joy in the presence of Jehovah Rapha.

The Lord's divine anointing oil recipe is recorded in Exodus 30:22-26. The ingredients of myrrh, cinnamon, calamus, cassia and olive oil are still available today. Of course, a dab of simple oil and a prayer of faith will work but having the scent directly from scriptures can make your healing journey more special. You could apply it every day as a prayer to God saying, "Show me the way to fill my lamp with oil so that my heart will forever be ready for your return!"

"Moses made the altar of incense out of acacia wood. It was square, a cubit long, a cubit wide, and two cubits high. Its horns were of one piece. And he overlaid with pure gold the top and all the sides and horns. Then he made a molding of gold around it. He made two gold rings below the molding on opposite sides to hold the poles used to carry it. And he made the poles of acacia wood and overlaid them with gold. He also made the sacred anointing oil and the pure, fragrant incense, the work of a perfumer."

Exodus 37:25-29

Have you ever picnicked on a sunny day with a wood fire pit burning fresh meat? Not only does your group get hungry from the smell but so do all the park goers in the area. Add the smell of fresh mowed grass with the remaining burning wood and you get the idea of the tabernacle incense. It's not only aromatic, but also warm and comforting. God created man in the image of God, so what God likes, we like!

The Lord wanted a special fire burning incense every morning and evening close to His mercy seat. "There I will meet with you, and from above the mercy seat, from between the two cherubim that are on the ark of the testimony I will speak with you about all that I will give you in commandment for the people of Israel" (Exodus 25:22).The Lord wanted to manifest His presence inside the tent, in the Most Holy Place, a veil away from the burning incense prepared by a perfumer. This is God's vibe, God's smell, and God's place to speak.

"I saw the Lord, high and exalted, seated on a throne; and the train of his robe filled the temple. Above him were seraphim, each with six wings; With two wings they covered their faces, with two they covered their feet, and with two they were flying. And they were calling to one another: 'Holy, holy, holy is the LORD Almighty; the whole earth is full of his glory" (Isaiah 6:1-3).

MEDITATE: The Lord commands angels to guard your way. He awaits you from a place of mercy. The Lord says, "Call to Me and I will answer you and tell you great and unsearchable things you do not know" (Jeremiah 33:3).

Day 150 | KINGDUIT

"Another angel, who had a golden censer, came and stood at the altar. He was given much incense to offer, with the prayers of all God's people, on the golden altar in front of the throne."

Revelation 8:3

Above is proof of how the bible interprets itself. The Old Testament Israelite tabernacle tent in the desert was the first temple. Then it was a pattern for the second temple made of stone. Then it was a pattern for the temple of Jesus' body. Then our bodies, and ultimately it all was a picture of heaven. The most consistent action of faith is represented by prayer. Jesus "always lives to intercede for us" (Hebrews 7:26). Similarly, we are told to pray without ceasing and from that lifestyle of worship is a sweet aroma. "But thanks be to God, who always leads us as captives in Christ's triumphal procession and uses us to spread the aroma of the knowledge of him everywhere" (2 Corinthians 2:14).

Not only do our prayers take us into the presence of God, but they also give us access to the counsel of God. In addition, our prayers are like an aromatic smell that spreads everywhere in this world, even all the way up to heaven to land in golden bowls mixed with incense on the altar in front of God's throne.

Our words, cries, requests, petitions, battle calls, praise, thanksgiving, and sacred communication with Almighty God are important, not only for us, but for the atmosphere of heaven. Of all the things we do as humans, prayer is powerful. King David said, "I call upon You, O Lord, come quickly to me. Hear my voice when I call to You. May my prayer be set before You like incense, my uplifted hands like the evening offering" (Psalm 141:1-2).

I believe biblical mental healing is the best, highest, and most transformative therapeutic effort towards soul-level healing that one can pursue. The wisdom of the Most High God is going to be the best solution for God's children. He is always at the mercy seat calling us to boldly approach His throne via incense-like prayers.

When we get to heaven, we will see God's throne, hear the choirs of angels singing, smell the incense from the golden sensors and behold the Lord upon His throne in front of golden bowls filled with our prayers. "Rejoice always, pray continually" (2 Thessalonians 5:17).

Altar of Incense

Write a letter to the Lord to clarify your understanding of prayers like incense before His throne in heaven. Thank Him for counting your life and heart cries with such high value. Seek wisdom to lead you to the next level of freedom and liberty in your mental health journey.

WRITE & PRAY: Start here, prayer write: Lord,

MONTH 6 - Garden Tending

Day 152 | KINGDUIT

"You are receiving the end result of your faith, the salvation of your souls."

1 Peter 1:9

The secular goal of therapy is to achieve better emotional and social functioning, and to positively improve and/or understanding life's challenges. Some people describe it as wanting to be filled with light and love, or to have peace. Many refer to mental health as a quest to live differently than their childhood or ancestors.

The Greek word for soul is psychon from psuche; breath, spirit, abstractly or concretely (Strong's 5590)[22]. The soul never dies, so it is the sum of your life now and for all eternity.

The root word psy is at the center of mental health practice. If you add ology, or the study of, you have psychology. Psychiatry is the healing of the mind that landed on the medicine side of mental health. A psychiatrist will prescribe medicine when the mental health counselor cannot. Psychology and psychiatry are modern scientific studies of human behavior that are less than two hundred years old.

Prior to this modern change, people were still practicing mental health the old-fashioned way, as Jesus taught the disciples, via demonic deliverance. "So, Jesus traveled throughout Galilee, preaching in their synagogues and driving out demons" (Mark 1:39).

When someone goes to a counselor, they are likely looking for a rescue or safety. Another word for rescue or safety is salvation. Our verse ties it all together stating that having our souls saved is the goal of our faith.

Secular mental health is not tied to faith or the Bible. We hope the secular mental health community offers pure healing, but you will find that America's National Board of Certified Counselors (NBCC)[23] constantly changes. So, if the nation devalues faith and the protection of children, so does the NBCC (which is currently pro sexual fluidity for children). This requires careful wisdom for the Christ follower prior to seeking professional secular help.

A bible-based healing points to freedom and godliness in this life to be prepared for Judgment Day. Bible centered health will lead the seeker on a path of righteousness and purity. "You are receiving the end result of your faith, the salvation of your souls."

"Examine yourselves to see whether you are in the faith; test yourselves. Do you not realize that Christ Jesus is in you-unless, of course, you fail the test?"

2 Corinthians 13:5

The process of soul salvation is searching, testing, examination, accountability to Holy Spirit led followers, fasting, repentance, and soul-searching before the Lord. We do this because "the human heart is the most deceitful of all things, and desperately wicked. Who really knows how bad it is" (Jeremiah 17:9)? The Lord promises full redemption, which means our lives must be redeemed, even our physical bodies. The only thing that remains in heaven is our soul.

There is no shame in the process of self-examination, even though the enemy loves to condemn us. The Lord is light and in Him there is no darkness. He blesses us when we freely welcome the light of Holy Spirit examination and soul revelation. As we seek, the Lord knows if we really mean it. He can clearly see if our hearts intend to turn away from the godlessness of our unredeemed lives.

There was a small-town pastor who led a young veteran to Christ, and he was totally saved. Prior to his salvation, the military man had been diagnosed with post-traumatic stress disorder (PTSD) by a government referred psychiatrist. He asked the pastor if he would attend and observe his counseling session. While attending the session, the psychiatrist was chain smoking and speaking crazy babble to his client. The psychiatrist turned to the pastor and said, "Well Pastor, what do you think?"

The pastor said, "I think you are way more screwed up than your client!"

The psychiatrist replied, "I think you are right; can you help me?" So, the man of God delivered him from a demon and exposed the psychiatrist to the Healer!

Our redemption is no joke; it came at the expense of the precious blood of Jesus Christ. Judgment Day is no joke, we will be held accountable for every part of our lives, even every careless word that we refuse to cleanse on earth. The good news is all confessed sin paired with repentance from our deceitful ways will be washed, cleansed, and be removed before Judgment Day.

Day 154 | KINGDUIT

"Therefore, with minds that are alert and fully sober, set your hope on the grace to be brought to you when Jesus Christ is revealed at His coming."

1 Peter 1:13

A liberated human soul has an alert mind and is fully sober. A clear and attentive mind can also be calm and peaceful. I see this as a picture of a warrior, one who is actively ready to move, even in chaotic surroundings while managing tasks in stealth mode. This doesn't mean someone has to know it all, it means they have mental clarity so they can peacefully figure out how to solve problems.

Christians are encouraged to set their hope on God's grace while waiting for His return. Mental freedom is connected to the return of Jesus Christ. It is very difficult to be alert and peaceful when there are daily struggles of fearful anxiety, bitterness, stress, and depression. Some are rooted in darkness, evil, unclean spirits, and the demonic. The unclean spirits that instigate negative feelings must be discerned and demolished straight away. These challenges are not part of God's plan, they oppose the blessing, joy and glory Jesus died to give all people.

Jesus is longing for a church (the bride of Christ) that is radiant and white as snow. Jesus is a good husband. When He ascended to heaven through the clouds, He didn't leave his people (the church) empty-handed, dull-minded, and without power. Jesus sent the Holy Spirit as the Helper. He gave us dynamic spiritual blessings and dynamite powerful authority to deal with every type of evil.

If we don't pursue Christ, activate a relationship with Holy Spirit, read the Bible until we love it, and pray regularly, then we will be weak and subject to the increasingly dark world. The days will continue to grow evil as we approach Jesus Christ's second coming.

My former spiritual ignorance, counselors/church staff refusing to teach how to overcome evil, and generational bondage pressed me to change. These massive mountains had to be moved, so I prayed until God showed me exactly the way to freedom on His terms. I used to struggle with the passage in James that tells us to consider it pure joy when we face trials. Now I know, those difficult paths led to my strengthening and deep-seated joy. I have direct access to God's throne room every day, He is glorious! He is worthy of every effort!

Psalm 90

"A prayer of Moses the man of God."

Moses wrote the first five books of the Bible, called the Pentateuch or the Torah. These books tell the origin story of planet earth, the natural world, the creation of man and woman, the heroes and the villains, the beginning of God's nation and the Law. But Moses also wrote Psalm 90.

Reading Psalm 90, you get a sense that Moses was going through a time of personal examination. Remember, Moses was raised by Egyptian royalty, so he was educated. Then he spent forty years in the desert after fleeing from his crime in Egypt. His back story is incredible and traumatic, even before Moses was born from the womb. Forty desert years gave him time to write and reflect with the Lord.

In Psalm 90 Moses writes about creation. He recalls that humans were created in dust and returned to dust. Moses thinks about death and being "swept away." He talks about the terror of God based on the light of God that exposes iniquities and secret sins. He wrote about wanting to be wise, seeking God's compassion and being satisfied with the unfailing love of God. Moses got the light show of the Ages which was the burning bush of God's voice, "I Am that I Am" in Exodus 3:7.

If you read the Bible through, you will see that great leaders had time alone with God. They sought the Lord to get things right and it equipped them to live for the Almighty, even if they failed.

We must never forget that God is Holy; He is an all-consuming fire. Us humans, we love fire because it comforts us, warms us, and has a divine beauty that can be found in nothing else. It also has a destructive force that is terrifying. That's because it is real. "By the same word the present heavens and earth are reserved for fire, being kept for the day of judgment and the destruction of the ungodly" (2 Peter 3:7).

MEDITATE: Slowly read Psalm 90 and then pray it over your life.

Day 156 | KINGDUIT

"As obedient children do not conform to the evil desires you had when you lived in ignorance. But just as He who called you is holy, so be holy in all you do; for it is written: "Be holy as I am holy."

1 Peter 1:14-16

Just like the Israelites are a nation called to be God's own special possession, so are Christians. The Jewish blessings are ours in Christ. When they rebelled, they were broken off. Since we're grafted into the same olive tree as the Hebrews, we stay humble, because unbelief still has consequences.

God carried the Jews out of Egypt on "eagle's wings and brought them to Himself" (Exodus 19:4). He said they were special! "Now if you will indeed obey My voice and keep My covenant, you will be my treasured possession out of all the nations - for the whole earth is Mine. And unto Me you shall be a kingdom of priests and a holy nation" (Exodus 19:5-6).

New Testament believers are called "a chosen generation, a royal priesthood, a holy nation, a peculiar people" (1 Peter 2:9). With that same distinction and blessing comes the call to holiness and purity. We are to be set apart, sacred, and holy like the Lord.

We have a better covenant with better promises than Israel does, so we pray they come to Yeshua the Messiah and will obey when they do. The Israelites did not have the Holy Spirit, individual access to the mercy seat of God (only special Levites at special times), access to the oil of the seven-fold Spirit represented by the lampstand and unlimited bread of His presence. They didn't have God's laws in their hearts and written on their minds, but we do plus much more. All these amazing supernatural gifts and rich inheritance come through receiving Christ. Receiving Christ is done with heart belief, confession of sin, confession of Christ as Lord, then the baptism of repentance and Holy Spirit. Salvation is only a call away but coming into the royal priesthood takes appropriation.

"But in fact, the ministry Jesus has received is as superior to theirs as the covenant of which He is mediator is superior to the old one, since the new covenant is established on better promises. For if there had been nothing wrong with that first, no place would have been sought for another" (Hebrews 8:7-8).

"Since you call on Father who judges each person's work impartially, live out your time as foreigners here in reverent fear. For you know that it was not with perishable things such as silver and gold that you were redeemed from the empty way of life handed down to you from your ancestors, but with the precious blood of Christ, a lamb without spot or defect."

1 Peter 1:17-19

We are responsible to purify our own souls via obedience to the truth (1 Peter 1:22). No one can do this for you. You are free to obey or deny Christ. Even a child who is tormented by negative thoughts must be willing to let go of bitterness and evil.

How will you know if you are totally free? Your life will express more love, power, and soundness of mind. Your character will bear the fruit of the Spirit: love, joy, peace, patience, goodness, kindness, gentleness, faithfulness, and self-control. The love you possess will be genuine love, even love for your enemies. That love will be a godly love that springs deeply from the heart.

When you don't have pure love, you won't condemn yourself, you will praise God that you are aware of another area in need of redemption, forgiveness, and cleansing. Soon your life will shine, inside and out. Then you will start to care about holiness and reverential fear. You will be willing to thoroughly cleanse yourself so that you can walk in a manner worthy of the Lord.

It won't be some type of religious pressure based on works and performance. In fact, it's possible that no one will notice because it will be a secret holy pursuit before the Lord's gaze. It will be your soul's expression of love and gratitude that becomes a good fight to overcome this dark world and everything that tries to set itself against the knowledge of God reigning over your life.

ART THERAPY DRAW: Draw nine pieces of fruit on a platter. Meditate and label the nine fruits of the spirit in Galatians 5:22. Look at yourself honestly, do you possess these character traits? Then risk asking an honest friend if they see God's fruit in your life.

Day 158 | KINGDUIT

Cautionary Tale

Jesus said, "As it was in the days of Noah, so it will be at the coming of the Son of Man. For in the days before the flood, people were eating and drinking, marrying, and giving in marriage, up to the day Noah entered the ark, and they knew nothing about what would happen until the flood came and took them all away. That is how it will be at the coming of the Son of Man" (Matthew 24:37-39). Jesus is warning us.

There was a fellowship gathering where families and friends came together to share a meal. One table had a visiting minister sitting at the table with friends and a family with many sons. The father asked everyone to share something that was going on in their lives, hoping each person could be heard and encouraged.

The time became sincere as each person talked about what burdened their heart. There was love and genuine care, but one son refused to speak and seemed disinterested. Then the next son shared and confessed feelings of torment and torture from spiritual oppression. The news took everyone off guard, so instead of commenting on the burden, the room got quiet. It seemed like no one knew what to do, so the next person shared. After everyone was done, the minister asked the father if he could talk privately to the son that shared his feelings of torment.

The father agreed, so the minister told the son that he didn't have to feel tormented, but surely Jesus could set him free that day. The son said he would like to be free but didn't know what to do since he could not overcome oppression.

The minister encouraged the young man to ask Holy Spirit when the oppressive things began. As the young man prayed, the minister silently prayed. Soon the young man told the minister the event in detail that was revealed by the Spirit. The minister asked the son if he would guard his heart/actions from that situation happening again going forward. The son said yes and with that willing spirit along with the minister's spiritual authority, the oppressive spirit was cast out in Jesus Name and the son was free and continued to live in freedom.

Holy Spirit revealed to the minister that the other son was also oppressed, but not willing to speak or share, so he lacked freedom.

CONSIDER & ASK: Do you tolerate feelings of torment and torture? Do you long for freedom? Are you willing to ask Holy Spirit to liberate you? Are you willing to trust the one sent your way to help support your request for freedom?

Day 159 | KINGDUIT

Be Holy as He is Holy Decree

SPEAK OUT LOUD & DECLARE

PRAY: Since God told me to be holy in all that I do, I can be holy. I am made with holy capabilities, and I will access holiness (1 Peter 1:16). My mind is alert and fully sober, I set my hope on the grace of God's revelation to me as Christ's return draws near (1 Peter 1:13). I am not ashamed of the gospel, because it is the power of God that brings salvation to everyone who believes: first to the Jew, then to the Gentile. God's salvation will fully save and rescue me as I believe (1 Peter 1:16). I will look intently into the Bible to examine my life. I will see the truth about myself and boldly run to the mercy seat of Christ to find grace. I praise Jesus for living to pray for me. I will reverently fear God, knowing my Father in Heaven provided the perfect sacrifice of Jesus to redeem my life. No matter what happened in the past with my ancestors, the blood of Jesus can heal all things.

I will become more aware of the fruit of the Spirit working in my character. I will grow in love, joy, peace, patience, goodness, faithfulness, gentleness, and self-control. When I don't possess these qualities, I will seek the Lord for wisdom about myself (Galatians 5:22). I will not deny the reality of the judgment of my Father in heaven. I will not be caught off guard, I will get ready for Jesus' second coming (Romans 2:3). I will seek Jesus for the salvation of my soul until I get a breakthrough. When God sends help my way, I pay attention, even letting others lead me. I will trust the Lord's guidance. Nothing is impossible with God. Even my trials are cause for joy. I will sing praises to God even when my emotions are low. The Lord is worthy of my praise and worship (Mark 2:23).

By faith, I turn away from greed, slander, deceit, gossip, wrath, revenge, vindication, guilt, shame, lying, stealing, bitterness and a lack of forgiveness. I am willing to begin the forgiveness journey of my healing (Mark 7:22).

God is my ever-present help. Jesus loves me and knows everything about me. Jesus understands. I will call for help when I am in need. I will cry, grieve, and mourn over the sin in my life. I will be forgiven and cleansed from all unrighteousness (Psalm 46). I thank Jesus for His faithfulness to complete the work He started in me. I am never alone in this life and in the life to come. I have confidence that Jesus will always be there for me no matter what happens. I will sing of His great love and fill myself with joy. I live, I move, and I have my whole being in the Lord (Acts 17:28).

I will spend time journaling my cares to the Lord:

"So, Jacob was left alone, and a man wrestled with him until daybreak. When the man saw that he could not overpower him, he touched the socket of Jacob's hip so that his hip was wrenched as he wrestled with the man. Then the man said, 'Let me go, for it is daybreak.'

But Jacob replied, 'I will not let you go unless you bless me.'

The man asked him, 'What is your name?'

'Jacob,' he answered.

Then the man said, 'Your name will no longer be Jacob, but Israel, because you have struggled with God and with humans and have overcome."

Genesis 32:24-28

Pursuing mental healing often deals with origin stories, or the narrative that tells how things started. Origin stories can be told about the beginning of cultural practices and are often in movies as the backstory of characters. The origin story can shed light on people's motives, intentions, or can be reasons to explain their behaviors.

In psychotherapy it's called Family System Therapy and uses a family tree graph to chart out each family member. From the chart the counselor and client can explore a variety of topics like culture, race, language, geography, traumatic events, faith, disciplines, vocation, economics, culinary, and much more.

The story above is a biblical origin story for the nation of Israel. Jacob got alone with God one day and relentlessly wrestled until God wrenched his hip. Then Jacob kept pressing in until he got a blessing! Apparently, God loved that wrestling match and, boom, started the nation of Israel through one feisty man.

ART THERAPY DRAW: Draw in bold the words "NAME CHANGE" and underneath it write out two words, "JACOB" & "ISRAEL." Then underneath Jacob write his name meaning, "He Deceives" and under Israel write the meaning, "Struggled with God."

"So, Jacob called the place Peniel, saying, 'It is because I saw God face to face, and yet my life was spared.' The sun rose above him as he passed Peniel, and he was limping because of his hip."

Genesis 32:30-31

Jacob was so blessed that he named the location of his God experience. He called it Peniel, which means "face of God."

My greatest hope for this devotional is that God will shine His face on you and that He settles upon you like the cloud and fire from the famous Israeli desert miracle. I hope the cloud will cover and comfort you and the fire will illuminate the truth and burn away impurities. I hope you have a relentless spirit like Jacob and are willing to wrestle with God over your origin story until you get the blessing and are endued with the power of the Most High God. Let it be so Lord!

May Gentile citizens of all nations seek God's blessing and then circle around modern Israel to bless Jerusalem unto eternal life! Shalom! Shalom for Israel!

Even if your origin story is rough, fret not because the blood of the everlasting covenant has the power to cleanse all things. Jacob's name means deceiver because he stole his brother Esau's inheritance blessing. That's the guy God chose to establish the people of God, Israel!

This is hope beyond hope, God can turn things around. And guess what, it did turn around because in Exodus 33 where Jacob meets up with Esau and they make peace. "As Jacob went on ahead and bowed down to the ground seven times as he approached his brother. But Esau ran to meet Jacob and embraced him, he threw his arms around his neck and kissed him. And they both wept" (Exodus 33:3-4).

Just a chapter prior in Exodus 32, Jacob was scared and pleading with God to rescue him from a possible attack by his brother Esau. He felt this way probably from his past deceptions he had with his brother. That's why he wrestled all night holding out for his blessing. For he was desperate for help!

MEDITATE: Read Exodus 32 & 33.

Day 162 | KINGDUIT

"Fight the good fight of faith. Take hold of the eternal life to which God has called you, which you have declared so well before many witnesses."

1 Timothy 6:12

Summarize your origin story & read it to somebody.

"Later, having traveled all the way from Paddan-aram, Jacob arrived safely at the town of Shechem, in the land of Canaan. There he set up camp outside the town. Jacob bought the plot of land where he camped from the family of Hamor, the father of Shechem, for 100 pieces of silver. And there he built an altar and named it El-Elohe-Israel."

Genesis 33:18-20

El-Elohe-Israel means God, the God of Israel. Jacob had been given tremendous blessings from God and peace with his brother. Now he was ready to settle his family. He took God's word seriously and built a family altar with the name he received from God, meaning he dedicated his new identity with a sacrifice.

New Testament believers don't have to sacrifice animals anymore because Jesus is the sacrificial Lamb of God. His one-time sacrifice on the cross took care of all sin for all of time. In gratitude, we offer our bodies as a living sacrifice by faith as an act of worship.

What's fascinating in this story is the geographical location. It is mentioned that this location in Shechem is where Jacob settled his family as Israel. When he died, his son Joseph inherited that land and commanded his bones be buried at the same plot, which Joshua later fulfilled. Then Jesus arrives at the same exact location, well over a thousand years later, to give living water to the Samaritan woman.

God preserved this location because it would be of great value to the people. Water wells like this are about seventy feet deep and hard to lose. That can also mean nothing is hard for God no matter how deep.

The mouth of Jacob's well is known as an authentic holy site and is currently located in Israel at a modern Greek Orthodox church. Think about this preservation of the story in Israel, where the bones of Joseph were laid and where Jesus revealed Himself as Messiah.

Jump two thousand years forward and Jacob's well is still protected, accessible, and producing clear, chilled drinking water! Eternal water indeed!

El-Elohe Israel

When Jacob's name turned to Israel, he built an altar to El-Elohe Israel, The Mighty One, the God of Israel. Did Jacob know at that time that Israel was to be a nation? He knew that instead of Jacob (deceives), he was to be named Israel (struggles with God). When he built that altar, it was a personal altar to basically say to God, you are El-Elohe Israel, you are the Mighty One, the God of Me! Or did Isaac know, you are the GOD OF ISRAEL!

Could I build an altar and call it El-Elohe Phebe, or could you build an altar called El-Elohe the Mighty One, The God of ____________________ (your name)? Could God do something on a national level with you? YES (Matthew 28:19)!

Jacob could have been told the bigger picture from his generational tree. There are things about our birth story that only our mother or father know. Still, God saw the divine purpose he had for Jacob. God knew about the twelve sons which would become the twelve tribes of Israel. God saw the fulfillment of His promise to Abraham in Israel, He saw a nation, He saw the Law, the Promise Land, the Temple, God saw a King and a Kingdom, and yes, God saw you!

Jacob was a true heart worshiper and devoted himself to the Lord by making a permanent altar to remind himself and his family that God is our God. Jacob was aligning his will to God's plan. The bible records Jacob's passion for his family and the fulfillment of God's purpose to his dying breath. The Lord filled Jacob's story with the names of God to show divine activity through Jacob's life.

When we struggle, it's hard to believe, but God has dreams for us too! He has been planning something epic, something in our future that is a part of the New Heavenly City of Jerusalem.

We are invited to be part of God's glory because we have been grafted into the divine olive tree through Jesus. The Bible says it this way: "Concerning this salvation, the prophets, who spoke of the grace that was to come to you, searched intently and with greatest care, trying to find out the time and circumstances to which the Spirit of Christ in them was pointing when he predicted the sufferings of the Messiah and the glories that would follow" (1 Peter 1:10).

Biblical Generational Tree

How well did Jacob know the Abraham, Isaac, and Jacob story while he was living in the middle of it? Was he told the promises God gave his grandfather Abraham? Did he understand how difficult his conception was, that his mother Rebekah was barren, and his father had to pray to the Lord until she conceived? Did he know that he and his brother Esau struggled with each other inside the womb? Did mother Rebekah tell Isaac that the struggle concerned her so much (no sonogram) that she "inquired of the Lord, 'Why is this happening to me" (Genesis 25:22)?

"He declared to her: Two nations are in your womb, and two peoples from within you will be separated; one people will be stronger than the other, and the older will serve the younger" (Genesis 25:23).

The bible says that Rebekah loved Jacob. Does this mean she told Jacob the prophecy above? We know that the Jewish community is big on prophecy and the oral traditions of storytelling. We also know that Esau was a hunter of wild game and out in the field while Jacob was cooking stew at home. Perhaps Jacob had more time to listen to his mother Rebekah and understand the national treasures inside his family system. Maybe if he was told the prophecy, he would have taken matters into his own hands and so the young deceiver planned the deception.

"One day, while Jacob was cooking some stew, Esau came in from the field and was famished. He said to Jacob, 'Let me eat some of that red stew, for I am famished.' (That is why he was also called Edom.)

'First sell me your birthright,' Jacob replied.

'Look,' said Esau, 'I am about to die, so what good is a birthright to me?'

'Swear to me first.' Jacob said.

So, Esau swore to Jacob and sold him the birthright. Then Jacob gave some bread and lentil stew to Esau, who ate and drank and then got up and went away. Thus, Esau despised his birthright" (Genesis 25:29-34). This story turns tragic in Genesis 27 to prove the reality of family drama and highlight the great need to take time to process your family tree before the Lord.

Day 166 | KINGDUIT

"See to it that no one is sexually immoral, or godless like Esau, who for a single meal sold his birthright. For you know that afterward, when he wanted to inherit the blessing, he was rejected. He could find no ground for repentance, though he sought the blessing with tears."

Hebrews 12:16-17

"Nothing in all creation is hidden from God's sight. Everything is uncovered and laid bare before the eyes of him to whom we must give an account" (Hebrews 4:13). Perhaps people only look at us for face value on the outside, but God looks at our body, mind, soul, and spirit. The Word of God is Jesus. It is the Word made flesh, and He cuts through our exteriors to divide our soul and spirit. He knows our thoughts and intentions of our heart.

When reading the story yesterday, perhaps you were mad that Jacob was so deceitful. Could it be that Jacob was mad that his firstborn brother disrespected the promises of God from his generational line? Could Jacob have discerned that Esau didn't really care about God and then prayed over the issue?

We don't know, but the New Testament tells us exactly what happened with Jacob and Esau in the Old Testament. God saw what was in Esau's heart, godlessness. Esau devalued the paternal blessing saying "what good is a birthright" in Genesis 25. God was offended so much that it is a huge warning for us today. Esau's fleshly appetite for stew was greater than his rich divine inheritance, that's why it is paired up with the flesh-based sexual immorality sin.

Fast forward in time to now and we live in the most widespread demonic attack of sexual immorality in the history of the world, so this story should get our attention. There is certainly an inheritance in store for us and if we practice godless immorality, we might lose the inheritance too. "Afterward, as you know, when he (Esau) wanted to inherit the blessing, he was rejected. Even though he sought the blessing with tears, he could not change what he had done" (Hebrews 12:17).

ART THERAPY DRAW: Draw a crying emoji

"See to it that you do not refuse him who speaks. If they did not escape when they refused him who warned them on earth, how much less will we, if we turn away from him who warns us from heaven? At that time his voice shook the earth, but now he has promised, 'Once more I will shake the not only the earth but also the heavens."

Hebrews 12:25-26

The blessing we are positioned to inherit is rich and glorious, abundant, and lavish, heavenly, and eternal, and beyond our imagination. If the Bible is saying, "see to it that no one is godless like Esau" in Hebrews 12:16, HE IS SERIOUS!

Because of the increase of wickedness in our world, we must renounce all involvement with godless activity and even godless ancestral activities that oppose the grace of God. No one can deny the increase of evil like violence, terrorism, occult, sexual immorality, human trafficking, witchcraft in movies, video games, books, and music. This is not only in adults and adult content, but also in children's content. There is a time and a place where there is no turn around or place for change. Now is the time to seek mental healing. Now is the season to renounce all godless ways, today is the day! There is no shame or condemnation in Christ Jesus, only mercy and forgiveness.

MY RENOUNCE LIST: Write down anything Holy Spirit brings to your mind and repent.

"For the grace of God has appeared that offers salvation for all people. It teaches us to say 'No' to ungodliness and worldly passions, and to live self-controlled, upright and godly lives in this present age" (Matthew 6:6).

Day 168 | KINGDUIT

Understanding of the Family Tree

Looking at our generational tree is some of the most revealing mental health work a person can pursue. Seeking wisdom regarding ancestry from a relationship or personal perspective can shed light on many things and bring clarity to your story. Take note, it can be a painful process because suppressed memories are difficult to recall.

WARNING: A full understanding of biblical forgiveness should be pursued and practiced prior to working on a family tree.

The wonderful thing about pursuing mental freedom alongside the Lord is that He knows when you are ready to deal with each memory. He has the divine wisdom to pace out each event to bring the greatest healing while watching over your soul. It's a delicate balance that is best done initially under the care of someone that is Holy Spirit centered and can lovingly guard a time of personal vulnerability. Even now, Holy Spirit might be bringing up a family issue that is not settled in your heart. Cast those thoughts and cares on the Lord, then ask Him to guard your heart.

ART THERAPY DRAW: Draw a tree with a root system underneath the trunk. Over the top of the tree write the following words, "PEOPLE – EVENTS - MEMORIES." Below the tree under the root system write the words, "ROOT ISSUES & HIDDEN MYSTERIES."

"Yet I am always with you; you hold me by the right hand. You guide me with your counsel, and afterward you will take me to glory."

Psalm 73:23-24

READ: Genesis 27: Family Tree Detail

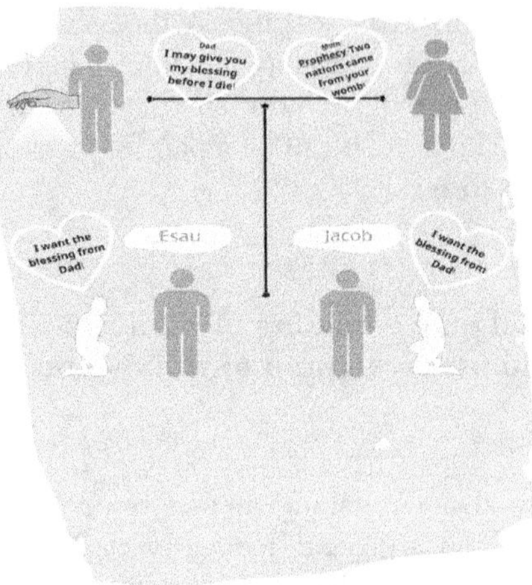

The above diagram is taken from the biblical scene in Genesis 27. God spoke to Abraham (Isaac's dad) this promise: "I will make you a great nation, and I will bless you; I will make your name great, and you will be a blessing" (Genesis 12:2). Isaac had two sons with Rebekah and they both deeply desired the father's blessing. The small family tree above shows internal thoughts of each family member. The boys bent at the knee to receive their father's hand of blessing over their lives. Fill in the emotional story, what happened? Try to explain what happened and tell someone this bible story.

Day 170 | KINGDUIT

Pray: Psalm 46 Over Yourself

God is your (my) refuge and strength, an ever-present help in trouble.

Therefore we (I) will not fear, though the earth gives way, and the mountains fall into the heart of the sea, though its waters roar and foam and the mountains quake with their surging.

There is a river whose streams make glad the city of God, the holy place where the Most High dwells. God is within her (me), she (I) will not fall; God will help her (me) at break of day. Nations are in uproar, kingdoms fall; He lifts His voice, the earth melts. The Lord Almighty is with us; the God of Jacob is our fortress.

Come and see what the Lord has done, the desolations He has brought on the earth. He makes wars cease to the ends of the earth. He breaks the bow and shatters the spear; He burns the shields with fire. He says, "Be still, and know that I am God' I will be exalted among the nations, I will be exalted in the earth."

The Lord Almighty is with us; the God of Jacob is our fortress.

This Psalm references Genesis 33:20 El-Elohe Israel, The Lord Almighty the God of Israel. Scripture is saying, The Lord Almighty is with us too! The God of Jacob is also our fortress. Hallelujah! Praise Jesus for our claim to biblical promises!

ART THERAPY DRAW: Draw a private picture of your mental health today. Start with a profile of a head and torso. Fill in the head with things that are on your mind. It can be a combination of godly thoughts and/or worldly thoughts. It can be things you want to get rid of or things you hope to be filled in your mind.

Day 172 | KINGDUIT

"You are a garden locked up, my sister, my bride; you are a spring enclosed, a sealed fountain. Your plants are an orchard of pomegranates with choice fruits, with henna and nard, with nard and saffron, calamus and cinnamon, with every kind of incense tree, with myrrh and aloes, with all the finest spices. You are a garden fountain, a well of flowing water streaming down from Lebanon."

Song of Solomon 4:12-15

As we move into the summer season, be inspired by this stunning allegory of a young girl from God's perspective. Note these short four verses, next to a whole garden inspired book, describing God's vision of female beauty. She is treasured, stunning, beloved, and protected. Take mental note of our modern contrast, how far away has much of humanity departed from this vision of female youth.

I read the above description and thought of a young girl. She was a client during my clinical work. The social workers couldn't reach her and gave me the case.

Clearly, by the look on her face, she was lost. No words, no response to anyone, only eyes wide open and gazing forward. I had limited time in that setting to work alongside her, so I silently prayed. My heart swelled with God's love, and I knew He had to break through to her, showing her she could trust me.

The Lord did the miracle and she found safety in our sessions. We unpacked a devastating trauma in her life. Like many young women of our day, she wasn't locked up in protection like verse 12, so the enemy got into the garden of her beautiful mind and heart. We unpacked her stories with talk therapy until His light of revelation shone into the dark places. As she healed, her eyes glistened with unspeakable joy. Her smile became wide with delight, her voice giggled, her heart was truly innocent and pure, and her words spoke of being a servant to her family.

One day, she asked me what I wanted. I told her I was in school and stressed about a final exam. She spoke the most loving, powerful words over me that filled my heart with hope like a spring burst open. I knew Jesus walked into the garden of her soul, touched her heart's fountain, and that sparkling water the Lord healed her with turned around and splashed on me!

GARDEN OF GOD

Imagine your life as a garden that God walked through. Just like God dwelled in the first Garden of Eden, the garden in Solomon's song describes the loveliness of God's garden. What would He find? Would He find the spring welling up to eternal life, would the waters be pure and sweet? Would he find trees of righteousness and plants bursting with fruitfulness? Would the garden be so well kept that an aroma spread through the air to refresh the atmosphere? Is the garden of your soul a love garden, full of flowers, fruits, and perfumes? Is the cooing of doves or singing birds sounding in the air? Is your soul longing for refreshment like the deer pants for water?

Song of Solomon or Songs of Songs is a highly descriptive love poem depicting the relationship between lovers. The setting within a garden can help us get a picture of God's high vision of love. Beholding God's vision is inspiration one can find to know what a healthy person's life can reflect. The natural world is a great place to use comparisons. The bible explains what happens when we lack proper vision by stating, "where there is no vision, the people perish" (Proverbs 29:18).

ART THERAPY PAGE: Grab your computer and open to a blank page, then copy and paste garden images that inspire you most. The most majestic trees, the best flowers, and the most luscious fruit. Then find spices that delight and animal life springing for joy.

Let this be a vision for yourself, a hope that God can cause you to abound in the fruitfulness of heart, mind, soul, and spirit!

Day 174 | KINGDUIT

"No good tree bears bad fruit, nor does a bad tree bear good fruit. Each tree is recognized by its own fruit. People do not pick figs from thorn bushes, or grapes from briers."

Luke 6:43-44

As Jesus compares people to good trees and bad trees, He also mentions thorn bushes and briers. Below is a sample of a bad tree. It's still standing, but it is covered in thorn bushes, briers, and huge circling choking vines. Truly it is a gray day for this tree as you look at the detail of the sharp thorns from the choking thorn vines.

When I bought a plot of raw land to beautify, I never imagined trees being so tied up. Jesus said it best, no picking from thorns! Ouch! Can I liberate this oak tree without a thorn piercing my skin? The project is taking years to beautify, as I get scratched, bitten by microscopic creatures, & skin rashes. It's taking time, so I keep working and talking to the Gardener. I am learning to trust the process.

"A good man brings good things out of the good stored up in his heart, and an evil man brings evil things out of the evil stored up in his heart. For the mouth speaks what the heart is full of."

Luke 6:45

The good and bad of our lives flows from our hearts. This verse says the heart has storage space. Someplace in our hearts that God only understands, is a collection of good things and evil things. What we can understand is that the mouth is the doorway to release the good and evil things. If you really start listening to your own words, you will start to hear what is in your heart. If you really want to understand someone else, keep your mouth shut and your ears wide open.

Proverbs 4:23 says, "Above all else, guard your heart, for everything you do flows from it." Biblical mental health says that the heart is the center, not the mind, and that the heart influences the mind.

"My son (daughter), pay attention to what I say turn your ear to my words. Do not let them out of your sight, keep them within your heart; for they are life to those who find them and health to one's whole body" (Proverbs 4:20-22). This promise is for wholeness, not only in our minds, but our whole body. Claim it by declaration! We can understand why the bible exhorts us to confess our sins to one another and pray to heal. The renouncing of transgression from the mouth is a remedy. Only God knows what impurities are inside our hearts, that is why we depend on Holy Spirit Helper to reveal things hidden in the heart.

Continue to pray that a Holy Spirit centered friend will come into your life that will serve in a priestly role of agreement in prayer for the promise of healing post confession. Are you being reminded of someone now? Perhaps you can mutually agree for forgiveness and cleansing together.

"If we claim to have fellowship with him and yet walk in the darkness, we lie and do not live out the truth. But if we walk in the light, as he is in the light, we have fellowship with one another and the blood of Jesus, his Son, purifies us from all sin. If we claim to be without sin, we deceive ourselves and the truth is not in us. If we confess our sins, he is faithful and just and will forgive us our sins and purify us from all unrighteousness" (1 John 1:6-9).

Day 176 | KINGDUIT

"What shall I do, then, with Jesus who is called the Messiah?' Pilate asked,

They all answered, 'Crucify him!'

...He had Jesus flogged, and handed him over to be crucified... They stripped him and put a scarlet robe on him and then twisted together a crown of thorns and set it on his head. Then they knelt in front of him and mocked him. 'Hail, king of the Jews!' they said. They spit on him and took the staff and struck him on the head again and again. After they had mocked him, they took off the robe and put his clothes on him. Then they led him away to crucify him."

Matthew 27:22, 26, 28-31

The chief priests grabbed the blood money Judas threw in the temple, then the people of Israel crowded before Governor Pilate and demanded the execution of Jesus by shouting "Crucify him!"

That same Satan who used Pharaoh to oppress the Jews had again deceived the people of Israel. This time to crucify Jesus, the perfect oak of righteousness (Isaiah 61:3). It's no wonder there was a thorny vine hanging around.

Imagine the psychological torment Jesus endured from the people he deeply loved. He had already been flogged, now they stripped him naked, set the thorny crown on his head, were screaming judgment, and publicly mocking him. Then they spit on him and repeatedly struck Jesus on the head again and again.

Jesus endured this violent trauma and devastating mental torment for your mental healing. "But he was pierced for our transgressions, he was crushed for our iniquities; the punishment that brought us peace was on him, and by his wounds we are healed. We all, like sheep, have gone astray, each of us has turned to our own way; and the Lord has laid on him the iniquity of us all" (Isaiah 53:5-6).

ART THERAPY DRAW: Draw a crown of thorns, get a red pen, and draw drops of blood on the thorns. Watch and sing: YouTube: Don Moen "By His Wounds" Live.

Honor Declaration

SPEAK OUT LOUD & DECLARE

There is no one like You Lord! You alone are holy; you are enthroned on the praises of Israel. Jesus is the only one in the history of the world that has paid it all for mankind. Dominion belongs to the Lord! You are the reigning King who is immortal, invisible, and the only true God over the nations (Psalm 22:3).

All glory, honor and praises belong to You! All you have done is worthy of praise, so I worship you today. I praise You and give you glory for your perfect sacrifice. As the heavens rejoice, so do I. You alone are worthy of my prayers and blessings all day long! Lord, you purchased the redemption of mankind, so therefore every tribe, language, people, and nation has been set free. Every mental issue has been healed by the blood of the Lamb (Revelation 5:9).

Thank you for coming to earth, and for taking on the form of man to understand my human experience. Thank you for understanding my mind, will and emotions. Lord, you understand psychological pain, you understand rejection, You have felt the torment and torture of a head beating, face spitting and of loud vicious screaming. You understand injustice in the face of innocence. You know all!

Lord, you have proven love by Your sacrifice. You have proven compassion by your suffering. Therefore, I lift my heart secrets to you. Do not let the darkness of these days overwhelm me. I trust in You. Help me to pour out my story before Holy Spirit. I will find supernatural healing, loving kindness, compassion, goodness, grace, power to change, and unending faithfulness.

I will make the effort, I will seek Your face, I will fight this good fight of faith because of You. I will see my heart secure, and my family divinely protected. I am strong, I am free.

"Blessed be the LORD God, the God of Israel, who alone does marvelous deeds. And blessed be His glorious name forever; may all the earth be filled with His glory" (Psalm 72:18-19). "May the LORD answer you in the day of trouble; may the name of the God of Jacob protect you. May He send you help from the sanctuary and sustain you from Zion. May He remember all your gifts and look favorably on your burnt offerings" (Psalm 20:1-3).

Day 178 | KINGDUIT

"I consider everything a loss because of the surpassing worth of knowing Christ Jesus my Lord, for whose sake I have lost all things. I consider them garbage, that I may gain Christ and be found in him, not having a righteousness of my own that comes from the law, but that which is through faith in Christ - the righteousness that comes from God on the basis of faith."

Philippians 3:8-9

Thankfully, not all the Jewish community turned away from Jesus. Saul, who was a Hebrew from the tribe of Benjamin, was a zealous law-centered Pharisee who met Jesus along the road. He bumped into the King of Glory and was blinded by His light. It changed him so much at the intellect part of his soul, like Jacob, that his name changed from Saul to Paul.

Paul remembered what they did to Jesus on the cross and was broken over it. He pursued redemption so much that he was willing to lose all things and suffer to know Christ. Paul truly desired total mental liberty and dedicated his life to the knowledge of Jesus, even if it meant hardships. He pressed into Christ so much that he wanted to hold on to the reality of Christ's sacrifice to strain toward the glory of redemption.

Basically, Paul understood the cost. Even though most of us don't pursue suffering like Paul, we are suffering these days. I met a faithful God-fearing wealthy lady who had hardships on many levels along with her children. She thought being good was enough, but she was still suffering.

There is much more than just the pursuit of mental health that can deliver us from today's struggles. When we take hold of what Christ did for us, we also get His glory and power made known in our lives. We get the same power Jesus was given to rise from the dead and live a life of honor. We take hold of that power to overcome the evil in the world that is oppressing and inflicting mankind. We obtain a faith-centered righteousness that is not about pleasing man or a religious system, but a righteousness that makes us right with God and man in our hearts. This righteousness cleanses us from the inside (thoughts, will, feelings). It makes us truly free!

"He has rescued us from the dominion of darkness and brought us into the kingdom of His beloved Son, in whom we have redemption, the forgiveness of sins."

Colossians 1:13-14

Have you ever considered that your struggle with sickness or mental health issues are coming from the dominion of darkness? Are you under a shadow of shame, fear or condemnation that makes you feel that you and everyone else is the problem? Are you puzzled that faith-based church attendance and church offerings are not changing the health and vitality of your family?

In Christ, your new identity is with the kingdom of His beloved Son. By faith, from salvation forward, your identity should focus on the kingdom of God, led by your Abba Father in heaven. The past is over, which means if your ancestry tree has struggled with godlessness, sickness, and sin, it is not where your gaze should be. Your gaze should be towards your citizenship in heaven where there is no lovelessness, darkness, sickness, sin, or death.

Have you considered that Christ in you means that you are in Christ? That means you are with Him in heaven right now. That means all infirmities of all kinds are ALREADY healed: past, present, and future. When Jesus was totally healed from His cross ordeal, so were you. When Jesus was completely resurrected, so were you. When Jesus went to the arms of His beloved Father in Heaven, so you fell in the center of divine love too. When Jesus shows up with His presence as you sit with Him in loving devotion, so there you are in heaven with Him as well! When Jesus came to earth and destroyed the works of the devil, now you have the power to continue to destroy the works of the devil too.

This is the glory of Christ in you! "To them God has chosen to make known among the Gentiles the glorious riches of this mystery, which is Christ in you, the hope of glory" (Colossians 1:27).

ART THERAPY DRAW: Draw a royal banner. Draw a crown on that banner. Celebrate with thanksgiving "CHRIST IN YOU, THE HOPE OF GLORY"

Day 180 | KINGDUIT

TO THE GARDEN WITH GOD

"I am the true vine, and My Father is the keeper of the vineyard. He cuts off every branch in Me that bears no fruit, He prunes to make it more fruitful. You are already clean because of the word I have spoken to you."

John 15:1-3

Prepare your mind & heart to seek the keeper of the vineyard this summer!

ART THERAPY DRAW: Draw a huge twig with a bunch of olives to represent the Holy Spirit oil that you will receive. Draw a huge twig with a bunch of grapes to represent the fruitfulness of your personal Garden of God!

"Remain in me, as I also remain in you. No branch can bear fruit by itself; it must remain in the vine. Neither can you bear fruit unless you remain in me."

John 15:4

The Lord promises that He will never leave or forsake us. God doesn't lie or fail in keeping His promises. The guaranteed deposit of Holy Spirit in our lives when we were born again, it was a royal sealed deal. Nothing can separate us from God's love, so clearly God does His part to stay with us, even if we walk away from Him. That's why the Bible often says, seek God!

He is asking us not to walk away but remain in Him. This is where our human will kicks in. He tells us to stay connected so that we continue to receive the nourishment of the true vine, Jesus. Without that root system connection, there is no hope for fruitfulness. God alone is our strength and our ever-present help in this life. We need him for the good things and hard things. We need love!

That's why we can never view the life of faith as a religious exercise or a system of works to win some type of special favor. That's not love, that's obligation. Our salvation was a big win; therefore, our devotion should always be because we love God, we need God, and we fear God. He is holy and we must receive the riches He provides to navigate this world system.

When the bible tells us to ask, seek, pray, and read the bible, the heart behind those actions is so we will be a glorious garden, abounding in fruitfulness (all those good emotions). This glorious life is our purpose and great joy. The reason why our will must get involved is because God never forces us by means of obligation or coercion. It feels like freedom and love that motivates us to get alone and seek Him until that liberty bell rings. Father, Jesus, and Holy Spirit are gentle, humble, and kind.

The devil is the control freak that brings heat, oppression, fear, and torment. If you dread your religious life or feel like you don't enjoy your faith, talk honestly to Jesus. If you can't read God's word to truly understand yourself or even get wisdom about the signs of the times and the promises of heaven, then ask, seek, and knock for wisdom. God has allowed both the wheat and the tares, the good seeds and the bad weeds, the darkness, and the light in the field of your life. Abiding in Jesus will help you navigate the truth leading to freedom!

MONTH 7 - Forgiveness Survey

SUMMER SEASON

GARDEN OF GOD

"I am the true vine, and you are the branches. The one who remains in Me, and I in him, will bear much fruit. For apart from Me you can do nothing."

John 15:5

Now is the time to heal! God has spread the net to alert all humanity that healing is available. It's hard to have a peaceful mind and a clean body if you are bitter and practice evil. This is God's world and I view the global mental health movement as His provision to counteract the darkness for the nearing end time harvest.

As millions seek help, the Lord also continues to purify His church and raise up healthy Christ-centered warriors for a good faith fight. Those who seek mental healing can find Jesus, the true vine, in the garden as an example of fruitfulness!

Remember, Jesus shed that first drop of redeeming blood from his head in Gethsemane's garden at the Mount of Olives. Jewish Jesus is the true vine/ olive root that Israel rejected. Some of Israel's branches were broken off leaving room for the Gentiles (non-Jews) of the world, called wild olive shoots, to be grafted in among the others. Gentiles now share in the nourishing sap from the olive root.

Based on Romans 11 Israel's "branches were broken off so that Gentiles could be grafted in. But they were broken off because of unbelief, and you (Gentiles) stand by faith. Do not be arrogant, but tremble. For if God did not spare the natural branches, he will not spare you either. Consider therefore the kindness and sternness to those who fell, but kindness to you, if you continue in his kindness. Otherwise, you will also be cut off. And if they (Israel) do not persist in unbelief, they will be grafted in, for God is able to graft them in again.

After all, if you were cut out of an olive tree that is wild by nature, and contrary to nature were grafted into a cultivated olive tree, how much more readily will these, the natural branches, be grafted into their own olive tree!

I do not want you to be ignorant of this mystery, brothers, and sisters, so that you may not be conceited: Israel has experienced a hardening in part until the full number of the Gentiles has come in, and in this way all Israel will be saved. As it is written: 'The deliverer will come from Zion; he will turn godlessness away from Jacob" (Romans 11: 19-26).

Day 183 | KINGDUIT

Divine Peace & Israeli Protection

PRAYER: Lord, your word says to pray for Jerusalem, especially in these days when there are assaults around every side of the nation. Deliver the Holy Land from Jihad rockets and war. "May those who love you be secure. May there be peace within your walls and security within your citadels. For the sake of my family and friends, I will say, 'Peace be within you. For the sake of the house of the LORD our God, I will seek your prosperity" (Psalm 122:6-9). High praises over Jehovah!

Bless the Gentile nations to stand with Israel. Even if their leaders don't. Send divine assistance like the ancient days, let there be miracles in the heavens over Israel. May the glory of Christ in Gentiles make the Jews envious to receive Jesus the Messiah. Protect the land, may the inhabitants be born again!

Oh Lord, watch over the Holy City, Jerusalem, the City of David, the Temple Mount, the divine furnishings, instruments of worship, and sacrifices. Clear away obstacles, leadership resistance and false worship. May the inhabitants of the land seek Jesus the Messiah!

Lord, you will go out and fight against the nations that oppose Jerusalem. Thank you, Lord, for one day your feet will stand on the Mount of Olives, east of Jerusalem that will form a great valley with half of the mountain moving north and half moving south. Lord, you will come again, and all the holy ones with you! Yes Lord, you will come again to secure Jerusalem with your glory, radiance, and living water. That living water will flow on that special day, and it will be full of light and no darkness. You Lord will be King over the whole earth as one Lord and your name will be the only name (Zechariah 14).

Enlighten the hearts of Your people Lord, the Jews, and the Gentiles of the world. Let us be ready!

ART THERAPY DRAW: Draw an Israeli flag. Ask the Lord to reveal His heart for Israel to you.

Day 184 | KINGDUIT

"If anyone does not remain in Me, he is like a branch that is thrown away and withers. Such branches are gathered up, thrown into the fire, and burned."

John 15:6

Why bad things happen to good people is confusing to many believers. It's hard to imagine the possibility of being thrown away and withering. But when evil and unbelief continue to exist, the God of Justice will not be silent, nor will He fail to act.

As the end of the age draws near, signs of the times point to an increase in darkness and negative behaviors amongst the people of the earth. Just like in the days of Noah, there was widespread wickedness. "Then the LORD saw that the wickedness of man was great upon the earth, and that every inclination of the thoughts of his heart was altogether evil all the time" (Genesis 6:5).

We must remember that our salvation and being grafted into the vine of Jesus Christ is the highest calling in the history of mankind. If we say we are Christ followers, and yet don't abide in the Lord, we will wither and become fruitless. That means, there is no proof we belong to the Lord.

Jesus said, "Not everyone who says to me 'Lord, Lord,' will enter the kingdom of heaven, but only the one who does the will of my Father who is in heaven. Many will say to me on that day, 'Lord, Lord did we not prophesy in your name and in your name drive out demons and, in your name, perform miracles?'

Then I will tell them plainly, 'I never knew you, away from me you evildoers" (Matthew 7:21-23).

If you are reading this, I pray we are still in a season of grace with time to repent. However, at the time of this writing, something has changed, and the nearness of Christ's return has God's people under urgency of preparation and readiness for His second coming. There have never been so many fulfillments of end-time bible prophecy, especially concerning the land of Israel. There has also never been so many Christian leaders and intercessors sounding alarms.

I can't urge you enough and beseech you by the mercy of God to repent and seek divine healing in preparation for the coming King!

BIG PICTURE GRAPHIC

Big Picture Graphic Explained

Because the Bible is a book, people often view it in a linear way. But if you look at the big picture graphic, it is a vertical view of the story of mankind. God so loved the world of humanity that he gave his son Jesus to come down from heaven to provide an escape from eternal death. Yet there is no way a human can jump up from earth to heaven.

Biblically, the earth is the first heaven, the sky is the second heaven and heaven itself starts in the third heaven. The way vertically up to the third heaven is the Jesus ladder. He is the only human in the history of mankind to live on earth without sin or moral corruption. Of all the good men and women in history, not one was without sin. Salvation's forgiveness of sin washes people unto the holiness necessary to enter the third heaven.

In the Bible the earth, the sky, and heaven are all called heaven. My guess is that wherever Jesus was, behold, you have heaven. Jesus was heaven on earth. Years ago, He ascended into the sky to pass up to heavens. He promised He will come down again to earth, with his feet standing on the Mount of Olives.

No one should desire to go down to the fire of hell; for it is eternal torture of the eternal soul. The pit of hell was designed for devils only, NOT HUMANS. The devil knows he is going to the flames and is mad. Since the fall of Adam and Eve in the garden, he has deceived mankind in evil ways, dragging humans mentally down.

Heaven is a holy place that mortal men can't enter. They need a holy Savior to grant them forgiveness of sin so they can be holy as God is holy and possess the imputed righteousness of Christ for third heaven access. "Jesus answered, 'I am the way and the truth and the life. No one comes to the Father except through me" (John 14:6).

So, what does this have to do with mental health? To obtain the gift of the super abundant life that Jesus promised His followers, we must believe we truly belong to heaven. Since we are seated with Christ in heavenly places, we have access to heaven's inexpressible and glorious joy along with a love that endures forever. Have you heard of that statement, "heaven on earth?" People say it to describe a moment of bliss that they think must feel like heaven.

Although we didn't live during the time of the Old Testament, those stories belong to us because Jesus is the Word, and He is in believers right now. Jesus came to earth during New Testament times, according to the Bible. Though a few thousand years have passed, we are still in New Testament times. The Bible covers history from the creation of the world to the end of the world. History still hasn't experienced the book of Revelation fulfilled, even though we are currently experiencing many of the last day events that are explained in the Bible. This is how we belong in the New Testament period of history.

The return of Christ is still on God's future calendar at this writing. We still have time to seek the Lord for mental freedom, peace, and holiness. As believers, we are blessed to embrace the whole counsel of God as our love letter and inspiration to find hope for liberty in all things, even the hard places.

Day 186 | KINGDUIT

"If you remain in me and my words remain in you, ask whatever you wish, and it will be done for you."

John 15:7

The promise above is that if your life is truly aligned to Jesus and the Bible, you will have everything you need to navigate this earth journey to prepare for eternity. If you truly know Jesus, you will seek Him and ask for all the things you need to obtain good mental health. Things like good friends, vocational purpose, a godly family, spiritual gifts to overcome evil, and even things that will support that lifestyle like housing and personal needs. When they arrive with blessing, you will rejoice with a grateful heart.

El Roi, the God who sees, knows exactly who has Jesus, The Word, on the inside. Someone can be brand new in Christ, just beginning their faith journey and Jesus already knows the seriousness of their seeking heart. A mentally healthy person talks to Jesus, then asks for whatever they need to live in peace. They receive those things by faith. Yes, just ask Jesus. As Holy Spirit moves, respond, and walk forward by faith.

As I walked along my healing journey, I realized I needed a mentor to show me some new things about Jehovah Rapha, the God who heals. So, I prayed for help. Then I felt like I needed to go to a faith-based conference, yet I sensed I'd meet an older lady there willing to mentor me. That's exactly what happened, and we've been prayer partners for years. She has a doctorate in ministry and showed me how to process many challenging mental health issues. Her most consistent message to me has always been, ASK JESUS!

ASK JESUS ANYTHING: Pray, write it down, or sing it for whatever it is that you need; just ask Jesus. He told you that you could "ask whatever you wish" in John 15:7, so go ahead and ask.

"This is to my Father's glory, that you bear much fruit, showing yourselves to be my disciples."

John 15:8

As we continue to walk through the Father's garden, under the Father's pruning, we can understand the big picture and look to see whether or not our lives bear fruit and connect to the true vine. The garden walk with the Father reveals more of what the life of faith in Christ looks like. No one else but the Trinity knows the true condition of our souls, so it would be great to look around, inspect, and examine ourselves to see who we are by our heart's fruit.

The end goal of man is to glorify God, the highest purpose an individual can accomplish. Read Psalm 145 to give you an idea what a high purpose looks like. Here are some attributes. Order them in importance on the second column to where they fit into your spiritual goals.

Garden List	**Order of Importance**
• Commandments	______________
• Spirit Fruit	______________
• Holy Spirit Oil	______________
• Love	______________
• God's Word	______________
• Peace	______________
• Jesus Vine Grafting	______________
• Daily Gratitude	______________
• Great Praises	______________
• Proclaim God's Power	______________
• Meditate God's Works	______________
• Sing Joyfully	______________

Day 188 | KINGDUIT

Tisha B'Av and the 3 Weeks

Close to this period in the summer, there is a Jewish holiday called "Tisha B'Av and the 3 weeks." It is an annual period of mourning when the Jewish community takes the time to reflect on the sad parts of their history. The Jews are keen on oral traditions and retelling the story of their ancestry, which includes some very sad and devastating events. The book of Lamentations expresses the suffering of God's people after the destruction of the holy city.

The Jews intentionally remember the destruction of their Temples of God. They remember those takeovers of the Temple when the Israelites went into exile to foreign lands and became slaves. They remember the worst of it, when the Babylonians put the first temple ablaze and then the Romans came in and destroyed the second temple. This holiday can serve as an example for the Gentiles of the world to learn from the Jewish community. They certainly know how to cry out to the Lord for help and redemption. They also contemplate the state of affairs in the world today and look for personal solutions.

"Nebuchadnezzar, king of Babylon, Nebuzaradan commander of the imperial guard, an official of the king of Babylon, came to Jerusalem. He set fire to the temple of the Lord, the royal palace and all the houses of Jerusalem. Every important building, he burned down" (2 Kings 25:8-9).

Had it not been for God's prophecies in the Bible, Israel would not be a nation today. USA President Truman was the first world leader to recognize Israel as a nation, so he pushed the plan with the United Nations in 1948 to proclaim a New State of Israel. That divine fulfillment set Israel back on track with the hope to rebuild the third temple and bring back the glory of God's Tabernacle.

We will spend several weeks preparing to seek God in the same way, by examining our lives and personal stories. We will let Holy Spirit show us the sad parts, the places where our families got burned by godlessness and evil. We will have the opportunity to make things right with Almighty God and rebuild our personal tabernacle to prepare for the second coming of the Lord.

MEDITATE: Can you identify with living in a nation under attack? Ponder Jewish history.

Forgiveness - Jesus's Cautionary Tale

If someone asked, what is one thing I can do as a believer to bring the quickest healing and best blessings into my mental health? Without a doubt, I would say forgiveness. In the Lord's prayer Jesus prays, "And forgive us our debts, as we also have forgiven our debtors" (Matthew 6:12).

Unforgiveness will produce bitter waters and clog the flow of Holy Spirit water more than anything else. Bitter waters make bitter tree roots. "See to it that no one falls short of the grace of God and that no bitter root grows up to cause trouble and defile many" (Hebrews 12:15). In addition, consequences of unforgiveness can result in torment.

ART THERAPY DRAW: Draw a bag of money labeled $10,000. Draw a coin labeled 100.

Jesus answered, "Therefore, the kingdom of heaven is like a king who wanted to settle accounts with his servants. As he began the settlement, a man who owed him ten thousand bags of gold was brought to him. Since he was not able to pay, the master ordered that he and his wife and his children and all that he had be sold to repay the debt. As this the servant fell on his knees before him. 'Be patient with me,' he begged, 'and I will pay back everything.' The servant's master took pity on him, canceled the debt and let him go" (Matthew 18:23-27).

NOTE: That $10,000 bag of gold is worth 3.48 billion dollars today.

Forgiveness - Jesus's Cautionary Tale (Part 2)

"But when that servant went out, he found one of his fellow servants who owed him a hundred silver coins. He grabbed him and began to choke him. 'Pay back what you owe me!' he demanded."

His fellow servant fell to his knees and begged him, 'Be patient with me, and I will pay it back.'

But he refused. Instead, he went off and had the man thrown into prison until he could pay the debt. When the other servants saw what had happened, they were outraged and went and told their master everything that had happened.

Then the master called the servant in. 'You wicked servant,' he said, 'I canceled all that debt of yours because you begged me to. Shouldn't you have mercy on your fellow servant just as I had on you?' In anger his master handed him over to the jailers to be tortured, until he should pay back all he owed. "This is how my heavenly Father will treat each of you unless you forgive your brother or sister from your heart" (Matthew 18:28-35).

ART THERAPY DRAW: Draw a bag of money labeled $100. Draw a bag of money labeled $1700. Draw a picture of a dried-up tree with no leaves and no fruit. Label it the "unforgiving tree."

KINGDUIT | Day 191

"For you know that it was not with perishable things such as silver or gold that you were redeemed from the empty way of life handed down to you from your ancestors, but with the precious blood of Christ, a lamb without blemish or defect."

1 Peter 1: 18-19

Since Jesus is the true vine that you have been grafted into, the most important tree in your personal garden is your Jesus olive tree. From those olives you will get the valuable oil preparing your entrance to the wedding feast. It is worth more than money because there is no amount of money that can buy your salvation, it is an extremely precious gift.

Just because it is given for free, it doesn't mean you can take it for granted. Our Father in heaven allowed Jesus to be sent down to earth from heaven as the priceless sacrificial lamb on your account. When we don't forgive others as Jesus has forgiven us, it makes our heavenly Father angry, so angry that He hands us over to torture.

Many believers still say, "I'll never forgive!" Many don't take the time to understand the value of being forgiven but suffering certainly can wake up the sleepy one who can't find freedom. The torture is more than just a prayer for help. It can lead someone to search out the value of forgiveness. Jesus alone provides forgiveness of sin.

It takes time in serious examination to forgive others from your heart. Some say unforgiveness manifests in physical sickness. Understanding the process of forgiveness is critical work in your faith. It will help deliver you of any type of torture you may be experiencing.

CONSIDER: Some people say, "I just can't do it," when they think of trying to forgive others that have done horrible things to them. Jesus knows you can't do it, that's why He sent Holy Spirit to help you. Look up Romans 5:5. Draw a picture of a heart and what God poured in your heart to help you forgive.

FORGIVENESS

Forgiveness, the word itself summarizes the power of its action. Take away the /ess/ at the end and you have forgiven. The two-part blessing of forgiveness is that if you practice forgiveness, you will be forgiven!

"In those days Jesus went out to the mountain to pray, and He spent the night in prayer to God. When daylight came, He called His disciples to Him and chose twelve of them. . .

Then Jesus came down with them and stood on a level place. A large crowd of His disciples was there, along with a great number of people from all over Judea, Jerusalem, and the seacoast of Tyre and Sidon. They had come to hear Him and to be healed of their diseases, and those troubled by unclean spirits were healed. The entire crowd was trying to touch Him, because power was coming from Him and healing them all. Looking up at His disciples, Jesus said: Do not judge, and you will not be judged. Do not condemn, and you will not be condemned, Forgive and you will be forgiven" (Luke 6:12,13,17-20, 37). From the lips of Jesus, the only way to be forgiven is to forgive. There is no mention that forgiving happens after one asks for forgiveness, the call is just to forgive. That means even if no one says sorry, we still forgive. What is mentioned is not to judge or condemn, but to forgive.

In this devotional, it is fitting that forgiveness is the start as we step into the garden. When Jesus talks about the good tree and the bad tree from his speech above, we hear about judgment, condemnation, and forgiveness. Basically, if we are judging and condemning others, we are not forgiving them and as a result, we will not be forgiven.

The concept of forgiveness is universal and global. The practice of forgiveness has been applied to multiple religions and even science. "Forgiveness isn't just practiced by saints or martyrs, nor does it benefit only its recipients. Instead, studies are finding connections between forgiveness and physical, mental, and spiritual health and evidence that it plays a key role in the health of families, communities, and nations. Though this research is still young, it has already produced some exciting findings and raised some important questions."[24]

"They had come to hear Jesus and to be healed of their diseases. Those troubled by unclean spirits were healed. The entire crowd was trying to touch Him, because power was coming from Him and healing them all."

Luke 6:18-19

Understanding why it is so important to forgive and why Jesus is the only one in history that can forgive sins is key. "In fact, the law requires that nearly everything be cleansed with blood, and without the shedding of blood there is no forgiveness" (Hebrews 9:2). Throughout history, people have understood that sacrifice leads to forgiveness. In other words, someone or something must pay. That's justice! One of the primary purposes of the first tabernacle temple was to prepare a sacrificial system to obtain the mercy of God, which is forgiveness.

It started with God in the Garden of Eden. After Adam's sin, there was a blood sacrifice. God did this because all the sudden Adam and Eve had a new set of leather clothes. God set up a justice system, someone or something must pay for wrongs done.

When God instructed Moses to tell the Israelites to put the blood of a lamb over the door frames of their homes so that the death angel couldn't kill their first born, he immediately did so. This is where the battle of good and evil collide because that death angel couldn't touch the blood of the lamb. That lamb sacrifice literally blocked the death angel's access to the door of real homes in Egypt.

Jesus took the sacrificial systems to the next level and became the once and for all sacrifice to redeem and deliver mankind from the power of death. Therefore, if you don't receive and apply the blood of Jesus over your life for forgiveness and extend God's grace to forgive others, you will not be protected from evil. In other words, evil will not see the blood of Jesus marking your life in the spirit world and attack you, which means torture.

After all, we are made from dust and are perishable, meaning we are dirty and can get messy in this world environment. All you must do is stop washing your body and well, you know. Keep up with the no washing and now you are subject to disease and sickness. There's pain and it affects how much you sleep, so your mind gets fuzzy, weird, and weak. Let that progress and your mind is subject to dirty, angry thoughts, bitter blaming others and now here come the unclean spirits.

Day 194 | KINGDUIT

"Looking up at His disciples, Jesus said: 'Do not judge, and you will not be judged. Do not condemn, and you will not be condemned, forgive and you will be forgiven."

Luke 6:37

Have you ever wondered why many lawyers are Jewish? They got the law first. "When Moses had proclaimed every command of the law to all the people, he took the blood of calves, together with water, scarlet wool and branches of hyssop, and sprinkled the scroll and all the people" (Hebrews 9:19).

How did we go from reading about Jesus' healing diseases and those troubled by unclean spirits in verse 18 to judging, condemning, and forgiveness in verse 19? It seems like the people got physical and mental healing and now Jesus looks up and starts talking to his disciples in legal terms.

"Righteousness and justice are the foundation of your throne; love and faithfulness go before you" (Psalm 89:14). Remember, Jesus lived in the kingdom of heaven with Abba Father and was sent to earth. The kingdom has a glorious king who sits on a throne with a foundation of righteousness and justice. "In the beginning God..." (Genesis 1:1). God is Elohim: the supreme God, magistrates, the God of Justice.

"Then God said, 'Let us make mankind in our image, in our likeness, so that they may rule. . ." (Genesis 1:26). Mankind is made in the image of the God of Justice so that they may rule. Are you getting a picture of a kingdom courtroom?

Read what is happening in that kingdom courtroom? "Then I heard a loud voice in heaven say, 'Now have come the salvation and the power and the kingdom of our God, and the authority of his Messiah. For the accuser of our brothers and sisters, who accuses them before our God Day and night, has been hurled down" (Revelation 12:10). As the accuser of God's children, the devil is condemning people day and night. He is not asking God to forgive them; he wants them to face a hellish judgment. Angry Satan devil serpent wants to destroy humanity. Those accusations are totally opposite God's throne of justice and righteousness. God loves, forgives, and does not condemn. Therefore, if we keep judging, condemning and not forgiving, then we are aligning with Satan. No matter how we feel, Jesus is telling us not to judge or condemn and to make sure we are forgiving all.

FORGIVENESS SURVEY

- PREPARE PART 1 -

Pursuing biblical mental healing in cooperation with the Lord is a serious endeavor. It is also very powerful! Therefore, we will slow down the pace to make sure this truth sinks deep down into the root system of your mind, heart, intellect, memories and will.

The Lord led me to this exercise I call FORGIVENESS SURVEY before I understood mental health/healing. I opened my soul to Christ alone as I prayed and prepared to partner with Holy Spirit to do the critical work of total forgiveness from the heart. I also closed my soul and guarded my heart from influences that tried to prevent me from seeking a forgiveness survey that inspects, examines, and waits upon Jehovah to reveal the truth about my heart.

This is NOT a religious exercise! In fact, while you pursue your own forgiveness survey, only tell your prayer partner who supports your obedience. This person can give you encouragement, accountability, and the power of agreement to bless your forgiveness journey.

You will be hiding alone with Jesus in the secret place of the Most High God. There you apply by faith the sacrificial blood of the Lamb to cleanse your soul, making yourself holy as the Lord is holy. This is you getting washed on the inside, whiter than snow to cover your scarlet red sins. This is you receiving divine removal of transgressions and iniquity from situations with yourself and others. This is faith work to allow God to remove sins so far away that they can never be recovered. This also means your confessed sins can never be brought to the courts of heaven by Satan the accuser.

"They triumphed over him by the blood of the Lamb and by the word of their testimony; they did not love their lives so much as to shrink from death. Therefore rejoice, you heavens and you who dwell in them! But woe to the earth and the sea because the devil has gone down to you! He is filled with fury because he knows his time is short" (Revelation 12:11-12).

FORGIVENESS SURVEY

- PREPARE PART 2 -

If the Lord doesn't lead you, it's because He knows your heart is not willing to forgive. He knows your heart and He doesn't force our will. We must force our own will. We decide to be willing. We speak to our own soul and command it to rise and obey the Lord!

King David understood this because he was a man of war and a warrior for God. He was burdened with rejection and vile threats on many levels, but God said David had a heart for him, and he certainly lived that out. This is how King David dealt with his own soul: "Contend, LORD, with those who contend with me; fight against those who fight me, take up shield and armor; arise and come to my aid. Brandish spear and javelin against those who pursue me. Say to my soul, 'I am your salvation" (Psalm 35:1-3)!

David was being an emotional male, pondering in his mind about all the violence of war and holy conquest. You don't get a weeping, crying soul description in the above verse, you get a mental battle soul struggle. You can read extensive bible stories about David embarking on battle after battle since his Goliath moment going forward and much of his life. He figured out the Lord would fight for him, and surely the Lord did just that as in written in Psalm 35.

One summer my husband was fuming with anger close to his breaking point. Nothing was happening negatively in our marriage, but I was the only person close to him to witness this situation. I might have said, "What is bothering you, why are you angry?" But instead, I prayed for him. That's when I realized how males generally express emotions with anger and females often show tears. Months later he told me what was happening. I teased him and said, "You're so emotional!" He didn't deny it but told me the Lord helped him and told him exactly what to do. It worked and in six months the issue was resolved!

"And do not grieve the Holy Spirit of God, with whom you were sealed for the day of redemption. Get rid of all bitterness, rage and anger, brawling and slander, along with every form of malice" (Ephesians 4: 30-31).

FORGIVENESS SURVEY

- PREPARE PART 3 -

Psalm 35 is an example of how real and honest we can be when we talk to the Lord. Below is a dialogue look at David's relationship with the Lord. He tells the Lord how he feels about his situation. Since the bible is designed to be useful to keep us on a righteous path, we can also tell the Lord our feelings.Remember our study of Joshua when he conquered people and lands in battle? Joshua tore down idolatrous temples and killed physical enemies. On the contrary, we don't fight with the weapons of the world. We demolish strongholds of thoughts, pretension, and arguments in our mind from our invisible enemy (2 Corinthians 10:4-5). This is the difference between physical and spiritual, but a battle, nonetheless. David's transparency and intimacy with the Lord is an example that can inspire us. Pray it out loud as a call for divine support.

Psalm 35: 1-10, 26-28 Of David

Contend with my opponents, O Lord; fight against those who fight against me. Take up Your shield and buckler; arise and come to my aid. Draw the spear and javelin against my pursuers; say to my soul: 'I am your salvation.' May those who seek my life be disgraced and put to shame; may those who plan to harm me be driven back and confounded. May they be like chaff in the wind, as the angel of the LORD drives them away. May their path be dark and slick, as the angel of the LORD pursues. For without because they laid their net for me; without reason they dug a pit for soul. May ruin befall them by surprise; may the net they hid ensnare them; may they fall into the hazard they created. Then my soul will rejoice in the LORD and exult in His salvation. All my bones will exclaim, "Who is like You, O LORD, who delivers the afflicted from the aggressor, the poor and needy from the robber?" May those who gloat in my distress be ashamed and confounded; may those who exalt themselves over me be clothed in shame and reproach. May those who favor my vindication shout for joy and gladness; may they always say, "Exalted be the LORD who delights in His servant's well-being." Then my tongue will proclaim Your righteousness and Your praises all day long.

ART THERAPY DRAW: Draw a picture of an oval. First title it SOUL, then draw a heart inside representing your feelings/emotions, a brain representing your memory, a light bulb representing your mind/intellect, and a door representing your will.

FORGIVENESS SURVEY

- PREPARE PART 4 -

When the Lord leads you to go into a season of healing, a commitment to Jesus in prayer will bless you to complete the work you start. The commitment is because it's difficult and the soul-searching work will bring tremendous healing, but it will also bring painful memories and spiritual resistance.

When you start the process, it will be emotional at a soul level. In this case, the emotions are good, don't push them away! For the men, the emotions aren't usually the ones that women deal with and express, but nonetheless, they are emotions. Emotions are more than just tears and crying. Emotions are also deep-seated anger, vengeance, revenge, regret, and remorse. Just because there are no tears and weeping, that doesn't mean emotions are not bubbling up.

Generally, women will tear up and cry starting a forgiveness survey. This is the soul's emotions surfacing. Generally, a man will start to ruminate and feel angry when they start a forgiveness survey. This is the soul's mind or intellect surfacing.

When heart/memory wounds or negative intellect start to come to your understanding, Holy Spirit will help you deal with these thoughts that are being made known to you through your mind. Then you can deal with them alongside Holy Spirit Helper.

The wonderful thing about taking a survey with the Lord is that it will be totally confidential. You can say anything in any way with any attitude, inflection, choice of words, or even sounds. No one can diagnose you or document your vulnerable story. No one will hold it against you or judge you. No one will record it to keep it hidden to punish you later. The Lord has already given us a soul anchor called hope to get us through.

"We have this hope as an anchor for the soul, firm and secure. It enters the inner sanctuary behind the curtain where our forerunner, Jesus, has entered on our behalf. He has become a high priest forever, in the order of Melchizedek" (Hebrews 6: 19-20).

ART THERAPY DRAW: Draw a small anchor here.

FORGIVENESS SURVEY

- PREPARE PART 5 -

It is important to prepare your heart as well as the time and place that you choose to sit with the Lord. You need that privacy. Once you start, it could take time, so don't rush it. The Lord knows how much time you need to process forgiveness every time you determine to seek Him for another forgiveness survey. If you need a break, whether days, weeks, or whenever, ASK JESUS.

When I first pursued forgiveness, I had hours alone in my bedroom uninterrupted. It was at night, so after I finished that session with Holy Spirit, I thanked Jesus and went to sleep looking forward to fresh morning mercy.

The Lord led me to this exercise I call FORGIVENESS SURVEY before I understood the mental health/healing. It seemed that once I obeyed the command to forgive and applied those biblical truths, the wisdom for total mental healing came my way.

Before you start the survey, carefully read through all the informational material in preparation for your faith exercise.

There will be a "BEGINNING FORGIVENESS PRAYER" to start your healing. Call a believer you trust in faith to let them listen via the power of agreement. There should not be any names/details mentioned during this time, just support by faith to prepare for your alone work.

"Therefore, confess your sins to each other and pray for each other so that you may be healed. The prayer of a righteous person is powerful and effective" (James 5:16). Your friend can witness your words and affirm your intention before you prepare for the forgiveness survey alone with Jesus. This will help align your heart to obey God's word regarding forgiveness. After the agreement prayer, it will be helpful to add a time of personal communion with the Lord and a speaking out loud of the Lord's Prayer. Your heart will be ready to begin the forgiveness exercise by faith. Thank the Lord for helping you be faithful to sincerely seek forgiveness.

ART THERAPY DRAW: Draw a road with a street name called "Forgiveness Lane."

Nehemiah's Survey – Part 1

"Nehemiah said to the king, "May the king live forever! Why should my face not look sad when the city where my ancestors are buried lies in ruins, and its gates have been destroyed by fire?"

Nehemiah 2:3

Remember in the Old Testament that battles over wicked land occupants ended up destroying the temple. The New Testament battle is over dark invisible spiritual forces that corrupt our souls. The kings in the Old Testament were human rulers, some godly and some evil. The New Testament King is Jesus, the King of the Jews, the King of Kings, and the Lord of Lords, the holy One.

The Jewish people in the Old Testament wanted shalom (peace) in the land and a glorious temple for worship to seek their national redeemer, the God of Israel. But evil kings brought on war, destruction and the temple kept getting destroyed while the Jews became captive slaves.

Nehemiah was sad and terrified over the reality that the city of his ancestors was ruined and burnt. He was so unsettled that he prayed to God of heaven seeking favor to take leave from his job in Persia to travel by horse to Jerusalem and inspect the damage.

Nehemiah was compelled to survey Jerusalem. His gut instinct and sad emotions proved true because the house of God was in ruins. He saw for himself the devastation of broken walls and burned gates. His life is a testimony of being a restorer of ruined cities.

ART THERAPY DRAW: Draw a simple stone wall with an open gate. Draw some stones broken up on the ground around the wall.

Proverbs 25:28 "Like a city whose walls are broken through is a person who lacks self-control."

Nehemiah's Survey – Part 2

A biblical chronological map/timeline of the Old Testament shows three tabernacles that were raised up and then destroyed.

Moses put up a Tabernacle Tent Temple in the desert, which was disassembled on the way to the Promise Land. King Saul didn't value the tabernacle, but King David brought glory to God by seeking plans for a stone temple that his son King Solomon built in breathtaking splendor.

Later, the Jews disobeyed God again and lost divine protection. Evil came in when Israel and Judah fell to idolatry. The temple was destroyed, gates were burned, and then the people of God were enslaved. Bye-bye beautiful gardens, oils, fruits, spices, splendor, glory, worship, harps, strings, lamb sacrifices and honor!

The Israelites had to flee to other countries and try to rebuild their lives. The Jews that loved God couldn't let Jerusalem out of their hearts. Moses taught them to pass on the law, commandments, and verbal history they knew to their children and then their children's children to preserve the glory of God.

It is a sad cycle that each generation struggles to overcome as world history unfolds. Even though evil seems to win at this game of life, God still made human beings in his own image. God is still love. "His love endures forever. Give thanks to the God of heaven. His love endures forever" (Psalm 136: 25-26).

"By the rivers of Babylon, we sat and wept when we remembered Zion. On the poplars we hung our harps, for there our captors asked us for songs, our tormentors demanded songs of joy; they said, 'Sing us one of the songs of Zion!' How can we sing the songs of the LORD while in a foreign land? If I forget you, Jerusalem, may my right hand forget its skill" (Psalm 137-1-5).

CONSIDER: NEHEMIAH TRAVELED over 700 miles via horse from Susa, Persia to Jerusalem, Israel TO SURVEY THE DESTRUCTION.

Nehemiah's Survey - Part 3

Without a doubt, Nehemiah was a lover of the God of heaven, a man devoted to Israel/Jerusalem! I believe if Nehemiah was a Gentile Christ follower today, he would have put the same effort into mental healing for himself as he did to rebuild walls and gates alongside his family. Surely, he would have looked back at his ancestral lineage to understand and survey (Sabar) what problems led to evil influencing his people. I'm certain Nehemiah understood Proverbs 18:10: "The name of the Lord is a fortified tower; the righteous run to it and are safe."

Here are some of Nehemiah's raw prayers taken from the Book of Nehemiah during his time of *Sabar inspection, examination and waiting upon the LORD for help during his time of crisis:

"O Lord, God of heaven, the great and awesome God who keeps his covenant of unfailing love with those who love him and obey his command, listen to my prayer! Look down and see me praying day and night for your people Israel. I confess that we have sinned against you. Yes, even my own family and I have sinned! We have sinned terribly by not obeying the commands, decrees, and regulations that you gave us through your servant Moses" (Nehemiah 1:5-7).

"Remember, O my God, all the evil things that Tobiah and Sanballat have done. And remember Noadiah the prophet and all the prophets like her who have tried to intimidate me" (Nehemiah 6:14).

As Nehemiah followed the LORD, God of heaven, his prayers were answered. His personal quest became a blessing that touched Israel!

Look up & Listen - YouTube: Yonina Jerusalem Mashup

National Survey

It only takes one willing person to strike a match that can set a whole family, nation, and world ablaze with the glory of God. Nehemiah was God's glory starter. What he did privately in the dark of night turned into a movement that got the whole nation on board to rebuild the ruins. When he got the green light from the LORD, he informed the "Jewish leaders - the priests, the nobles, the officials or anyone else in the administration" (Nehemiah 2: 16). He got a positive response and soon the whole nation was willing to seek the LORD corporately.

"The people assembled again, and this time they fasted and dressed in burlap and sprinkled dust on their heads. Those of Israelite descent separated themselves from all foreigners as they confessed their own sins and the sins of their ancestors. They remained standing in place for three hours while the Book of the Law of the Lord their God was read aloud to them. Then, for three more hours they confessed their sins and worshiped the Lord their God. . . they cried out to the Lord their God with loud voices" (Nehemiah 9:1-4).

"What a gracious and merciful God you are! Every time you punished us you were being just. We have sinned greatly, and you gave us only what we deserved. Our kings, leaders, priests, and ancestors did not obey your Law or listen to the warnings in your commands and laws. So today we are slaves in the land of plenty that you gave our ancestors for their enjoyment! We are slaves here in this good land. The lush produce of this land piles up in the hands of the kings whom you have set over us because of our sins. They have power over us and our livestock. We serve them at their pleasure, and we are in great misery." The people responded, 'In view of all this, we are making a solemn promise and putting it in writing'" (Nehemiah 9:31, 33-34, 36-38).

The Lord stated his desires to Moses when He said, "have them make a sanctuary for me, and I will dwell among them" (Exodus 25:8). The divine turnaround necessary to get on track with God's plan was setting up the sanctuary. It worked and the walls and gates were rebuilt.

Consider one man's heart, willing spirit, obedience, and actions turning into a national blessing. Are you willing to survey your bodily temple alone with God and wait upon Jehovah to see the fruit of your obedience?

My Survey

Are you seeing the connection between Israel and yourself? Just like Paul prayed that the eyes of your heart would be enlightened to know the hope of your calling, I'm praying for the same light to burst forth into our times and our hearts.

Remember, God is the same yesterday, today and forever. Do you understand that we belong in this great story of the people of God too? Note the book of Hebrews is in our biblical time, the New Testament, and we are "surrounded by such a huge crowd of witnesses" (Hebrews 12:1). It's like a cloud of former faith people that have gone before us in the divinity of Almighty God.

It started with Adam and Eve, then through the line of God's people all the way to the Hebrews. Moses led out in the big redemption plan and built a formal house of God for the people to seek Jehovah. The Jews finally made it to the Promise Land and became the Jerusalemites. Just like us, they struggled to keep God's standard of holiness and fell. They fell so hard they killed Jesus, so gardener God cut them off the olive tree and gave the Gentiles a chance to worship the Lord.

We have an advantage over the ancient Jews. That advantage is that Christ is in our bodily tent as our hope of glory. Like the Jews, we have also built a place of worship to seek God, however it is not in a temple made of stone. We seek God in our hearts by having the mind of Christ, the communion of the blood of the covenant, Holy Spirit Helper, and God the Father (our Abba).

Therefore, we must survey the condition of our part of God's temple (living stones). We must be holy as God is holy and clean things up. This is an impossible task apart from the spotless blood of the Lamb of God, Jesus, who takes away the sin of the world. Only this sacrificial blood can wash away our sins, transgressions and empower the removal of unclean spirits that influence our lives. Since Jesus is the one sent from heaven and authorized to forgive sins, we seek Jesus and Holy Spirit to reveal hidden, repressed, heart deceit, denied, and double-minded sins stuck in our soul.

This process is our survey! Like Nehemiah took personal time as a layman to survey Jerusalem at night, we draw near to God alone, and survey soul wounds, false belief systems and broken things needing divine repair. It will be difficult, personal, and includes generational sin that has controlled our family systems.

"A good man brings good things out of the good stored up."

Luke 6:45

Call your faith-based friend (someone without heavy leadership responsibilities) to help you agree in prayer. Basically, you are making yourself accountable to this friend by committing to go through your personal forgiveness survey. Their role is to listen to your intention to seek time with the Lord for forgiveness and be willing to spend a moment to listen to you recite the prayer of commitment listed on the next page.

Having a friend to agree in prayer brings in the promise of healing to support your forgiveness survey. If they are Holy Spirit centered, He will remind them to call you a few times and encourage you or offer to pray over you as you go through this season of healing in your life. They don't need to know any details; the LORD has the ears for the details of your life story.

Perhaps, you can say something like, "God keeps showing me new situations or people I need to forgive, and it is difficult. Thank you for praying for me!" Are you being reminded of someone now? Ask the Lord to show you a good time to reach out to them. Perhaps it is someone you know who is pursuing mental healing as well and you can mutually agree to pursue forgiveness and cleansing before the Lord.

"If we claim to have fellowship with him and yet walk in the darkness, we lie and do not live out the truth. But if we walk in the light, as he is in the light, we have fellowship with one another and the blood of Jesus, his Son, purifies us from all sin. If we claim to be without sin, we deceive ourselves and the truth is not in us. If we confess our sins, he is faithful and just and will forgive us our sins and purify us from all unrighteousness" (1 John 1:6-9).

This simple time of fellowship is like the above verse, walking in the light of His love while knowing that another human supports your difficult journey along the path of righteousness. When we confess our sins to another, it brings about the humility that can welcome God's mercy and grace in our times of need. Godly agreement can also be sharing commitments that we will obey or complete assignments.

SURVEY COMMITMENT – Part 1

PRAY: Jesus, you didn't die in vain, you died to provide forgiveness and redemption for all mankind. Forgiveness isn't an idea, it is a command that says, "Forgive and you will be forgiven" (Luke 6:37). I realize I must forgive, but I don't know how, the pain is too difficult! How can I find the strength to do it Lord?

Our "hope does not put us to shame, because God's love has been poured out into our hearts through the Holy Spirit, who has been given to us" Romans 5:5

I cannot forgive, but Holy Spirit's power in me can do it as I align my will. I don't want to be psychologically prisoned and tortured, so I choose to forgive as an act of my will. I don't want others to grieve over my refusal to forgive. Right now, Jesus, I let go of those on my upcoming forgiveness survey; I will forgive them for the situations, events, actions, and words. I will talk to Jesus about each situation. Jesus, I will spend the time necessary to do a forgiveness survey of my life. I will let go of the painful memories and trust You to be my God of Vengeance! You said, "It is mine to avenge; I will repay," and again, "The Lord will judge his people" (Hebrews 10:30).

Even though I know this process will hurt, I want freedom more. I want the oil of Holy Spirit to anoint my life and the living waters to wash my heart, mind, body, emotions, soul, and spirit. Thank You, Jesus, for going to the Mount of Olives, and then paying the price on the cross for my forgiveness and my ability to forgive others.

As for forgiving myself, help me Lord, to ask for forgiveness from you. Especially in the areas where I have made mistakes that I don't feel that I am worth forgiveness. I don't want to judge, condemn, criticize, or shame myself or those who hurt me anymore. I want to love and be loved by You. Have mercy on me, Lord, so that I can have mercy on others.

You will be faithful to complete this forgiveness work. Your ways are not my ways, your ways are higher. They go all the way up to heaven. Come down by Your Holy Spirit and help me Lord. Help me to believe your instructions and cleanse my unbelief. Cleanse me and wash me. Grant me a willing spirit.

SURVEY COMMITMENT – Part 2

PRAY: As I prepare my heart, forgive me for all the times I've been angry and resentful. Lord, come and turn my bitter waters sweet for all the times I withheld forgiveness. And when I feel offended again, help me to become a forgiving person, who forgives again. Prepare me to grieve, mourn and wail over the hurts that I swept under the rug. Give me the courage to face it before you. You will show me the right timing. Help me separate a time and place to process my forgiveness survey.

Because of the cross, I am already healed! Let me flow into the river of forgiveness so that I will allow the pain to be washed out and away from me. Redeem my life from the pit and restore health to my psychological wounds.

Heal me, Oh Lord and I will be healed. I will find freedom. I will overcome. I will have joy, and all this subconscious pain will surface and be removed as far as the east is from the west. As an act of my will, this work will produce oil in my life and prepare me for an abundance of healing! I will be ready for your return! I will see your glory!

Thank You Jesus! Thank you, Abba Father! Thank you, Holy Spirit!

In Jesus Name, let it be so and AMEN!

CLEANSING ACTION: Breathe, go outside, take a walk, and thank God for his wonderful mercy.

FORGIVENESS SURVEY

- INSTRUCTIONS -

The Forgiveness Survey has sixteen parts (16). We will spend sixteen (16) days reviewing how each part can be experienced. Remember, this is a simple pattern that can be adapted for your personal relationship with the Lord. It is a guide to help you process a season seeking Jesus for forgiveness.

After we review the sixteen (16) parts, the whole survey will be listed on the seventeenth day. It might be good to print out that whole survey or possibly write out your own notes for the sixteen (16) points review. The days of review will give you time to think and prepare yourself for the moment when you will sit before the Lord, give Him access to your life events/memories and begin to process your forgiveness survey.

Pursuing heart level forgiveness should become a habit that will activate a cleansing pattern that will keep your heart free from the warfare and mental entanglements of unforgiveness.

"But encourage one another daily, as long as it is called 'Today,' so that none of you may be hardened by sin's deceitfulness" (Hebrews 3:13).

FORGIVENESS SURVEY REVIEW

- PART 1 -

1. Set a time and find a quiet place with no people around. Turn off all phones/alarms/electronics. Holy Spirit loves an undivided heart. Distracted or half-hearted devotion isn't the best plan.

What kind of place can you go to feel totally alone, yet emotionally safe? Can you arrange for your current home to be empty for the day or evening? Would you be more comfortable to find a room or space that is not connected to your home? Would you like to sit on a chair, by a desk, on a bed or in nature?

FORGIVENESS SURVEY REVIEW

- PART 2 -

2. Align your WILL to God's work (Psalm 51:12) and commit to stay in that space until you sense a release from the Lord. Say out loud, "I WILL OBEY YOU, LORD, DURING THESE MOMENTS."

Beginning a holy practice often meets opposition! Don't be surprised if you finally find your perfect spot, you get settled and then little distractions come along to discourage you. You must stick around for yourself no matter what comes along and keep seeking the Lord until the process flows.

ART THERAPY DRAW: Draw a mountain with an ant pushing a rock up one side of the mountain. Label the rock "memories." Draw a red flag on top of the mountain representing the cleansing blood of Jesus. On the other side of the mountain, draw a rock labeled "divine removal." Then next to it on the downside put up a big wave to represent God's Sea of forgetfulness.

FORGIVENESS SURVEY REVIEW

- PART 3 -

3. Have tissues close by and a notebook to write down any special wisdom you receive.

Everyone is different and expresses emotions in different ways. Forgiveness is a grieving process, so tissues come in handy. So does a bottle of water and a notepad. You will be surprised by things that come to your memory and the emotional component that makes you forget some interesting details. Write it down!

ART THERAPY DRAW: Draw a picture of a notebook or a journal and a pen. Put a label that says "Forgiveness Notes" on the top of the notebook.

FORGIVENESS SURVEY REVIEW

- PART 4 -

4. Ask Holy Spirit to bring ANY memory of people, places, events, or things that you had not intentionally forgiven from your heart, including forgiving yourself.

Holy Spirit is all knowing and all present. He was there when you were formed in your mother's womb. There are things about your life that might be revealed to you during your forgiveness survey or wisdom that you may need to ask certain people to help you recall that period in your life. Welcome Holy Spirit into your survey!

ART THERAPY DRAW: Draw a picture of a dove representing Holy Spirit Helper, your loving companion during this time. Draw a picture of a head with several wheels inside representing different parts of your soul (mind/will/memory/emotions/heart).

FORGIVENESS SURVEY REVIEW

-PART 5 -

5. The feeling is like sitting on a beach, with slow wave after wave of memories washing over you. With each wave, forgive that situation.

"Jesus got up, rebuked the wind and said to the waves, 'Quiet! Be still!' Then the wind died down and it was completely calm" (Mark 4:39). When you process your forgiveness survey with Jesus, He knows exactly how to handle these waves of emotions, so let them calm down and bring you to a place of shalom peace.

ART THERAPY DRAW: Draw a simple picture of a beach with a horizontal line when the sand meets the waves. Then draw moving lines to represent the calm ocean waves. Draw a big heart sitting on the shore in the sand, representing your body. That's you, sitting on the beach with the Lord, close by are His waves washing away your pain.

FORGIVENESS SURVEY REVIEW

- PART 6 -

6. As the pain bubbles up inside you, acknowledge it before the Lord.

Pain is a normal part of healing and health. Pain can be an indicator that confirms a healing need. Don't be afraid of it, let it bubble up and surface with Jesus because he says; "Come to me, all of you who are weary and burdened, and I will give you rest. . . I am gentle and humble in heart. . ." (Matthew 11:28-29).

ART THERAPY DRAW: Draw another picture like the beach scene yesterday, and/or add bubbles inside your heart. As you are willing to continue the forgiveness survey as the Lord reveals new areas of pain inside that need forgiveness and cleansing. It feels like bubbles of memories or emotions surfacing from the inside.

It's okay, that's Holy Spirit helping you remember things that hurt your soul.

MONTH 8 - Father's Glory

FORGIVENESS SURVEY REVIEW

- PART 7 -

7. When you feel the heart pain and deeply grieve, tell the Lord your feelings in detail and describe to Him the situation (let your thoughts/ emotions flow out freely).

Some don't cry, that's a form of repression. Tears exist for a reason, to release emotional pain. In the pain, be glad for tears! "Deep calls to deep in the roar of your waterfall; all your waves and breakers have swept over me. By day the LORD directs his love, at night his song is with me - a prayer to the God of my life" (Psalm 42:7-8).

ART THERAPY DRAW: Draw a huge lemon. Put a face on the lemon and big tears coming out of the eyes to symbolize releasing emotions through tears.

FORGIVENESS SURVEY REVIEW

- PART 8 -

8. Speak out loud your willingness to forgive with a sincere heart.

The sword of the Spirit is the word of God, which is intended to be our mouth speaking truth. Obey God's command to forgive by verbally speaking out the words; "Lord I forgive ______________for ____________________________________."
This not only heals our soul, but it also defeats the enemy, our accuser. "The tongue has the power of life and death, and those who love it will eat its fruit" (Proverbs 18:21).

ART THERAPY DRAW: Draw a profile picture of a head. Draw a brain inside the head and oil dripping on top of the head to represent Holy Spirit. Draw lines going out from the mouth with the words, "LORD, I FORGIVE . . ."

FORGIVENESS SURVEY REVIEW

- PART 9 -

9. Fill your lungs by breathing in and then exhale, and again, breath in and then exhale. Receive God's promises of forgiveness and purification. "If we confess our sins, he is faithful and just and will forgive us our sins and purify us from all unrighteousness" (1 John 1:9).

Often emotional expression makes people get winded from a feeling of being upset. Don't forget to practice breathing to gather yourself. Take deep breaths in to fill your lungs and exhale. Repeat. Quiet yourself in the Lord and give yourself a soaking time of rest and peace. Whisper words of thanksgiving and praise for the faithfulness of the Lord to carry you through.

ART THERAPY DRAW: Draw the word BREATHE in huge letters. This represents the time of taking cleansing breaths to gather yourself.

FORGIVENESS SURVEY REVIEW

- PART 10 -

10. Continue to breathe and then wait for the peace of God to confirm your faith action.

There are moments in the forgiveness survey when there is a holy pause. Let the Lord do his part to remove, cleanse and purify your soul. Take a drink of water, slow down, breathe and let your body recover from the thoughts/emotions. God knows how to give you breaks before He reveals more information to process.

ART THERAPY DRAW: Draw your interpretation of a holy pause. It might seem like nothing is happening, but the Lord is doing His part to wash your soul.

FORGIVENESS SURVEY REVIEW

- PART 11 -

11. Thank the Lord and even sing praises of gratitude.

After you breathe and catch your breath, let the moment rest. In between Holy Spirit memory reminders, give thanks for divine help over your survey. If a song of praise bubbles into your thoughts, start singing and humming a sound of gratitude. This is the secret place of the Most High, soak it in. Oh, how He loves you!

ART THERAPY DRAW: Draw musical notes moving through a beautiful sky.

FORGIVENESS SURVEY REVIEW

- PART 12 -

12. Stay in the moment - let the waves of forgiveness wash away all sin and pain into His sea of forgetfulness (Micah 7:19).

Experience the compassion of the Father in the midst of this process. His love is great and high, He knows how you were formed. If you have heard Holy Spirit remind you of things to process forgiveness, praise Him for helping you. You are experiencing "BIBLICAL MENTAL HEALING"!

"As far as the east is from the west, so far has he removed our transgressions from us." (Psalm 103:12).

ART THERAPY DRAW: Draw a hand waving goodbye to the burdens as they float away at the deep end of the ocean.

FORGIVENESS SURVEY REVIEW

- PART 13 -

13. By faith, appropriate (make one's own) the blood of Jesus Christ for emotional healing. Receive the washing of that area of your soul white like snow (Isaiah 1:18).

Apply the blood by faith with a declaration of your mouth. Say something like, "I thank you LORD for your cleansing blood! Thank you for giving me freedom from burdens. Thank you for removing my offenses. Thank you for carrying me through this time of mental survey. I receive my obedience blessing!

ART THERAPY DRAW: Draw a red string going up to heaven.

FORGIVENESS SURVEY REVIEW

- PART 14 -

14. Tell the Lord that you will keep forgiving each situation you remember along the way up to 70x7 times (Matthew 18:22) as He leads. Doing this work doesn't erase memory, it washes the heart. So going forward when you remember events, say something simple like, "Thank you Lord, I forgive ______________________________ again."

If you are determined, you will continue to obey again and again. This is the work of faith. This is the sanctification process, the real life of faith. Some people that come up in your memory are easy to forgive and let go, some are difficult and painful. Determine to keep forgiving until you are free of negative emotions!

ART THERAPY DRAW: Draw a huge math equation of the Biblical numbers 70X7= FORGIVENESS. How many times does that equal?

FORGIVENESS SURVEY REVIEW

- PART 15 -

15. After you gather yourself, if you are willing to continue, ask the Lord to bring to your memory another situation you need to process forgiveness.

You can say something like, "Lord, that was very hard, I can't do this without your grace and Holy Spirit. Stay with me Lord as I process these painful memories." You will know if your heart can go on or you need a break. If you are not sure, ask the Lord, "Anything else you want to show me?" It might be little things that drop off fast.

ART THERAPY DRAW: Draw two jars next to each other with an arrow between them. Put sad and angry faces in the jar on the left. Make the arrow pointing to the right jar. Put hearts of love in the jar on the right.

FORGIVENESS SURVEY REVIEW

- PART 16 -

16. Repeat the process.

We forgive others because the Lord forgives us. The Lord made sure humanity had an endless supply of forgiveness on the cross. He took on the curse of sin so we wouldn't be cursed in life and eternity. Continuing to forgive purifies us and allows more of the light and life of the LORD to fill our hearts and give us love.

ART THERAPY DRAW: Draw radiating sun rays coming out of heavenly clouds with a repeat symbol in the middle.

THE FORGIVENESS SURVEY

1. Set a time and find a quiet place with no people around. Turn off all phone/alarms/electronics. Holy Spirit loves an undivided heart. Distracted or half-hearted devotion isn't the best plan.

2. Align your WILL to God's work (Psalm 51:12) and commit to stay in that space until you sense a release from the Lord. Say out loud, "I WILL OBEY YOU, LORD, DURING THESE MOMENTS."

3. Have tissues close by & a notebook to write down any wisdom you receive.

4. Ask Holy Spirit to bring ANY memory of people, places, events, or things that you had not intentionally forgiven from your heart, including yourself.

5. The feeling is like sitting on a beach, with slow waves after waves of memories washing over you. With each wave, forgive that situation.

6. As the pain bubbles up, acknowledge it before the Lord.

7. When you feel the heart pain and deeply grieve, tell the Lord your feelings in detail and describe to Him the situation (let your emotions flow out freely).

8. Speak out loud your willingness to forgive with a sincere heart.

9. Fill lungs with breath and exhale, breathe and exhale. Receive God's promises of forgiveness and purification. "If we confess our sins, he is faithful and just and will forgive us our sins and purify us from all unrighteousness" (1 John 1:9).

10. **Continue to breathe and wait for the peace of God to confirm faith action.**

11. Thank the Lord and even sing praises of gratitude.

12. Stay in the moment - let the waves of forgiveness wash away all sin and pain into His sea of forgetfulness (Micah 7:19).

13. By faith, (make one's own) the blood of Jesus Christ for emotional healing. Receive the washing of that area of your soul white like snow (Isaiah 1:18).

14. Tell the Lord: "I will keep forgiving each situation you remember along the way up to 70x7 times" (Matthew 18:22) as He leads. Doing this work doesn't erase memory, it washes the heart. So going forward, say something simple like, "Thank you Lord, I forgive ____________ again" when you remember events.

15. After you gather yourself, if you are willing to continue, ask the Lord to bring to your memory another situation you need to process forgiveness.

16. Repeat the process.

"I will exalt you, my God and King; I will praise your name for ever and ever. Every day I will praise you and extol your name for ever and ever. Great is the Lord and most worthy of praise; his greatness no one can fathom."

Psalm 145:1-3

Your forgiveness testimony is valuable to Jesus. His earthly mission was a project of determination to provide total forgiveness for your whole life.

WRITE IT OUT: Write a description of the forgiveness survey from your perspective.

Day 226 | KINGDUIT

"Anyone you forgive, I also forgive. And what I have forgiven - if there was anything to forgive - I have forgiven in the sight of Christ for your sake, in order that Satan might not outwit us. For we are not unaware of his schemes."

2 Corinthians 2:10-11

The Apostle Paul understood the forgiveness survey so much that he was willing to forgive people in the church that had offended other people. Paul cast the forgiveness net way out. God knows it is easy to take up other people's offenses, so we keep forgiving and cleansing our hearts so that we can walk in love towards others.

The verse above gives us another good reason why we should keep forgiving, because Satan is a divider of people. If we don't forgive, we lose the unity, and the love God wants for the people of God. Unity and love bring tremendous blessing and much anointing oil. Remember, we need to be filled with Holy Spirit oil every day!

"How good and pleasant it is when God's people live together in unity! It is like precious oil poured on the head, running down on the beard, running down on Aaron's beard, down on the collar of his robe. It is as if the dew of Hermon were falling on Mount Zion. For there the Lord bestows his blessing, even life forevermore" (Psalm 133).

ART THERAPY DRAW: Draw a figure that represents you. Then draw oil from heaven pouring onto your head and draw heavenly dew surrounding your life/body. Label it "MOUNT ZION BLESSINGS."

"For land that drinks in the rain often falling on it and produces a crop useful to those for whom it is tended receives the blessing of God. But land that produces thorns and thistles is worthless, and its curse is imminent, in the end it will be burned."

Hebrews 6:7-8

According to Jesus, we are like the trees/vines in a summer garden. The untended tree/vine is going to have weeds, obstructions, overgrowth, or thorns trying to keep it from fruitfulness. Just like trees or vines can be choked and twisted with vines or thorns, so can people. There can also be dark vines with sharp thorns. Negative influences in life can feel like choking or thorny vines that pull.

A life in order allows a heavenly influence to be the keeper of their vineyard (John 15:1). With Jesus' help, entanglements can be removed from the inner circle of close relationships that choke out the life of God.

A life out of order will not display the glory of God made evident by a fully surrendered life. There won't be the blessing of oil producing olives or sweet fruit.

Often family systems, close relationship systems or even those who access your life through work or social media can wrap around your mind in unhealthy ways. Some people are controlling, some are co-dependent, some are too needy, some think you are the source, some are mean spirited, and some demonically harass.

When a person decides to pursue biblical mental healing, the other people in their life are affected by that person's freedom. A call to liberty or freedom in Christ can often mean someone has to cut ties, put up boundaries, stand tall and refuse to be entwined in unholy dependency or activities. On the other hand, close relationships of dependency like marriage and parenting, are designed to blossom into God-centered interdependence and support.

A surrendered heart welcomes pruning. The Lord will certainly make your garden extraordinary. By remaining in the true vine, you will give the wisdom, grace, mercy, power, nourishment, and abundant blessings to overcome anything in your path.

CONSIDER: Can you think of someone who has their garden in order? How do you see God's blessings and fruitfulness in their lives?

Day 228 | KINGDUIT

Jesus said, "You are My friends if you do what I command you. No longer do I call you servants, for a servant does not understand what his master is doing. But I have called you friends, because everything I have learned from My Father I have made known to you. You did not choose Me, but I chose you. I appointed you to go and bear fruit - fruit that will remain - so that whatever you ask the Father in My name, He will give you. This is My command to you: Love one another."

John 15:14-17

Regulations, examinations, testing, and evaluations are a part of society. They keep culture, business, and leaders in check to prosper.

The doctors maintain licensure. The farmers keep the crops by managing weeds, critters, and soil testing. The physical therapist gets evaluated for healing procedures. The pilot's skills are upgraded and examined to maintain flying qualifications. Even children have examinations in school.

If society is held accountable by laws and rules, how much more should Christ followers welcome Holy Spirit to examine them to keep a steady walk on the narrow path of holiness that leads to eternal life. When your spirit is willing, you will have moments when Holy Spirit shows you the true condition of your heart.

There was a lady who was a customer service agent and said she loved people. One day she served a group of people that were relentlessly demanding and rude, so she was worn out by serving them. The same group showed up again, expecting extra care, so she gave again.

On the third visit, the group was horrible. The customer service agent couldn't take it and went on break. This trial exposed her limit, so she confessed to the Lord her heart lacked love and asked for forgiveness.

The obedient life gives access to the Father in heaven through Jesus. It sets us up to receive blessings after blessings because we are invited to ask for whatever we need. How will we know our progress? By the love we have for others, even those we must forgive repeatedly. As we keep forgiving, the fruit of love will grow, manifesting at a soul level bringing great peace.

KINGDUIT | Day 229

"Now may the God of peace Himself sanctify you completely, and may your entire spirit, soul, and body be kept blameless at the coming of our Lord Jesus Christ. The One who calls you is faithful, and He will do it."

1 Thessalonians 5:23-24

If we trust in the Lord, we get blessings from heaven. "Blessed be the Lord from Zion, He who dwells in Jerusalem. Hallelujah" (Psalm 135:21)! Our God reigns, speaks, listens, breathes, and loves us so much that we can experience a dynamic relationship with Him that is real.

The promise above is for the God of peace Himself to sanctify you completely! This promise is beyond wonderful and worthy of a personal holy hug of AMEN! It covers our ENTIRE SPIRIT, SOUL AND BODY, a head-to-toe promise!

Do you feel "called" to participate in this mental healing devotional? Did the One and Only God of peace call you to healing? If the answer YES? Then thank the God of peace Himself for being faithful to do it!

When we respond to His word with obedience, we get His heavenly promises fulfilled in our lives. May amazing shalom cover your life as you seek Him. May change grace you at a spirit, soul, and body level. The promises in the bible are endless and obtainable as we willingly apply the truths and follow the directives of His will.

God is faithful to pour out abundance on many levels. During this season of mental healing, the abundance is often in the revelation of the heart. It is a call to action to confess or forgive followed by healing peace and comfort in the soul. As you move up into more glory, you will be aware of a divine shift in your life that feels like a blessing from Zion, the heavenly Jerusalem.

ART THERAPY DRAW: Draw two hands doing a pinky promise. Label one hand "God's Promise" and label on the other hand "Our Willingness." Remember, God gave you power over your will, so He can't make you do anything. Biblical Mental Healing is a partnership with the Wonderful Counselor and Your Willing Spirit.

Day 230 | KINGDUIT

"You were taught, with regard to your former way of life, to put off your old self, which is being corrupted by its deceitful desires; to be made new in the attitude of your minds; and to put on the new self, created to be like God in true righteousness and holiness."

Ephesians 4:22-24

Secular mental healing might call the above verse Behavior Therapy. The one seeking mental health must change their behavior and start acting and thinking differently. The counselor can't do that work, each person seeking a change must do the work. Complaining, blaming others, finding fault, soaking in bitterness, and being mad at the world does nothing good.

The world needs people who are taking responsibility for oneself along with the power of the human spirit to change. The people that make these difficult changes should be admired, for they use the power of their will to be different. When they start behaving in love and peace, they will get the fruit of their changed behavior. The missing piece is the divine cleanse that comes from seeking counsel from the "Wonderful Counselor, Mighty God, Everlasting Father, Prince of Peace" (Isaiah 9:6).

The believer in Jesus Christ has the greatest advantage because the blood of the lamb washes their soul, so the enemy has no ground for accusation in the courts of heaven. With Christ on the inside, not only does a life change, but a manifestation of glory also radiates.

CONSIDER: What behaviors in your life need changing?

"Jesus replied, 'Blessed rather are those who hear the word of God and obey it."

Luke 11:28

If you took the forgiveness survey seriously, you should be feeling a fresh cleansing on the inside. This can be a new pattern to continually seek Jesus. As life goes on and new situations tug at your heart strings, you can quickly go to the Lord for cleansing so you can keep your heart pure and free.

There is one more step to be done and that is sealing your healing with the word of God! Being clean and empty of sin is wonderful, but the end goal is to be filled with Holy Spirit and the fruitfulness of the Spirit of the Living God. The new fill up is a must!

FILL UP, FILL UP, FILL UP

Your new insides are love, joy, peace, patience, goodness, kindness, gentleness, and self-control. In addition, the light of Christ fills believers like Isaiah 11:2: "The Spirit of the Lord will rest on him - the Spirit of wisdom and of understanding, the Spirit of counsel and of might, the Spirit of the knowledge and fear of the Lord."

As you read the "speak out & declare" filling up prayers they will bless your healing work with abundance. Your speaking tongue has the power of life, therefore declare it. To start, say out loud; "By the eternal covenant of the blood of Jesus Christ, I am forgiven, cleansed and sealed by the power of Holy Spirit! In Jesus Name, AMEN!"

ART THERAPY DRAW: Draw two jars next to each other with an arrow between them. Put white snowflakes in the jar on the left representing your forgiveness cleansing. Make the arrow pointing to the right jar. Put a Bible, the Cross, and a Dove inside.

Day 232 | KINGDUIT

<u>Filling up Fruitfulness for Abba Glory</u>

SPEAK OUT LOUD & DECLARE

Jesus, you chose me and appointed me to bear eternal fruit. (John 15:15). I have the fruit of Holy Spirit. I have <u>love</u>. As the Father loves me, I love others. I obey God's command to love; I remain in love. I walk in love, above all, because I love others deeply, my love covers a multitude of sin (1 Peter 4:8).

I have <u>joy</u>. I sign joyfully. I consider it pure joy whenever I face trials of many kinds because they perfect me, even in enduring hardships. (James 1:2).

I have <u>peace</u>. Jesus freely gave me His peace so my heart would not be troubled or afraid. I am a peacemaker, I sow in peace, then I reap a harvest of righteousness. The peace of Christ rules in my heart, I am called to peace" (James 3:18).

I have <u>patience</u>. I choose to be completely humble and gentle, patiently bearing with others in love. I still myself before the Lord and wait patiently for Him to move on my behalf (Ephesians 4:2).

I have <u>goodness</u>. I strive to be a good tree with good fruit. I do good deeds daily, even using money to do good things (1 Peter 3:11).

I have <u>kindness</u> and continue in kindness. I consider the kindness of God that continually leads me to repentance. I am kind and tender-hearted. I am forgiving. I speak kindly and show extraordinary kindness to others (Romans 11:22).

I have <u>faithfulness</u>. I am full of faith. I live by faith. My faith and actions work together. I am justified by faith. I put my faith in Jesus Christ (Hebrews 10:38).

I have <u>gentleness</u>. I have the meekness and gentleness of Christ. I have a gentle spirit. I deal with others gently, even foolish, and lost people, I bear with their weaknesses and patiently pray for them (2 Corinthians. 10:1).

I have <u>self-control</u>. I make every effort to add self-control to my faith. Like an athlete exercising self-control in all things, so I control myself so that I can run in God's race and win (Galatians 5:23).

KINGDUIT | Day 233

Filling in the Light of Christ

SPEAK OUT LOUD & DECLARE

Jesus, you are the light of the world. As I follow you, I will never walk in darkness, but I will have the light of life. In Christ, I am the light of the world. I put my light on display to enlighten everyone in my home. I also let my light shine before others, that they may see my good deeds and glorify my Father in heaven. Jesus, your hand is upon me, you will lead me by the Spirit of the Lord. I trust you, Sovereign LORD, you alone know my way (Matthew 5:14).

The Spirit of the LORD says to me; "Do not be afraid or discouraged" because he is the Lord of Hosts and will protect me. I will be strong in the Lord and in his mighty power (Ephesians 6:10). "I keep asking that the God of our Lord Jesus Christ, the glorious Father, may give me the Spirit of wisdom and revelation, so that I may know him better" (Ephesians 1:17).

"I pray that the eyes of my heart may be enlightened in order that I may know the hope to which he has called me, the riches of his glorious inheritance in his holy people, and his incomparably great power for us who believe. That power is the same as the mighty strength he exerted when he raised Christ from the dead and seated him at his right hand in the heavenly realms, far above all rule and authority, power and dominion, and every name that is invoked, not only in the present age but also in the one to come" (Ephesians 1:18-21).

As I grow in the Spirit of understanding, I have knowledge to use words with restraint, I am even-tempered. Lord, fill me with wisdom and understanding, and all kinds of skills to carry out your divine purpose in my life. The Lord's counsel instructs me with divine plans. Teach me your ways, your knowledge, and your instructions. I ask for the counsel of my enemies to fail and amount to nothing (Psalm 27:11). I seek your strength Lord, mightier than the thunder of the great waters, mightier than the breakers of the sea - the LORD on high is mighty in my life (Psalm 93:4).

I humble myself because I fear the LORD. I submit to God Almighty, maker of heaven and earth. I fill up in the fear of the LORD by hating evil and wicked ways. The fear of the LORD is the beginning of wisdom, so I choose to pursue wisdom, understanding and follow His ways (1 Peter 5:6).

"While Jesus was sitting on the Mount of Olives, the disciples came to him privately. 'Tell us', they said, 'when these things will happen and what will be the sign of Your coming and of the end of the age?"

Matthew 24:3

The disciples wanted to find Jesus, so they went to the Mount of Olives. It was the place of anointing, prayer, Jewish history, suffering, and the exact place of the 2nd coming of Jesus Christ. Jesus loved the summit Mount of Olives, which overlooked the temple. This was where he privately went to commune with Abba Father. He had just wept and lamented over Jerusalem because the Jews were unwilling to accept their Messiah. Can you imagine human Jesus completely undone, lamenting, and weeping like a mother "hen longing to gather her chicks under her wings" (Matthew 23:37)? Crying out, "O Jerusalem, Jerusalem!" It is sad that incarnate Jesus, God himself, was crying over rejection. Despite the awesome things Almighty God did for Israel through Moses up to this point in history, it turned into religious hypocrisy, greed, self-indulgence, wickedness, impurity, and sin.

Imagine the Wonderful Counselor running to the Mount of Olives to talk to Abba Father in heaven? That is what Jesus did, and scripture tells why Jesus was upset. He saw the future destruction of the temple again, a consequence for wicked living. "Do you see these things?' Jesus replied. 'Truly I tell you, not one stone here will be left on another; everyone will be thrown down" (Matthew 24:2).

The disciples asked, "when will these things happen" (Matthew 24:3)? Jesus answered in detail about OUR TIME IN HISTORY, RIGHT NOW, THE END TIMES!

Jesus answered, "See to it that no one deceives you. For many will come in my name claiming, 'I am the Christ,' and will deceive many. You will hear of wars and rumors of wars but see to it that you are not alarmed. These things must happen, but the end is still to come. Nation will rise against nation, and kingdom against kingdom. There will be famines and earthquakes in various places. All these are the beginning of birth pains. Because of the multiplication of wickedness, the love of most will grow cold. But the one who perseveres to the end will be saved" (Matthew 24:4-8, 12-13).

"Now learn this lesson from the fig tree. As soon as the branches become tender and sprout leaves, you know that summer is near. So also, when you see all these things, you will know that He is near, right at the door."

Matthew 24:32-33

If Jesus wanted the disciples in his day to learn lessons from the summer garden, how much more should we learn our lessons? We are called to be ready for the second coming of Jesus Christ at any hour. We already learned how important it is to have our spiritual lamps filled with Holy Spirit oil, now we can understand from the words of Jesus why this is so important.

"No one knows about that day or hour, not even the angels in heaven, nor the Son, but only the Father. As it was in the days of Noah, so it will be at the coming of the son of man. For in the days before the flood, people were eating and drinking, marrying, and giving in marriage, up to the day Noah entered the ark. And they were oblivious, until the day the flood came and swept them all away. So, it will be at the coming of the Son of Man. Two men will be in the field: one will be taken and the other left. Two women will be grinding at the mill: one will be taken and the other left. Therefore, keep watch, because you do not know the day on which your Lord will come" (Matthew 24:36-42).

We are the disciples of Jesus Christ and are also called to observe the signs of the times like a gardener observes the fruit. No doubt, the gardener doesn't want to miss the harvest season. This can mean life or death for families depending on food provision. In our case, partnering with the true vine, Jesus, by daily tending to Holy Spirit is like filling our lamps with oil. Our sweet, love-based connection to Jesus keeps the flow of wisdom alive. Our prayers change our lives, homes, and nation.

As the days get darker, it will be difficult to persevere without the Lord. The goal of our faith is the salvation of our souls because we need healthy souls to survive the last days. From the place of psychological health, comes spiritual fortitude. This means the mind is clear, the emotions are stable, the will is steadfast, and the heart is pure. Now the eyes can see clearly what is happening, the ear can hear the Spirit of the Living God speak words of wisdom to understand the times.

BIBLICAL MENTAL HEALTH

"Because of the increase of wickedness, the love of most will grow cold, but the one who stands firm to the end will be saved" (Matthew 24:12-13).

"But about that day or hour no one knows, not even the angels in heaven, nor the Son, but only the Father" (Matthew 24:36). Jesus doesn't tell us the exact day and time of his return. however, he does tell us that life on earth will be very difficult. If he is saying that wickedness will make people lose love, Jesus understands that an evil, wicked, negative, violent, greedy, and perverse environment makes people lose heart. It is hard to love anyone, even a perfect God if your environment is depressing and dark. Even animals grieve and moan under oppression.

The pursuit of biblical mental healing will get your heart and mind ready to face anything. The anointing oil from a flourishing garden life will keep you lathered in a God romance. It will enlighten your path to extinguish darkness. A ripe, seasonally fresh batch of spiritual fruit will sweeten any home or workplace. Proper spiritual nutrition will heal the daily pressures, strengthen the temple, and empower more seeking, praying, and singing to keep the aroma of Christ ablaze. Now you can stand firm with confidence that with Christ in you, there is hope for a glorious finish to the race of faith. Now you can be a part of the solution for the nations and the world. Nothing can stop you if you abide in Christ!

While we still have time in the garden season. Let's review the different ways change happens in a believer's life that can motivate us towards a continued willingness to receive full mental redemption.

"The path of the righteous is level; you, the Upright One, make the way of the righteous smooth. Yes, LORD, walking in the way of your laws, we wait for you, your name and renown are the desires of our hearts."

Isaiah 26:7-8.

"In that day this song will be sung in the land of Judah: We have a strong city; God makes salvation its walls and ramparts. Open the gates that the righteous nations may enter, the nation that keeps faith. You will keep in perfect peace those whose minds are steadfast because they trust in you. Trust in the LORD forever, for the LORD the LORD himself, is the Rock eternal."

Isaiah 26:1-4

God is the faithful One to make a strong city. God will make the walls and gates stable. We have discussed methods the Lord uses to fortify our lives, like discipline. Next, we will discover how the works of darkness can lead to growth and wisdom for change. Even though people feel shame from discipline, pruning or attacks, I have learned that trials and difficult hardships can be blessings worthy of gratitude.

We started with discipline, the humbling process when Holy Spirit reveals sins and transgressions. We learned about repentance and aligning the will to seek the Lord for cleansing. Then we went into detail concerning forgiveness to be purified, which can also manifest in bodily healing. The experience was a diligent and unending pursuit for total forgiveness to gain a willing spirit for the biblical mental healing journey.

As we continue to explore the garden of our lives, we can realize that pruning can be some of the best ways to make our lives tremendously fruitful. Every prize-winning gardener hacks back the vine and fruit trees every year to continue to produce the highest and best quality produce. The gardener doesn't do it to punish the trees and vines, the gardener prunes to bless and bear more glorious and delicious fruit that will nourish themselves and others.

We can get to the point of our journey that any correction or pruning from the Father is divine attention fully based in love and ever-increasing blessing. That means mental accountability every day and, in every way, even from a kind friend or family member. Even a momentary thought can harm and needs cleansing. Words that speak death should be challenged and gracefully corrected with words that elevate self and the listener. Next, we will look at some of the work of the enemy. This is necessary to outwit and even punish the deeds of darkness!

Day 238 | KINGDUIT

"Jesus told them another parable: 'The kingdom of heaven is like a man who sowed good seed in his field. But while everyone was sleeping, his enemy came and sowed weeds among the wheat and went away. When the wheat sprouted and formed heads, then the weeds also appeared. The owner's servants came to him and said, 'Sir, didn't you sow good seed in your field? Where then did the weeds come from?'

'An enemy did this,' he replied."

Matthew 13:24-28

One thing I often say to myself to help maintain the courage to overcome the enemy is, "the devil is a COWARD!" He is always hiding, masquerading, and doing things in the dark where no one can see. Cowards are afraid, they play on weak ones or little ones, and they hide.

Why do they hide? Because if you don't see them and things go wrong, others are likely to blame people or even you for an error. The enemy won't outrightly show himself because he hates people and wants them to turn on each other instead of him. If he keeps sowing bad seeds while in hiding, people will keep destroying each other with judgment and false accusations while he mocks and accuses us before God at how foolish we are for falling again.

The enemy also wants us to stay ignorant and dumb. Darkness especially thrives when we don't read the bible. When this happens, we don't learn how powerful we are to stop the enemies' schemes in a snap. So, keep tending the garden of your life and Holy Spirit will reveal every demonic plot set against you. Keep seeking total healing and your "mind of Christ" will grow sharper. When Holy Spirit teaches you to be an overcomer, you will be able to clean enemy weeds out of your garden before they cause you and your family trouble.

One breakthrough came through reading scriptures forty days. I didn't understand it, but when the Lord told me to read scriptures out loud between midnight and three am, it was likely keeping enemy weeds out of my garden for at least forty days. That was enough for me to leap forward on my healing journey and continue to pursue Christ to seek full redemption over the decades as I relentlessly pursued liberty.

KINGDUIT | Day 239

"Then Jesus left the crowd and went into the house. The disciples came to him and said, "Explain to us the parable of the weeds in the field."

He answered, 'The one who sowed the good seed is the Son of Man. The field is the world, and the good seeds stand for the people of the kingdom. The weeds are the people of the evil one, and the enemy who sows them is the devil."

Matthew 13:36-39

Jesus told the parable of the wheat and the weeds to the crowds to expose one of the enemy's tricks, which is to sow weeds at night while the workers slept. The disciples took it a step further and sought Jesus for more understanding.

Can you picture this parable of a farmer's field? No doubt a farmer isn't going to plant weed seeds in his field, he's going to plant the best wheat seeds to produce an excellent harvest. He will desire good wheat seeds to make delicious bread, bread that can sustain and prosper the life of his family and community.

His enemy isn't going to trespass on the farmers property in plain sight in daylight, he might get killed. His enemy will sneak in at night when everyone is sleeping and cause trouble.

Our enemy is the devil. Have you ever wondered why the devil is depicted carrying a pitchfork? A pitchfork is a pronged farm tool with a handle, a clear confirmation of the biblical weed seeder.

On days when you are trying your best to be good for your Father in the Kingdom of Heaven, rest assured that He is the God of Justice and will punish "everything that causes sin and all who do evil" (Matthew 13:42).

ART THERAPY DRAW: Draw a garden with a moon to represent the night. Draw a red devil with a pitchfork in the garden, smiling.

Day 240 | KINGDUIT

"I pursued my enemies and overtook them; I did not turn back till they were destroyed. I crushed them so that they could not rise; they fell beneath my feet."

Psalm 18:37-38

"The weapons we fight with are not the weapons of the world. On the contrary, they have divine power to demolish strongholds. We demolish arguments and every pretension that sets itself up against the knowledge of God, and we take captive every thought and make it obedient to Christ."

2 Corinthians 10:4-5

David wrote Psalm 18 when the Lord rescued him from all his enemies and from King Saul's multiple assassination attempts. David said the Lord removed his enemies because of his cries for help. He was willing to physically move out to battle with great courage and faith. Psalm 18 gives an incredible description of exactly how David was delivered from evil during his Kingdom journey. His victory was accomplished with a bronze bow, a shield and divine intervention.

We also get divine intervention when we cry out to the Lord and physically open our mouths with spiritual authority in Christ. Our words execute explosive power like dynamite paired with the sword of the Spirit which is the word of God.

King David desired the Lord's praises over the nations, victory, and unfailing love in his life and for all his descendants. Yes, all Christians too! We have "adoption to sonship through Jesus Christ . . ." (Ephesians 1:5). We have been grafted into the olive tree and abide in Jesus, the true grapevine. We have the shield of faith for victory!

ART THERAPY DRAW: Draw a King's Crown and a Jewish Star.

"...and the enemy who sows them is the devil. The harvest is the end of the age, and the harvesters are angels.

As the weeds are pulled up and burned in the fire, so it will be at the end of the age. The Son of Man will send out his angels, and they will weed out of his kingdom everything that causes sin and all who do evil. They will be thrown into the blazing furnace, where there will be weeping and gnashing of teeth. Then the righteous will shine like the sun in the kingdom of their Father. Whoever has ears, let them hear."

Matthew 13:38-43

Pursuing mental health and healing can be like tending the garden of your soul. We are exhorted to stay connected to Jesus the olive root while also abiding in Jesus the true vine so that we will be fruitful and even evict the serpent out of our garden.

When we are filled with Holy Spirit, we have the gift of discerning spirits to know when evil spirits are trying to influence and wreak havoc in our garden. We must fight the good fight against those evil influences by using our authority in Christ, the same authority that raised Christ from the dead.

If people who are in our field of influence belong to the evil one, then we need to activate our invisible sword with His mighty power. We can overcome evil with good and fight a spiritual battle by faith. The power to demolish everything that sets itself against the knowledge of God has already been given. With the increase of evil in our history, we must shield ourselves while we hide in the secret place of the Most High. Remember, God will fulfill his promises to us as we are willing to obey the Word of God with faith and action. Rest assured, there will be a day of reckoning when the Son of Man will weed out all evil and evildoers. There will be justice and there will be eternal punishment.

Then, the Kingdom of Heaven will be filled with the Father's garden of beauty, and we will shine bright forever, and God will wipe away all our tears.

Supreme God of the Heavens & Earth

SPEAK OUT LOUD & DECLARE

Dear Father, you are in heaven, and your name is Holy. You are the Lord my God, the Supreme God of the heavens above and the earth below. You are the lover of my life. You are my gardener, cutting off every branch in me that bears no fruit. Even the branches that bear fruit, you prune so that I will be even more fruitful. Thank you for Your great care and lovingly tending my life like a glorious garden of God. Abba Father, Supreme God, thank you for beautifying my garden to make sweet aromas with joy. You are the keeper of Your covenant of love, thank you. May I love you deeply from the heart and keep your commands (John 15).

The Bible says you look at the soil of my life and ask, "How is the soil?" Is it fertile or poor? Though you are full of compassion and mercy, you will still be the Judge standing at my door! May I be willing to forgive, remove the bitter roots, weed seeds, and fruitless deeds of darkness from my being. Let me be found grafted in the Jesus' olive root. May my growth cultivate oil for my lamp, oil that remains so my light shines bright. May Israel witness our love for Heavenly Father and Yeshua and be provoked to long for divine restoration!

Find my branches abiding in the vine of Jesus, bearing much fruit, bringing glory to the Kingdom of Heaven. Find me willing to pull out the weed seeds to evict evil roots choking my harvest. I will do my best to bring fruit from my healing journey, lasting fruit. I will bring good things out of the good stored in my heart to cultivate the new Holy Spirit wine outpouring for these days.

May I put action into my faith so that I am alive on the inside and full of strength and courage like Joshua. May I be encouraged in heart and united in love. Give me the full riches of complete understanding in order that I may know the mystery of God in whom are hidden all the treasures of wisdom and knowledge (John 15:9).

When the days are dark and I discern evil, I will put up a good fight of faith to turn the tables and bring about change. I will raise my voice; I will sing and proclaim the faithfulness of Almighty (1 Timothy 6:2). "The Lord will march out like a champion, like a warrior he will stir up his zeal; with a shout he will raise up the battle cry and will triumph over his enemies" (Isaiah 42:13). Holy is His name, now and forever! AMEN!

Pray yesterday's prayer again & sing praises!

YouTube - Holy Forever - Jen Johnson, Bethel Music

ART THERAPY DRAW: Draw fireworks to represent the glory of God's goodness over your life.

MONTH 9 - Unquenchable Love

KINGDUIT | Day 244

"My beloved has gone down to his garden, to the beds of spices, to browse in the gardens and gather lilies."

Song of Solomon 6:2

January is the beginning of a global calendar. But according to the Bible, the month of September is the beginning of God's calendar for the Jewish New Year. That's because it is the birthday of the Universe, when God created the heavens and the earth. We will learn about Rosh Hashanah in September to understand how we fit in the story of our ancestors. This will go all the way back to the Garden of Eden originating with Adam and Eve.

This Biblical mental healing devotional is intended to plant your mind into redemption found in the Bible with an end goal of soul-level salvation. We have reviewed the history of God's people from the beginning to the end, both Jew and Gentile. This has laid the foundation of how mankind has experienced redemption along with the rise and falls of the human experience, from a personal and national perspective.

"When the righteous thrive, the people rejoice; when the wicked rule, the people groan" (Proverbs 29:2). Your negative mental health can be influenced by a wicked government, and contrary to that your mental thriving and healing can lead to national healing or global restoration.

This historical time finds many suffering at psychological levels, while people of faith long for peace. We have seen the results of disaster trauma, demonically oppressed nations, and evil influences every day. Even children long for joy and security. Many have fled to the isolated life of off-grid homesteading, where they live quietly and search for community.

The Jews had to trek through the desert to find Almighty God, then learn to lean on Him until they could move into a peaceful society. That is still God's plan: to seek Him, find Him, be redeemed by Him, and then glorify Him!

Looking into God's garden in the Song of Solomon will illustrate a healthy life with the beloved bridegroom. It is like a love-centered, vibrant well-spring on the inside that represents God's mysterious global plan on the outside.

Day 245 | KINGDUIT

"I am my beloved's, and my beloved is mine; he browses among the lilies."

Song of Solomon 6:3

Truly, God still walks around the garden like he did in the Garden of Eden. The spring easter lily is a picture of Christ by representing his purity, innocence, and rebirth. The white lily flower is both beautiful and sad as it rises and falls back into the dirt to bloom again. As little-Christ followers, like lilies, can experience the resurrection and life of Christ on the inside. The Song of Solomon Garden is so lovely, beautiful, fruitful, passionate, and aromatic that men may want to shy away from this utopian environment, but they shouldn't.

God's garden is centered in covenant love, the love between God and Israel, the church, and you. It's about God's love for men and women, boys, and girls. It's the everlasting love of God that endures forever. The love of dreams where peace abounds with grace and beauty are at every corner. God's love is so strong it dies for people. This love will form a majestic troop and go to war. This love is so relentless it burns and blazes, longs and waits. It will burn until all the impurities come out to reveal gold, and then, the love hammers. This love hammers like a master sculptor until a masterpiece forms to display in the garden. It will result in a golden ark-like rescue vessel where angels appear and hover. This garden of love is unquenchable, so nourished and flourishing that even an ocean can't stop this love from breaking through. Yes, it's for men too!

When our beloved El Roi, the God who sees, comes down from heaven by His Spirit to browse in the garden of our soul and gather lilies, we intentionally get still in the presence of the Lord and let him tend to our hearts, souls, and spirits.

We make room in our hearts and open the door to His knocking, no matter what chamber He desires to abide in. From the most intimate places of our identity, sexuality, purpose, and stories to the secret places of our dreams and desires.

Knowing we belong to our beloved God gives reason for deep-seated joy. Hopefully, a healing season of grace is made available by your willing spirit to cultivate your heart garden for the kingdom of heaven. Yes, this love, the greatest love of all, is inside the human heart. Creator God made it ready on the 6th day.

KINGDUIT | Day 246

"Like a lily among thorns is my darling among the young women. Like an apple tree among the trees of the forest is my beloved among the young men."

Song of Solomon 2:2-3

God's man is described like a fruit tree. "Like an apple tree among the trees of the forest is my beloved among the young men. Let him lead me to the banquet hall and let his banner over me be love. I delight to sit in his shade, and his fruit is sweet to my taste, and let his banner over me be love" (Song of Solomon 2:3-4).

The male garden is full of the delight of provisions and victory. A man on a conquest to rule and reign out of a spirit of love is certainly victory. The conquering spirit to male love is that it is a holy pursuit. Therefore, you won't discern control, lust, or greed in this love. The leadership of the man of God will take you to the banqueting hall of the King of Kings. Calling all biblical males!

This pure love is kingdom centered via a holy conquest. It raises a banner of God's love. This love is out in the mountains like a gazelle looking at the times and seasons, watching the fig tree, hiding in the secret place of the Most High, and delighted to sit in the presence of God by tending to the garden of his life, waiting for the right time to move out for the Kingdom.

"You prepare a table before me in the presence of my enemies, you anoint my head with oil, my cup overflows. Surely Your goodness and love will follow me all the days of my life, and I will dwell in the house of the Lord forever" (Psalm 23:5-6).

ART THERAPY DRAW: Draw mountains and label them "MOUNT ZION."

Day 247 | KINGDUIT

"My dove in the clefts of the rock, in the hiding places on the mountainside, show me your face, let me hear your voice; for your voice is sweet, and your face is lovely."

Song of Solomon 2:14

When King David, the warrior lover, longed for fellowship with the Lord, he was led to a place of still waters to rest in green pastures. His soul was restored to be led further by God on a path of righteousness for the sake of the kingdom.

God walks around longing for fellowship with his children. Can you imagine the Lord looking at your face and listening for your voice? When we seek after Him and He finds us posturing ourselves to be with him, He says our faces are lovely and our voices are sweet. It is humbling to think that we do something for our Lord, but we do! We bring joy and delight to Him. He wants us to find solitary hiding places as we seek Him. He wants to bless us in His presence!

Jesus said in Matthew 6:6, "When you pray, go into your room, close the door and pray to your Father, who is unseen. Then your Father, who sees what is done in secret, will reward you." This type of seeking the Lord is not a religious activity. It is a private, personal, heart-warming, secret meeting with our Beloved God.

After these words, Jesus teaches the crowd of God seekers the Lord's prayer starting with, "Our Father in heaven, hallowed be your name, your kingdom come, your will be done, on earth as it is in heaven" (Matthew 6:9-10). This type of praying is about the kingdom of heaven coming down on earth. That means your love relationship with the Lord is about something heavenly. The garden of your soul is being cultivated for the kingdom of heaven on earth.

"How lovely is your dwelling place, Lord Almighty! My soul yearns, even faints, for the courts of the Lord; my heart and my flesh cry out for the living God. Even the sparrow has found a home, and the swallow a nest for herself, where she may have her young- a place near your altar, Lord Almighty, my King and my God" (Psalm 84:1-3).

"Catch for us the foxes, the little foxes that ruin the vineyards, our vineyards that are in bloom."

Song of Solomon 2:15

You will find as you encounter the Lord in your hiding place, He truly is captivated by your face and words. Your heart will melt with a longing for more love and holiness. God intended for this to happen in your heart because his kindness leads you to turn away from what hinders your 'garden of God' life.

You will also realize you just can't be holy like God is holy. That's when you will ask Him to catch the foxes in your vineyard that ruin fruitfulness. Foxes are known to dig up gardens, which keeps them from harvest. God knows how to catch the things that hinder you because He loves you and watches over your life.

Even Jesus had to deal with the foxes that tried to ruin the garden of his soul's heavenly mission. "At that time some Pharisees came to Jesus and said to him, 'Leave this place and go somewhere else. Herod wants to kill you.'

Jesus replied, 'Go tell that fox, I will keep on driving out demons and healing people today and tomorrow, and on the third day I will reach my goal" (Luke 13:31-32).

Jesus knows that religious leaders like Pharisees can be the ones trying to keep people away from blessings. Yes, even the disciples (God's men) tried to hinder children from seeking Jesus. If you are honest with yourself, there are times that even you hinder others and yourself from seeking God.

"Then the little children were brought to Jesus for Him to place His hands on them and pray for them. And the disciples rebuked those who brought them. But Jesus said, 'Let the little children come to me, and do not hinder them, for the kingdom of heaven belongs to such as these.' And after He had placed His hands on them, He went on from there" (Matthew 19:14).

The kingdom of heaven is so valuable that we must protect it. We ask the Lord to catch the foxes so our garden can be fruitful for the Father's glory! We are sensitive to ways we may hinder divine progress.

Day 249 | KINGDUIT

"Daughters of Jerusalem, I charge you by the gazelles and by the does of the field: Do not arouse or awaken love until it so desires."

Song of Solomon 2:7/3:5/8:4

God's garden is a place of fruitful holiness which includes sexual purity. Even though weeds are allowed to remain in the world, true worshippers have removed the enemy weeds. Holy living is a sure way to be ready for the coming harvest. As you may have noticed, this exact verse is repeated three times in Song of Solomon. You can imagine its importance. It is a warning and charge from God to hold sexual love until one's wedding night. Mental healing includes freedom from fornication, adultery, perversion, and sexual abuse. Being aroused and awakening love does have a time and place before the Lord. If you read Song of Solomon, you understand sexual intimacy in God's way, with the bride and the bridegroom. The nakedness of lovers is delightful and beautiful inside a devoted biblical marriage.

The book of Song of Solomon is an allegory about God's love for the Israelites and His sacred covenant of love. It is also a poem about unashamed marital eros (sex) love. Fruitfulness in marriage is a picture of Christ and the church. The big wedding supper of the Lamb is coming. A healthy person has love; a love for God and love for others by showing respect, honor, and purity. "Make every effort to live in peace with everyone and to be holy; without holiness no one will see the Lord. See to it that no one falls short of the grace of God and that no bitter root grows up to cause trouble and defile many. See that no one is sexually immoral…" (Hebrews 12:14-16).

You can't talk about liberty without mentioning sexuality. Don't let a wicked and perverse generation deceive you into thinking ANY type of sexual impurity outside of biblical marriage is a good thing, because it's not. If someone is into sexual perversion, they love lust, not love. If someone secretly looks at the uncovered man, woman, boy or girl, it is a sign of hate in the heart and will bring a curse. Covering or protecting nakedness is a blessing. Read about nakedness in Genesis 9:18-27.

Holy love never looks at nakedness outside marriage and pure caregiving. Love covers, love guards, love keeps, and love protects. Love charges, promises, swears, and makes an oath to wait on God.

"If she is a wall, we will build towers of silver on her. If she is a door, we will enclose her with panels of cedar."

Song of Solomon 8:9

God's idea of pure love is protection and fortification from the entrance of immoral influence. The lover and bride's garden are kept safe and secure from predators. Ancient silver walls and cedar panels were strong to protect ladies from any sexual activity until the wedding night. Christ longs for the church to radiate purity for the soon coming marriage supper of the Lamb.

Jesus said this, "Truly, truly, I tell you, I am the gate for the sheep. All who came before Me were thieves and robbers, but the sheep did not listen to them. I am the gate. If anyone enters through Me, he will be saved, he will come in and go out and find pasture. The thief comes only to steal and kill and destroy. I have come that they may have life and have it in all its fullness" (John 10:7-10).

Jesus knows that sexual immorality is one of the plots of the thief to steal, kill and destroy young people, individuals, and families. The bible calls sexual immorality godlessness. Perversion has led to a massive amount of trauma and mental torment these days. If counseling office walls could tell the stories, there would be great lamenting over godless perversion.

Our generation certainly knows that society has been horrifically and violently corrupted by a demonic whore. The bible calls her "the great prostitute." For those of us who have been ashamed and broken by any type of sexual perversion, know that the Lord our God will avenge this evil while making His bride white and clean.

"Hallelujah; Salvation, and glory, and power belong to our God, for true and just are his judgments. He has condemned the great prostitute who corrupted the earth by her adulteries. He has avenged on her the blood of his servants. . .For the wedding of the Lamb has come, and his bride has made herself ready. Fine linen, bright and clean, was given her to wear" (Revelation 19:1-2, 7-8). God the Avenger has a plan for his church bride!

ART THERAPY DRAW: Draw a wall with silver towers and a cedar door.

Day 251 | KINGDUIT

"How is your beloved better than others, that you charge us? My beloved is radiant and ruddy, outstanding among ten thousand."

Song of Solomon 5:10

This type of conversation questions the devotion of a loved one has for a spouse out of reverence for Almighty God, the lover of our souls. Is Jesus the Messiah worth our promises, oaths, and vows to keep ourselves free from transgression? Is Jesus worthy of holiness and sanctification? How is Jesus better than the gods of this world or the great whore?

Think about why Jesus is worth seeking personal purity while you wait for Him to return to earth. Has the love of God felt heavenly/eternal/glorious to your soul? Is the garden of your soul being cultivated for the kingdom of heaven on earth? The bride responds by saying:

"My beloved is radiant and ruddy, outstanding among ten thousand. His head is wavy and black as a raven. His eyes are like doves by the water streams, washed in milk, mounted like jewels. His cheeks are like beds of spice yielding perfume. His lips are like lilies dripping with myrrh, His arms are rods of gold set with topaz. His body is like polished ivory decorated with lapis lazuli. His legs are pillars of marble set on bases of pure gold. His appearance is like Lebanon, choice as its cedars. His mouth is sweetness itself; he is altogether lovely. This is my beloved, this is my friend, daughters of Jerusalem" (Song of Solomon 5:9-16). One day we will see him face to face and behold his beauty. Truly the avenger will come down out of heaven as a heavenly warrior. His eyes are ablaze as he prepares to mount a white horse to strike down the nations. He is already pouring out his Spirit upon all flesh to prepare us for his return. True worshippers are here now, worshiping in spirit and truth day and night. They sing and proclaim Yeshua the Messiah! Don't miss out, pursue soul salvation every day. Get ready by joining the praise!

WORSHIP: Listen - YouTube: Yeshua Jesus Image Michael Koulianos

"Place me like a seal over your heart, like a seal on your arm; for love is strong as death, its jealousy unyielding as the grave. It burns like fire, like a mighty flame."

Song of Solomon 8:6

Why is love so emotionally powerful? Why has love and passion driven so many to therapy? This passage sounds extreme, but history has proven its truth, love is as strong as death. Love is fierce, even to the grave. Love flashes like fire and warms with beauty. But it also can be destructive like jealousy and ruin lives. Countless are the love songs. How can the God of perfect love have anything to do with jealousy?

Jealousy is generally viewed as a negative emotion, but there is a jealousy that is positive, emanating from the heart of God and motivated by blessing. "The Lord spoke to you face to face out of the fire on the mountain" (Deuteronomy 5:4). This blazing fire of love is where Moses received the Ten Commandments, which were given to protect the people. "Hear O Israel, the statutes and ordinances that I declare in your hearing this day. Learn them and observe them carefully. . .I am the Lord your God, who brought you out of the land of slavery. You shall have no other gods before me. You shall not make for yourself an image in the form of anything in heaven above or on the earth beneath or in the waters below. You shall not bow down to them or worship them; for I, the Lord you God, am a jealous God, punishing the children for the sin of the parents to the third and fourth generation of those who hate me, but showing love to a thousand generations to those who love me and keep my commandments" (Deuteronomy 5:1,6-10).

Don't forget, Creator God made male and female in His image, as His treasured possession. He is jealous for us to receive His love. He is jealous for you, meaning He wants so badly for you to be loved by Him. That is why He is not willing to let us go to the enemy and the other gods/idols of the world. Discipline and punishment are meant to inspire the turn around. God loved Israel so much he was jealous for them to live in the covenantal blessings of His promises.

But Israel kept turning to idols repeatedly, that's why God sent his son Jesus from heaven to earth to remedy the situation on the cross of Calvary. Then they killed Jesus, but He is coming again with "eyes like blazing fire and many royal crowns on His head" (Revelation 19:12). Does this return sound like love to you?

Day 253 | KINGDUIT

"Many waters cannot quench love; rivers cannot sweep it away. If one were to give all the wealth of one's house for love, it would be utterly scorned."

Song of Solomon 8:7

Jesus is the man who left all the riches of a heavenly kingdom for love. He left the honor, wealth, purity, and splendor of the kingdom of heaven to become a human born in an animal stable and died with his heart crushed and body destroyed. The floodgates of the passion of Christ are so massive, it covers whosoever will receive His love!

The bride above is speaking about her experience with the beloved. She wants to be sealed over her lover's heart. She explains the consuming nature of this divine covenantal love like many waters.

Of all the natural disasters, water is inescapable and relentless. But the waters of trials and betrayal is no match for the love God had and still has for Israel. Many waters cannot quench God's love for you and His church. God adores his Romans 11:17 "wild olive shoot," gentile bride, that has been grafted into the olive root, sharing the nourishing sap with the hope of making Israel envious one day soon. Jesus's once and for all sacrifice of redeeming love truly paid it all. His love will wash, cleanse, and redeem any willing person, family, or nation.

If you know His love, you know that no matter what the storm is trying to rain on you with, His love will always be there. Truly you can say with King David the psalmist, "Because Your love is better than life, my lips will glorify you. I will praise you as long as I live, and in your name, I will lift up my hands" (Psalm 63:3-4).

This love song, the Song of Solomon, ends with the bride understanding that her vineyard is within her own will to give. She then chooses to give abundance to her beloved King as she also shares with those who have helped tend her garden.

The bridegroom then calls out to "you who dwell in the gardens with friends in attendance, let me hear your voice" (Songs of Solomon 8:13)! God is love and He is calling you! Can you hear him?

"Above all, love each other deeply, because love covers over a multitude of sins" (1 Peter 4:8).

KINGDUIT | Day 254

"Jesus replied: 'Love the Lord your God will all your heart and will all your soul and with all your mind,' This is the first and greatest commandment."

Matthew 22:37-38

If you have sincerely engaged with Jehovah Rapha throughout this mental healing devotional, my hope is that you have experienced the deep love of God. I pray His love has empowered you to ascend on the mountain of His high ways to discover that divine love, power, and a sound mind is freedom. Without a doubt, the proof of divine mental healing is an increasing and abounding love manifesting in and throughout your life. Love is the remedy and love is the goal.

"And so, we know and rely on the love God has for us. God is love. Whoever lives in love lives in God, and God in them" (1 John 4:16). Even unbelievers believe that love is a high calling. Musicians find success in singing about love. Love has the power to heal like no other force in the world.

Even though most can agree on the concept of love, it's the acting out in our own lives and then towards others that can be challenging at times, especially if you don't come from a loving upbringing. Feeling loved by family, friends and coworkers has lost ground in these days of social media, progress, and self-love.

To those reading for information purposes, I suggest to "taste and see that the Lord is good; blessed is the one who takes refuge in him" (Psalm 34:8). God's love can change your life and enrich your mental health daily!

The pursuit of divine love can be the most humbling and blessed kind of emotions to experience. The humble part is that the Most High God, King and Creator of the universe, loves someone like you and me. The brokenness of the human experience paired with the beautiful depth of Christ's eternal and unending love brings a comfort to the soul that is unmatched by anything.

Making the effort to love God with your heart, soul, and mind will not only bring mental healing, but has the power to restore your life and purpose as you step into a space of hope that makes anything possible in this life.

WORSHIP: Listen - YouTube: Reckless Love Cory Asbury

Day 255 | KINGDUIT

<u>Pray for Love</u>

I pray that out of His glorious riches He may strengthen me with power through His Spirit in my inner being so that Christ may dwell in my heart through faith. And I pray that I, being rooted and established in love, may have power, together with all the Lord's holy people, to grasp how wide and long and high and deep is the love of Christ, and to know this love that surpasses knowledge - that I may be filled to the measure of all the fullness of God. Now to him who is able to do immeasurably more than all I ask or imagine, according to His power that is at work within me, to Him be glory in the church and in Christ Jesus throughout all generations, for ever and ever! Amen.

Ephesians 3:16-21

ART THERAPY DRAW: Draw a tree that has roots tied to hearts. Surround the tree with glorious rich like jewels symbolic of kingdom wealth.

Greatest Commandment: LOVE

SPEAK OUT LOUD & DECLARE

Jesus, you said the first and greatest commandment is to love the Lord my God with all my heart and with all my soul and with all my mind. Jesus, you said the second greatest commandment is to love my neighbor as I love myself (Luke 10:27). As I partner with Jehovah Rapha to heal myself, I will have greater love to love others freely. I put on love above all else. I value love, my love will cover a multitude of sins. Because of the Lord's love, I love others, proving my discipleship. Because you first loved me, I love others earnestly (Colossians 3:14).

Even when the culture stirs up hatred and strife, I put on love to cover up the offense. I have come to know and rely on the love of God for me. God is love. As I live in love, I live in God and God lives in me. This is how love is made complete in me so that I will have confidence on the day of judgment. I will be like Jesus in this world. My love banishes fear. As my love is perfected through the healing power of Jesus, my love drives out fear, because fear has to do with punishment (1 John 4:16-18). I demolish the spirit of fear because it opposes the love of Christ in me.

Jesus loved me first, therefore I love myself. If I refuse to love and forgive others, I lose my claim of loving God. If I say I love God yet hate others, I am a liar. I cleanse myself of the godlessness of being unloving. As I seek God's love more, my love for others increases.

I have confidence in my love as His child because I carry out his commands. His commands are not burdensome. My love for God will lead me to overcome the world. The atoning sacrifice of Jesus continues to empower my life of loving God. God's merciful, gracious, patient, abounding steadfast love enriches my life daily. God is faithful to keep steadfast love with me as I continue to keep his commandments. My obedience will carry on to a thousand generations because the Lord my God is love!

I have the power to love my enemies, do good to them, and lend to them without expecting to get anything back. Then my reward will be great, and I will be a child of the Most High (Luke 6:35). As the Father loves Jesus, Jesus loves me, and I remain in Christ's love!

Day 257 | KINGDUIT

"Then the man and his wife heard the sound of the Lord God as he was walking in the garden in the cool of the day. . ."

Genesis 3:8

As we move towards the end of Summer, we will take a break to understand Rosh Hashanah and Yom Kippur in our quest for vitality. Walking from our garden of God all the way back to the original Garden of Eden will bring great revelation. God already created paradise instead of a formless, empty, and dark surface of deep waters in the universe. "The Spirit of God was hovering over the waters. And God said, 'Let there be light,' and there was light" (Genesis 1:2).

No matter where you are on your healing journey, Almighty God has the power to bring light into any dark situation around your life. He did it before and He can do it again! If you feel oppression from the dark side, the Lord God still walks in the middle of your garden. He still speaks to us to call out looking for you to engage His heart and Spirit, even when you hide. He still intends to punish the enemy for his deceptions while he washes you with His waterfalls of endless love.

"The LORD decrees His loving devotion by day, and at night His song is with me as a prayer to the God of my life."

Psalm 42:8

Rosh Hashanah Begins Sunset

We finally caught up to the Jewish calendar's New Year. Rosh Hashanah begins at sunset in the nation of Israel. Happy Birthday Universe! God literally started time itself when he created man to mark the start of the Jewish New Year.

"Then God said, 'Let Us make mankind in Our image, in Our likeness, so that they may rule over the fish in the sea and the birds in the sky, over the livestock, and over all the creatures that move along the ground.'

So, God created mankind in His own image; in the image of God, He created them; male and female He created them.

God blessed them and said to them, 'Be fruitful and increase in number; fill the earth and subdue it. Rule over the fish in the sea and the birds in the sky and over every living creature that moves on the ground.'

Then God said, 'I give you every seed-bearing plant on the face of the whole earth and every tree that has fruit with seed in it. They will be yours for food. And all the beasts of the earth and all the birds in the sky and all the creatures that move along - everything that has the breath of life in it - I give every green plant for food.' And it was so" (Genesis 1:26-30).

It's no coincidence that the Lord is leading us back to the beginning of time, back to the garden, back to the blessing of fruitfulness and dominion. We are reminded that the Lord is the King of the Universe, the Most High God, maker of heaven and earth. The Lord reigns and is worthy of our joy in proclaiming that the Lord is King forever!

CONSIDER: As we draw closer to the return of Christ, consider making yourself aware of the Jewish calendar and the Jewish festivals. This will enlarge your understanding of the Bible and the way God works at redeeming people and nations.

Day 259 | KINGDUIT

"Blow the trumpet in Zion; sound the alarm on my holy hill. Let all who live in the land tremble, for the day of the LORD is coming. It is close at hand."

Joel 2:1

The Jewish community is still blowing the shofar for the new year, which is a ram's horn. The trumpeting represents a sound that highlights many aspects of our heavenly king and kingdom. This starts with the provision of the first sacrifice of redemption and continues all the way to the return of the bridegroom. The Jewish community desires to rightly launch a new year, therefore they give value to the celebration. The "Head of the year" focus is to seek peace and prosperity in the coming year. The Jewish people even read prayers that include all the inhabitants of the world.

Understanding the Jewish calendar can bring blessings for all people, especially biblical Christians. To seek wisdom concerning the end of days will prepare us for the trumpet call to all mankind, an alarm sent from heaven. It will mark humanities redemption when Jesus comes again. He will set his feet on the Mount of Olives and usher in the unshakable kingdom.

"For the Lord himself will come down from heaven, with a loud command, with the voice of the archangel and with the trumpet call of God, and the dead in Christ will rise first" (1 Thessalonians 4:16). This day will shake all the heavens and earth, along with mankind, with a glory and consuming fire. Many bible scholars believe the season of this historic day will be in the month of September.

As we align our will to the pursuit of divine healing, it will surely prepare us in the best way for the coming end of days event. What shall we do in other nations while Israel celebrates Rosh Hashanah?

We seek the promise of God for full redemption and follow the exhortation of the bible to "keep on loving one another as brothers and sisters" (Hebrews 13:1). We do this by being kind, hospitable, remembering those who suffer, honoring marriage, staying sexually pure, refusing to bow to the idolatry of money, and holding fast to the Word of God.

All these exhortations build into a life of love, power, and a sound mind. "Shana Tova!" May you have a good and sweet Hebrew New Year!

Rosh Hashanah Ends Nightfall

"Praise the Lord, my soul; all my inmost being, praise his holy name. Praise the Lord, my soul, and forget not all his benefits - who forgives all your sins and heals all your diseases, who redeems your life from the pit and crowns you with love and compassion, who satisfies your desires with good things so that your youth is renewed like the eagle's."

Psalm 103:1-5

Like us, the Jewish community focuses on the power of prayer individually and corporately. They also consider humanity as a whole during Rosh Hashanah, so we who are Gentile believers should also consider the nation of Israel and Jerusalem.

We activate our willingness to align our wills to the Word of God and pray to our Father in Heaven. We take time for ourselves to praise the Lord and proclaim His faithfulness over our lives, our families, our nations, and the nation of Israel.

Many groups have set up day and night prayer and worship services to align with the Bible by praying corporately for Israel. When we bless Israel, we bless ourselves.

We seek the Lord and proclaim, "For Zion's sake I will not keep silent, for Jerusalem's sake I will not remain quiet, till her vindication shines out like the dawn, her salvation like a blazing torch. The nations will see your vindication, and all kings your glory; you will be called by a new name that the mouth of the Lord will bestow. You will be a crown of splendor in the Lord's hand, a royal diadem in the hand of your God" (Isaiah 62:1:3).

MEDITATE: Write out the word equation:

GOD'S PROMISE = OUR WILLINGNESS.

Think about the way God has worked among people throughout history. The benefits of forgiveness, healing, redemption, love, and compassion are for those who worship, praise, speak out, and pursue the Lord.

Day 261 | KINGDUIT

"How awesome is the Lord Most High, the great King over all the earth! He subdues nations beneath us, and peoples under our feet. He chooses our inheritance for us, the pride of Jacob, whom He loves. Selah

God has ascended amid shouts of joy, the Lord with the sound of the horn. Sing praises to God, sing praises; sing praises to our King, sing praises!

For God is King of all the earth; sing profound praises to Him."

Psalm 47:2-7

The hard work of pursuing soul-level mental healing requires times of rest. A selah (pause) followed by seeking the Lord with prayers and singing is a good plan. Part of the healing process requires filling up the soul with the goodness of God, His holy word and the high praises of worship and singing.

Balancing these things is part of a biblical lifestyle. Often pursuing mental healing comes with resistance, a painful recalling of the past, brokenness, tears and even suffering. Some of us are going against the grain of our family life and culture by pursuing biblical mental healing. Our willingness to look at ourselves in consideration of God's holy word can truly rend the heart. It is a mixture of sadness while experiencing the human condition but also great grace and joy that Jesus will never leave us or forsake us as we walk through life's shadows.

The joy of fellowship with Christ along with the fruitfulness of freedom is wonderful. Just like Jacob wrestled with God over his life situation and received tremendous blessing as a result, so will we!

James 1:23-25

"Anyone who listens to the word but does not do what it says is like someone who looks at his face in the mirror and, after looking at himself, goes away and immediately forgets what he looks like. But whoever looks intently into the perfect law that gives freedom and continues in it - not forgetting what they have heard but doing it - they will be blessed in what they do."

"And the Lord God planted a garden in Eden, in the east, where He placed the man He had formed. Out of the ground the Lord God gave growth to every tree that is pleasing to the eye and good for food. And in the middle of the garden were the tree of life and the tree of the knowledge of good and evil."

Genesis 2:8-9

When I designed the outline of this devotional to focus on the garden for the summer season, I didn't know the Lord would lead us to the Garden of Eden, but here we are!

On my personal healing journey, my mentors encouraged me not to limit my pursuit of healing to my own generation, but to ask Holy Spirit if there was anything in my family line that needed redemption prayers. I thought "why not?"

The Jewish people have history recorded all the way back to the Garden of Eden. Here, Gentile believers are grafted into that olive root. The Garden of Eden is a picture of God's utopian plan for mankind! If we study this special garden, we might understand ourselves better. God's idea was to place Adam and Eve in the garden to behold its natural beauty, the delightful food it produced, and above all else, the companionship of God.

God also placed two special trees, the tree of life and the tree of the knowledge of good and evil. Even though this garden was paradise for the man and woman, they were also given a specific set of instructions for the way to behave in God's garden. They had a lot of freedom, but they also had severe warnings and limitations. Adam and Eve did not heed the warnings and were banished out of God's garden. Angels with flaming, whirling swords guarded the way to the tree of eternal life so mankind could find the needed salvation to experience garden paradise.

That is the ultimate origin story for all mankind, and it can relate to us today? So many of us are looking to take an epic journey to the most gorgeous nature destinations where waterfalls abound, animals live, and an abundance of fresh produce that can refresh our body. People are still looking for their soul mates so they can relax without shame to enjoy intimacy and wedded bliss. They also don't want deception by a crafty serpent beast bent on a takedown.

Day 263 | KINGDUIT

"Now the serpent was more crafty than any beast on the field that the Lord God had made. And he said to the woman, 'Did God really say, 'You must not eat from any tree in the garden?"

Genesis 3:1

The very first demonic attack came to the woman. It was an attack of words to cause Eve (the mother of the living) to question God's word. Perhaps the serpent was afraid of the man, so as cowardly as he is, he deceived the woman. Have you wondered what is going on that seems so anti-women? Why is womanhood under resistance? Why are men trying to become women? Why does the abuse continue even in sport?

The serpent knows how tender God feels about the woman. God even uses a woman to represent the nation of Israel and the New Testament church in the Bible. The serpent/devil/dragon is therefore hell set against God's woman.

From the first chapter to the last book of the Bible, we read about a woman under attack, especially from dark forces. That can help us to understand that the issue is spiritual in nature. God told the serpent that the seed of the woman would crush him. "Cursed are you above all livestock and all wild animals! You will crawl on your belly, and you will eat dust all the days of your life. And I will put enmity between you and the woman, and between your offspring and hers; he will crush your head, and you will strike his heel" (Genesis 3:14-15).

This battle is real. Unfortunately, secular counselors and therapists don't mention spiritual warfare. Even churches stay away from the issue, which often makes the one who is being counseled feel like they have serious mental problems. "Dear friends, do not be surprised at the fiery ordeal that has come on you to test you, as though something strange were happening to you" (1 Peter 4:12).

The more you mature in the knowledge of God and the pursuit of Biblical Mental Healing, the more sound minded you will be. This power will equip you to overcome every dark force that attempts to steal your peace and mental clarity. As you keep striving and seeking the Lord, you will overcome! God will absolutely win in the end. Revelation Chapter 12 is a fascinating future reality and a must read to understand the amazing salvation, power, and authority of God's Messiah.

"God did say, 'You must not eat fruit from the tree that is in the middle of the garden, and you must not touch it or you will die.'

'You will certainly not die,' the serpent said to the woman.' For God knows that when you eat from it, your eyes will be opened, and you will be like God, knowing good and evil."

Genesis 3:3-5

This verse is the origin story of the first deception, a lie! The lie came first to the woman and passed to the man. Here is Jesus' commentary on the serpent: "He (the devil) was a murderer from the beginning, not holding to the truth, for there is no truth in him. When he lies, he speaks his native language, for he is a liar and the father of lies" (John 8:44).

A mark of being a good counselor is no condemnation, compassion, empathy, and sincerity. These traits are often obtained from therapists that have been through traumatic events in their own life and have healed. The Bible calls Jesus a wonderful counselor in Isaiah 9:6, then it records some of the traumatic hardships in detail that Jesus faced with his generational family, the Jews.

There was a heated argument where the Jews accused Jesus of having a demon. Jesus replied by calling them liars, illegitimate children, and that they belong to their father the devil. In response, the Jews picked up stones to kill him. Whoa!

If ever you think you can't pray to Jesus or seek Him because you feel too sinful in contrast to His holiness, think again. He understands human conflict and knows all the lies the devil has sown into the garden of your life.

During a faith-centered mental healing season, I sat in group therapy to uncover struggles, which were the lies we believed about ourselves or the Lord. Often, we were challenged with God's word in Genesis 3:11 when He said, "Who told you that . . . ?" The point being was to expose the reality that we had been deceived by the devil's lies many times during our life. It was an unsettling revelation that I found to be true. When I got home, I studied the Bible and asked Holy Spirit for myself how the serpent lied in the Garden of Eden to destroy the married couple's peace and blessing.

Day 265 | KINGDUIT

"Adam named his wife Eve because she would be the mother of all the living. And the Lord God made garments of skin for Adam and his wife and clothed them.

And the Lord God said, 'The man has now become like one of Us, knowing good and evil. He must not be allowed to reach out his hand and take also from the tree of life and eat and live forever."

Genesis 3:20-22

God created a garden where "Adam and his wife were both naked and they felt no shame" (Genesis 2:25). This picture is like a little child who is innocent, pure, and undefiled, just like Jesus said the kingdom of heaven is. That is what God created for mankind, a glorious place of no shame or condemnation, a place of mental purity and freedom. They walked and talked with God, and so, they lived in paradise.

The serpent slithered in with his lies and created such a big problem that Adam and Eve lost their paradise. God had to save the tree of life for all of mankind and everyone's future heavenly garden.

As mankind evolved without the garden relationship with the Lord, they shifted towards listening to the serpent more than the Lord. That is why the Bible says the "heart is deceitful above all things and beyond cure. Who can understand it" (Jeremiah 17:9)?

The Lord can and will help us understand our hearts! "I the Lord search the heart and examine the mind, to reward each person according to their conduct, according to what their deeds deserve" (Jeremiah 17:10).

"Then the angel showed me the river of the water of life, as clear as crystal, flowing from the throne of God and of the Lamb down the middle of the great street of the city. On each side of the river stood the tree of life, bearing twelve crops of fruit, yielding its fruit every month. And the leaves of the tree are for the healing of the nations."

Revelation 22:1-2

Since the Garden of Eden's earthly closure, the tree of life has been sought after by historians and archeologists. Make no mistake, the Lord God has preserved the tree of life out of his love for the coming redemption of Israel and the church. Those who are in Yeshua Messiah can look forward to enjoying the tree of life for all eternity!

The tree of life can be compared to a life lived inside the blessings of God. "Blessed are those who find wisdom, those who gain understanding, for she is more profitable than silver and yields better returns than gold. She is more precious than rubies; nothing you desire can compare with her. Long life is in her right hand; in her left hand are riches and honor. Her ways are pleasant ways, and all her paths are peace. She is a tree of life to those who take hold of her; those who hold fast will be blessed" (Proverbs 3:13-18).

It's real, the fruitful life of righteousness that comes from abiding in the vine of Jesus Christ and being grafted into the olive root tree of Israel is one of God's great and merciful mysteries that will be revealed at the coming of the Son of Man. If you are reading this devotional, you still have time to repent, turn to God, and love the Lord with all your heart, soul, mind, and strength.

Yes, it takes effort, but seeking the Lord for a renewed mind is the most rewarding and transformative personal quest a man or woman can pursue, higher than any other endeavor!

YOM KIPPUR

The Jewish community prepares for the traditional Old Testament religious practice of Yom Kippur; however, Jesus already fulfilled the promise of God in a new way. The Jewish community still looks for their sins to be atoned for, therefore Yom Kippur is the high holy day leading up to the Day of Atonement. These religious activities give hope for the cleansing of the soul. A scapegoat is necessary in their practice, so the animal sacrifice atones for the sins of the people.

"We all like sheep, have gone astray, each of us have turned to our own way; and the Lord has laid on him the iniquity of us all" (Isaiah 53:6). "For Christ did not enter a sanctuary made with human hands that was only a copy of the true one; he entered heaven itself, now to appear for us in God's presence. Nor did he enter heaven to offer himself again and again, the way the high priest enters the Most Holy Place every year with blood that is not his own. Otherwise, Christ would have had to suffer many times since the creation of the world. But he has appeared once for all at the culmination of the ages to do away with sin by the sacrifice of himself" (Hebrew 9:24-26).

In the bible, shedding of blood was the only way for sins to be forgiven, so God ordered the Jewish priest to send a goat into the wilderness after having laid hands on the animal to pass the sins of the people upon it. A scapegoat is a term taken from the bible to describe a person who unfortunately takes the blame for other people's wrongs. Whether it is a subconscious blaming of abuse or for reasons of outright deception, being scapegoated is torture.

The idea of scapegoating in mental health is some of the most hurtful pain people deal with because the person being blamed for the wrongdoing is often a person who is innocent. Certainly, Jesus was blameless while He carried the punishment and sorrows of mankind.

CONSIDER: Whatever has happened in your life to make you feel like a scapegoat, know this, Christ took it all upon himself because of His love for you. He can identify with your pain, and you can find comfort in the arms of Jesus. He is the man of sorrows and is familiar with all grief.

YOM KIPPUR = DAY OF ATONEMENT

HOLIEST DAY OF THE YEAR

"This day of atonement will be made for you, to cleanse you. Then, before the Lord you will be clean from all your sins. It is a day of sabbath rest, and you must deny yourselves; it is a lasting ordinance."

Leviticus 16:30-31

Even though many people who are Jewish deny Jesus as the Messiah, they continue to practice this Levitical Covenant. "Whatever is set aside from the holy offerings the Israelites present to the Lord I give to you and your sons and daughters as your perpetual share. It is an everlasting covenant of salt before the Lord for both you and your offspring" (Numbers 18:19).

Some Jewish people still fast and pray. This removal of fleshly comfort helps them deny self and seek the Lord. They pray and ask the Lord for forgiveness.

At the Old Testament Temple, the priests sacrificed animals, calling them scapegoats. "He is to lay both on the head of the live goat and confess over it all the wickedness and rebellion of the Israelites - all their sins - and put them on the goat's head. He shall send the goat away into the wilderness in the care of someone appointed for the task" (Leviticus 16:21). The laying of hands on the animal is to put all their sins on the animal because someone or something must pay for sin. It is a religious system based on works.

For the Christ follower, there is no religion, we have grace. "For it is by grace you have been saved, through faith - and this is not from yourselves, it is the gift of God" (Ephesians 2:8).

Religion says, "Look at what I did God!" The credit goes to the man or woman putting forth religious effort. Faith says, "Look what Jesus did!" All the glory and honor go to our scapegoat Jesus Messiah! Isaiah 53 describes in detail the story of Jesus as the suffering servant. Receive His sacrificial gift leading to the immeasurable grace of total forgiveness and experience this amazing love! Jesus, once and for all time paid it all! Hallelujah!

SPEAK OUT LOUD & DECLARE

Prayers for Israel

PRAY: Brothers and sisters, my heart's desire and prayer to the God of the Israelites is that they may be saved (Romans 10:1). Let us not be ignorant of this mystery so that we may not be conceited: Israel has experienced a hardening in part until the full number of the Gentiles has come in and in this way all Israel will be saved. As it is written: The deliverer will come from Zion; he will turn godlessness away from Jacob (Romans 11:25-26).

For Zion's sake I will not keep silent, for Jerusalem's sake I will not remain quiet, till her vindication shines out like the dawn, her salvation like a blazing torch. The nations will see your vindication, and all kings your glory; you will be called by a new name that the mouth of the Lord will bestow. You will be a crown of splendor in the Lord's hand, a royal diadem in the hand of your God. No longer will they call you Deserted or name your land Desolate. But you will be called Hephzibah, and your land Beulah; for the Lord will take delight in you, and your land will be married. As a young man marries a young woman, so will your builder marry you; as a bridegroom rejoices over his bride, so your God rejoices over you (Isaiah 62).

You are my King and my God, who decrees victories for Jacob. Through you we push back our enemies; through your name we trample our foes. I put no trust in my bow, my sword does not bring me victory; but you give us victory over our enemies, you put our adversaries to shame. In God we make our boast all day long, and we will praise your name forever (Psalm 44:4-8).

You who answer prayer, to you all people will come. When we were overwhelmed by sins, you forgave our transgressions. Blessed are those you choose and bring near to live in your courts! We are filled with the good things of your house, of your holy temple. You answer us with awesome and righteous deeds, God our Savior, the hope of all the ends of the earth and of the farthest seas, who formed the mountains by your power, having armed yourself with strength, who stilled the roaring of the seas, the roaring of their waves, and the turmoil of the nations (Psalm 65:2). May God be gracious to us and bless us and make his face shine on us so that your ways may be known on earth, our salvation among all nations. May the people praise you, God; may all the people praise you (Psalm 67:1-3).

KINGDUIT | Day 270

"As for you, you were dead in your transgressions and sins, in which you used to live when you followed the ways of this world and the ruler of the kingdom of this world and the ruler of the kingdom of the air, the spirit who is now at work in those who are disobedient."

Ephesians 2:1-2

The Bible is historically layered from the Old Testament to the New Testament to Heaven. Hell, the literal earth, and the heavens are layered similarly from bottom to top with hell below, the first heaven of earth, the second heaven in the air and the third heaven where Jesus is along with those in the faith who have already passed away/died. Apostle Paul mentions the third heaven saying, "I know a man in Christ who . . . was caught up to the third heaven" (2 Corinthians 12:2).

ART THERAPY DRAW: Fill in the blanks below, starting with the #1 location labeled as eternal HEAVEN, label #2 AIR, label #3 EARTH, label #4 eternal HELL.

Read the scripture above, then fill in on the second column list below where the "ruler of the kingdom of this world" belongs. Write in your name next to the "EARTH" line. Write the name "JESUS" next to the heaven line. Draw a flaming fire next to line 4.

1. ______________________________ ______________________________

2. ______________________________ ______________________________

3. ______________________________ ______________________________

4. ______________________________ ______________________________

This is a positional diagram and can begin to help you understand how to fight the good fight of faith. Remember in battle, the high position gives the best vision for victory.

Day 271 | KINGDUIT

"I pursued my enemies and overtook them; I did not turn back till they were destroyed. I crushed them so that they could not rise; they fell beneath my feet."

Psalm 18:37-38

King David was a warrior and lover seeking to establish God's Kingdom on earth. He had a heart for the Lord and spent his whole life pursuing Jehovah. First as a young man, next a worshiping shepherd, and then a warrior using earthly weapons to defeat flesh and blood enemies. He killed Goliath out of passion for Israel, then continued to conquer and finally became a king. He sought the Lord for a divine blueprint for day and night worship in a stone temple. He couldn't start a building project during a war season, so as soon as God gave him rest from his enemies, he received the architectural temple designs. David overcame kingdom battles in order to prepare a habitation for God's glory.

This biblical pattern remains. "Yet a time is coming and has now come when the true worshipers will worship the Father in the Spirit and in truth, for they are the kind of worshippers the Father seeks" (John 4:23). First comes worship, and then the overcoming of evil to prepare for a glorious tabernacle tent body. Jesus gave his disciples, including us, all authority in heaven and on earth (Matthew 28:18). We have a mighty sword of the Spirit. We have all power, which is the same power that raised Christ from the dead to defeat every type of evil influencing our lives.

In Daniel 10, Daniel went vegetarian to mourn and pray in order to defeat a demonic prince in the air over the kingdom of Persia. Likewise, we don't conquer flesh and blood, we fight a supernatural spiritual battle (Ephesians 6:10-18). Paul exhorted us to demolish everything set against God's ways until God's enemies are crushed like David did in the earth realm from Psalm 18.

MEDITATE: Ask the Lord to give you a desire and understanding on how to be an overcomer. Using God's authority paired with our divinely powerful Spirit sword is a big part of mental victory. King David fought until the land had peace. Pray for a warrior spirit to be a part of your life so that your land, your spiritual house, and your family can live in peace. Jesus did not die in vain, He died so that you can be totally free.

THE FEAST OF TABERNACLES

"But when the time of the Feast of the Jewish Tabernacles was near, Jesus' brothers said to him. 'Leave Galilee and go to Judea, so that the disciples there may see the works that you do. No one who wants to become a public figure acts in secret. Since you are doing these things, show yourself to the world.' For even his own brothers did not believe him.

Therefore, Jesus told them. 'My time is not yet here; for you anytime will do."

John 7:2-6

All the special Jewish holidays have been fulfilled in Christ except the Feast of Tabernacles. When Jesus' brothers were trying to get him to go to the Feast of Jewish Tabernacles, Jesus refused. His time to attend the Feast of Tabernacles has still not arrived. This festival marks the promise of the Messianic Kingdom when Jesus comes back to earth as a conquering King.

Jesus will come back as a bridegroom looking for His bride. But we are not ready because the Bible says we will be clothed in garments of righteousness, white and clean. This is a picture of a spotless glorious bride/church. I think we can all agree that the early 21st century church needs additional healing and divine cleansing.

Without a doubt, the Jewish community is preparing and longing for the fulfillment of the Feast of Tabernacles, the most holy feast! Preparations are being made and it's fascinating to watch bible prophecy unfold in our generation.

For the Gentile church, we are also preparing ourselves for Christ's return, the wedding supper of the Lamb. This is the harvest of souls. By making ourselves glorious on the inside by pursuing the salvation of our souls, our anointing increases to fulfill the great commission.

"Then the angel said to me, 'Write this: Blessed are those who are invited to the wedding supper of the Lamb!' And he added, 'These are the true words of God" (Revelation 19:9).

Day 273 | KINGDUIT

"And God raised us up with Christ and seated us with him in the heavenly realms in Christ Jesus in order that in the coming ages he might show the incomparable riches of his grace expressed in his kindness to us in Christ Jesus."

Ephesians 2:6-7

"THE POWER is the same as the mighty strength he exerted when he raised Christ from the dead and seated him at his right hand in the heavenly realms, far above all rule and authority, power and dominion, and every name that is invoked, not only in the present age but also in the one to come. and God placed all things under his feet and appointed him to be head over everything for the church, which is his body, the fullness of him who fills everything in every way" (Ephesians 1:19-22).

MONTH 10 - Resilient Warriors

FALL SEASON

SOUL HARVEST

KINGDUIT | Day 274

"But you, man of God, flee from all this and pursue righteousness, godliness, faith, love, endurance and gentleness. Fight the good fight of faith. Take hold of the eternal life of which you were called when you made your good confession in the presence of many witnesses."

1 Timothy 6:11-12

The biblical world view of liberty and mental freedom involves a fight, a good fight of faith. This points to the battle of good versus evil in life with a need to act to get the victory.

Most of the secular ideas of freedom centers around wealth and pursuing riches. Many people believe that if you have a large treasury, then you will be free. They pursue money, but money cannot purchase peace or happiness. In fact, some of the most peaceful people in the world have abandoned material things.

"But godliness with contentment is great gain. For we brought nothing into the world, and we can take nothing out of it. But if we have food and clothing, we will be content with that. Those who want to get rich fall into temptation and a trap and into many foolish and harmful desires that plunge people into ruin and destruction. For the love of money is a root of all kinds of evil. Some people, eager for money, have wandered from the faith and pierced themselves with many griefs" (1 Timothy 6:6-10).

Biblical vitality speaks of riches in the context of the knowledge of Christ, "in whom are hidden all the treasures of wisdom and knowledge" (Colossians 2:3). True wealth is knowing the Prince of Peace while reaping the rewards of wisdom and understanding. Our heavenly home has wealth that will last for all eternity. Therefore, chasing the kingdom will reap the greatest riches. If you have a need for provision, ask your Father in heaven and you will find Him faithful to satisfy all your physical needs.

Consider the harvest season of this mental healing year. Make it a priority to seek the abundance that leads to a true bounty of freedom and personal mental shalom.

Are you willing to pursue the higher ground and fight the good fight of faith?

Day 275 | KINGDUIT

"Then Haman said to King Xerxes, 'There is a certain people dispersed among the peoples in all the provinces of your kingdom who keep themselves separate. Their customs are different from those of all other people, and they do not obey the king's law, it is not in the king's best interest to tolerate them. If it pleases the king, let a decree be issued to destroy them."

Esther 3:8-9

"Mordecai had a cousin named Hadassah, whom he had brought up because she had neither father or mother."

Esther 2:7

Queen Esther was willing to fight a good fight when she realized that if she didn't, her Jewish culture in Persia might perish. Her personal life had already been devastated by personal loss and trauma. As a young girl, she basically lost everything, like many Jewish people through the ages. *According to Judaism's Midrash interpretation, her mother and father died surrounding her birth.

Traumatic events often cause people to shut down. Who can blame them or point fingers, so we give more grace because we all know life can be hard. Everyone goes through seasons of loss and grief, but we should never give up on life, family, or nation. Even though loss is devastating, God is greater and knows the beginning from the end. As biblical people of the past faced terrifying situations, time and again the Lord called them to take up arms, fight the good fight and press toward the high calling.

"Brothers and sisters, I do not consider myself yet to have taken hold of it. But one thing I do: Forgetting what is behind and straining toward what is ahead, I press on toward the goal to win the prize for which God has called me heavenward in Christ Jesus" (Philippians 3:13-14).

*Encyclopedia of Midrash, 2005, Esther. Rabbah 6.5; Megillah 13a

---

ART THERAPY DRAW: Draw a picture of a Queen with a golden scepter. Consider how one girl with influence saved a nation.

"Esther won the favor of everyone who saw her. She was taken to King Xerxes in the royal residence in the tenth month, the month of Tebeth, in the seventh year of his reign."

Esther 2:15-16

The idea of taking up arms is a topic that is not common in modern church services, yet when you read the historical narrative of God's nation of Israel and the Jewish people, time and time again they are trying to escape oppression or defending themselves to find freedom from their enemies and live-in peace.

The young Queen Esther lived in a period when the Jewish people were hated by local leaders. She understood this so she hid her Jewish ancestry from her husband, the king, to prevent being hated herself. "Dispatches were sent by couriers to all the king's provinces with the order to destroy, kill, and annihilate all the Jews - young and old, women and children - on a single day, the thirteenth day of the twelfth month, the month of Adar, and to plunder their goods" (Esther 3:13-14). Immediately the Jews became victims and fell into a state of grave mourning at the impending disaster and destruction.

Esther, with the help of her uncle, realized she had a position of influencing authority. So bravely, she used her position to try to stop the executive order. The king couldn't stop it, but he could issue another edict to give the Jews a way out.

"The king's edict granted the Jews in every city the right to assemble and protect themselves; to destroy, kill, and annihilate the armed men of any nationality or province who might attack them" (Esther 8:11).

ART THERAPY DRAW: Draw your spiritual weapon. How can you destroy and annihilate demonic oppression?

"If it pleases the king," Esther answered, 'give the Jews in Susa permission to carry out this day's edict tomorrow also, and let Haman's ten sons be impaled on poles.'

So the king commanded that this be done."

Esther 9:13-14

DESTRUCTION EDICT

Jesus is the King of the Jews, the King of Kings and the Lord of Lords throughout time and eternity (Rev 19:16). He is still commanding that the enemies of God's people be destroyed. Because of His great love for His people, He does not appreciate when the enemy tries to steal, kill, and destroy God's children. In fact, Jesus came to earth to destroy the devil's work and now that He is in heaven, He is expecting His children to take up their spiritual swords of the Spirit (Word of God) and destroy the things that set themselves up against God's ways.

He didn't like the bullies in the Old Testament times, and He certainly does not like the devil's schemes in this New Testament era (Ephesians 6:22). A believer's high position of being seated with Christ in heavenly realms gives them the authority and power to defeat any and every dark foe.

Even though you may feel like the past traumatic events in your life have hindered you or somehow disqualified you, that simply is not true. If anyone was in a low place, it was Esther the abandoned by death orphan. She seemed to be a nobody, but in the eyes of the Lord and King Xerxes, she was a Queen with the potential to save the beloved Jewish people. It did not matter that no one except her uncle saw this potential in her. What mattered was that the Lord was able to move heaven and earth to position her for triumphal victory. Of course, it worked because Almighty God is Mighty to save individuals and nations. Jesus allowed the devil's spear to pierce his heart on that cross so that full redemption could be imparted to the world. Part of the redemption is empowering His bride church with the sword of the Spirit as their weapon, for the here and now destruction edict.

Do you have the courage of Esther to usher in victory over your life, people, and nation?

"The enemies of the Jews hoped to overpower them, but now the tables were turned, and the Jews got the upper hand over those who hated them. The Jews assembled in their cities in all the provinces of King Xerxes to attack those determined to destroy them. No one could stand against them, because the people of all the other nationalities were afraid of them.

The Jews struck down all their enemies with the sword, killing and destroying them, and they did what they pleased to those who hated them."

Esther 9:1-3, 5

The providence of God placed Esther in a strategic position during a time of great need. Her faith and courage to raise her voice to secure a divine turn around worked.

Any time a child of God partners with Abba Father, there is going to be victory. God is the Most High God, exalted over the heavens and the earth. That means everything Almighty God does, works! The amazing thing is that God has chosen to use common people, including the youth, through the bible and even world history to become vessels of divine turnaround time and time again.

In this devotional, we have read many stories of people like Moses, Joshua and Joan of Arc that demonstrate the power of one obedient person willing to lead out nations. This divine pattern is still at work today, but even more so. Before Jesus left earth to go to heaven to reunite with his Father, he gave the disciples ALL the authority. Not just the early disciples, but the disciples of every season of life.

"Jesus replied, 'I saw Satan fall like lightning from heaven. I have given you authority to trample on snakes and scorpions and to overcome all the power of the enemy, nothing will harm you. However, do not rejoice that the spirits submit to you, but rejoice that your names are written in heaven" (Luke 10:18-20). The snakes and scorpions are references to evil spirits. Most Old Testament battles were flesh and blood while New Testament battles are fought against dark, evil spiritual forces.

ASK: Ask Jesus for help to defeat the most burdensome area of your mental health.

CAUTIONARY TALE

There were two different groups that met in a city. Each group found a meeting spot and gathered on a regular basis, enjoying common interests and fellowship.

One group of believers gathered to study the Bible. They started with a blessing prayer, opened the Word of God, read a bible study guide, discussed the topic, and afterwards shared refreshment with drinks and snacks. During fellowship, a single mother shared her concerns for her teenager caught up in magic and witchcraft. The group listened to her burden and was kind to the mother. They said they would pray for her, but no group prayer was spoken, no divine authority utilized, nor heavenly fire released. After their time of sharing, they went home.

Another group in that city met together to practice witchery and sharpen their supernatural powers. They met on a group chat, got together to light candles, set up altars, and taught hexing. They set intentions to interfere with public movements they didn't support by engaging the spirit world. They formed a bond of agreement and called on the powers of darkness to cast spells.

It just so happened that one of the girls from the bible study and one of the girls from the wiccan group worked together in a DEI (diversity, equity & inclusion) managed business. One day during lunch break they started a conversation and shared their group stories. The wiccan girl teased the Christian saying, “Our group laughs at Christians because they rarely use their powers!”

The Christian girl was confused and asked what she meant. The wiccan replied, “You can pray, but I bet you don't know how to activate the authority of Jesus. Since Christians don't use their God given power, wiccan's keep hexing you with no resistance!” She got up and walked away leaving the Christian girl speechless.

Which group had more power to activate change in their community during their meeting? The group that talked about the bible or those who united with the rulers, authorities, powers of this world's darkness and the spiritual forces of evil (Ephesians 6:12)?

“Thrones were set in place, and the Ancient of Days took His seat...His throne was flaming with fire, and its wheels were all ablaze. A river of fire was flowing, coming out before Him” (Daniel 7:9).

"Therefore, I urge you, brothers and sisters, in view of God's mercy, to offer your bodies as a living sacrifice, holy and pleasing to God - this is your true and proper worship."

Romans 12:1

Just like in Esther's time, the enemy executes plans with intentions to steal, kill and destroy. Nonetheless, God doesn't leave his people defenseless. His people follow the pattern of Christ and offer their own bodies as a sacrifice on the altar of God. They run to the throne of grace to receive help and mercy in their time of need.

That's exactly what Esther did to save the Jews. The edict against them set them up to be as good as dead, so Esther called a prayer fast for support and willingly offered herself as a sacrifice.

". . .Mordecai sent back Esther this reply: 'Do not think that because you are in the king's house you alone of all the Jews will escape. For if you remain silent at this time, relief and deliverance for the Jews will arise from another place, but you and your father's house will perish.'

Then Esther sent this reply to Mordecai: 'Go, gather together all the Jews who are in Susa, and fast for me. Do not eat or drink for three days, night or day, I and my attendants will fast as you do. When this is done, I will go to the king, even though it is against the law. And if I perish, I perish" (Esther 4:13-16)!

Esther's willing sacrifice led to a divine turn around that saved the Jews. It is the action that turns desperate situations around and ushers in divine deliverance. The reason why it works is because it is not based on human performance but is based on the mercy of God and His love that endures forever.

God's people don't construct merciless altars with idols and objects like the pagans.

"For great is the Lord, and greatly to be praised; He is to be feared above all gods. For all the gods of the nations are idols, but it is the Lord who made the heavens. Splendor and majesty are before Him; strength and beauty fill His sanctuary" (Psalm 96:4-6).

Day 281 | KINGDUIT

"Esther also was taken to the king's palace and entrusted to Hegai, who had charge of the harem. . . Every day Mordecai walked back and forth near the courtyard of the harem to find out how Esther was and what was happening to her."

Esther 2:8,11

Only God knows what went on inside the pagan king Xerxes's harem house. All we read is that many young women were bathed, perfumed, and brought into his house. We find Uncle Mordecai pacing back and forth to see if Esther is okay.

That's enough for me to shut my eyes and start pracing (prayer-pacing) myself. The takeaway is Esther certainly had a traumatic youth; there was epic parental loss, suffering and then this.

Until this writing, I had never considered the similarity of Queen Esther and Joan of Arc. They both were orphaned by the death of their parents, both common girls, both divinely given a position to influence kings, both were used to utterly save their nation from extinction, and both are still celebrated today. Could it be that there are more "Old Testament types" meant to rise up in the New Testament era to liberate nations? Could it be you?

You may say, "No, I'm too messed up, my back story isn't credible, my family is common, and I don't know any powerful people. On top of that, I always carry the trauma of my past with me!" That may be true, but God! It is hard to understand, but the Lord often uses people that nobody cares about, including family, that have gone through difficult trauma. Look at King David and Joseph. How many brothers rejected them both and even hated them? How about the constant oppression they were under for many years?

Real life stories from the bible are meant to help people realize that traumatic events are common, and painful. To read about how the events really can get stuck in the soul of a woman or man can bring hope. There is nothing happy about the traumatic events themselves. People were devastated, tortured, terrified, seared and deeply wounded - that's real trauma and it hasn't stopped inflicting people. Nonetheless, intentional study of God stories to read how God redeemed things can bring liberty.

WORSHIP: YouTube: -Natalie Grant - I Am Not Alone

PURIM

Queen Esther's story was written to be useful for your life. Even though the way her life started was tragic, God used her uncle in her life. God put her uncle Mordecai in her life as a type of Holy Spirit to lovingly guide her and watch over her. He guided her on a path to become a woman of great help and influence for her people. He guarded her life with tender love, even when Esther had to endure hardship.

When the moment came for Esther to make a big difference in saving her life and the lives of a whole nation, Mordecai urged her to find the strength to move. He persuaded her to take quick action. Esther's partnership with Holy Spirit led Mordecai to be that influence to her, and her faith and courage totally worked! A national and personal trauma was released, and a miraculous deliverance was accomplished.

As a result, a celebration took place called Purim. Jews still celebrate Purim's victory every March!

CONSIDER: Can you relate your mental health to a partnership with Holy Spirit to help you get victory over all your enemies? Write down a list of issues that need a divine intervention.

Day 283 | KINGDUIT

"He heals the brokenhearted and binds up their wounds. He determines the number of the stars and calls them each by name. Great is our Lord and mighty in power, His understanding has no limit. The Lord sustains the humble but casts the wicked to the ground."

Psalm 147:3-6

Trauma therapy is part of the modern counseling movement. It was introduced in the *Diagnostic Statistical Manual (DSM-3) in 1980 relating to civilian and military combat, which included Post-traumatic Stress Disorder.[25] Prior to that it was also connected to war and human abuse.

On the other hand, the concept of trauma in the bible is thousands of years old beginning with Eve's psychological deception. That incident was so traumatic that it passed to the next generation and manifested itself in sibling murder. Therefore, not only has the bible addressed trauma for centuries, but it has provided the remedy for trauma going forward in history.

Did you know that the bible is a flawless document? "And the words of the Lord are flawless, like silver purified in a crucible, like gold refined seven times" (Psalm 12:6). That means all impurities have been removed. If the bible says the Lord heals the brokenhearted, then He can and will. Because the Bible is alive, it is literally Jesus. Go to the Lord with the Bible in hand and a sincere heart. Jesus Himself will meet you there. He will call your name with understanding of every detail of your life. "He calls His own sheep by name and leads them out" (John 10:3).

Who can repair emotional wounds? What person has that power? The answer is only the Lord. The reference to the stars being named, points to Abraham and the Lord's promise for numerous descendants. Those descendants will be "like stars in the sky." What other god calls you by name? None, only Jesus! Muslims even admit Allah doesn't know their name, even when they pray five times a day.

"Great is our Lord and mighty in power, his understanding has no limit. The Lord sustains the humble but casts the wicked to the ground" (Psalm 147:5-6). Whatever the case, whether past trauma, war trauma, relationship/ family trauma, accident trauma; you are known, heard, understood, and divinely defended.

"Anyone who listens to the word but does not do what it says is like someone who looks at his face in a mirror and, after looking at himself, goes away and immediately forgets what he looks like. But whoever looks intently into the perfect law that gives freedom and continues in it - not forgetting what they have heard but doing it - they will be blessed in what they do."

James 1:23-25

Of all the people that have lived and died on the face of the earth, there is no group of people prior to the 21st century that has spent more time looking at themselves in mirrors. We have mirrors with light and magnification that will show us every fine detail of our face, we can even split hairs. The mirror gazing gives clear vision to the reality of appearance.

Are you interested in the appearance of your soul? If so, an intentional and consistent look into the Bible will reveal things that give personal soul reflection. The blessing promised from looking intently into the laws of the Lord will give freedom, even freedom from some of the most challenging traumatic situations. It's not easy because God's tools are sharp, divisive, and painful at times.

Some traumas are multigenerational, historical, human abuse related, accidental trauma, war/combat related, and national trauma. The Lord has a way of bringing understanding through the stories, history, songs, wisdom, and instruction. They can become personal and identifiable in life as needed for remedy. "For the word of God is alive and active, Sharper than any double-edged sword, it penetrates even to dividing soul and spirit, joints and marrow; it judges the thoughts and attitudes of the heart" (Hebrews 4:12).

Jesus was "a man of sorrows, familiar with suffering" (Isaiah 53:1). His Father in heaven ordained his life to be a testimony of trauma and divine resilience from conception to death, for the ministry of comfort to all. Jesus' human and fleshly experience combined with his all-knowing, all-powerful, and all-present ability, enables him to provide perfect counsel and the healing to the broken hearted, no matter how extreme the trauma story. "Where can I go from your Spirit? Where can I flee from your presence" (Psalm 139:7)?

Day 285 | KINGDUIT

"Here is my servant, whom I uphold, my chosen one in whom I delight; I will put my Spirit on him and he will bring justice to the nations. He will not shout or cry out or raise his voice in the streets. A bruised reed he will not break, and a smoldering wick he will not snuff out."

Isaiah 42:1-3

Jesus is the trauma expert and Holy Spirit is our supernatural Helper. They know how to heal mental wounds, be compassionate, not to break a bruised soul, and know not to put out one's fire who only has a little smoke remaining. His understanding is limitless. God Almighty chose Holy Spirit to do many of the fine and tender actions needed to restore the soul. We must all read and meditate on the Bible because Jehovah Rapha, the Healer, is inside the text. Only by reading the text will you find the specific things necessary to minister to your personal pain. Keep reading Isaiah 42 to gain understanding beyond measure.

One of the biblical terms for trauma is tribos: a beaten track, a path (Strongs 5147). Interestingly, the phonetic spelling is tree-bos. It is a "rut/path that is formed from constant use. The intended biblical use of tribos is that one creates a path, or a route established by the Lord, where people can best know Him. This is also a regular path that all saints must travel in their spiritual journey (romance) to know God. So, how is your love path with God connected to trauma? Often, suffering leads us to the Lord and creates a fellowship walk. Paul called it "the fellowship of his sufferings" (Philippians 3:10). While studying traumatology I reviewed an MRI of a PTSD soldier's brain. There was a rut, a fixed neural network separated like a path. That is the part of traumatic memory that gets fixed in your mind and won't go away. Medical intervention can't fix it, but bodily healing using the will can change your brain.

John the Baptist was sent to proclaim redemption. He was a "voice of one calling in the wilderness, 'Prepare the way for the Lord, make straight paths (tribos) for him" (Matthew 3:3/Isaiah 40). That message still rings loud and clear! YOU must mentally rub via biblical meditation a straight rut in your mind for Jesus. Clear things up, He's coming again!

"Is this the kind of fasting I have chosen; to lose the chains of injustice and untie the cords of the yoke, to set the oppressed free and break every yoke?"

Isaiah 58:6

Biblical Trauma Therapy:

- Aligning the will or being willing to process the trauma
- Pushing away fearful emotions that keep one from addressing the trauma
- Identifying the traumatic event
- Believing that "the Lord will guide you always; he will satisfy your needs in a sun-scorched land and will strengthen your frame. You will be like a well-watered garden, like a spring whose waters never fail" (Isaiah 58:11).
- Committing to being a person who WILL rebuild, raise-up and repair the broken places in the mind with Holy Spirit's help

In summary, the process is about your intention to heal your traumatic memories and holistically partner with Holy Spirit to remove the trauma from your mind. When the bible calls Christ the burden-bearer out of Matthew 11:28, it means Christ takes the burden from you and replaces it with peace and rest. When that release exchange happens, the shalom of God descends upon your mind. From there, by your will, you determine to fill up, rebuild, restore, repair, or replace that mental space with positive words, biblical promises, and new thoughts.

This divine supernatural experience is an amazing and powerful mental healing. miracle! When the Lord takes a horrible burden out of your mind and gives you shalom, it evokes a response of humility and gratitude combined with a desire to help others. When oppressed thoughts are replaced with freedom, things change.

"Then your light will break forth like the dawn, and your healing will quickly appear; then your righteousness will go before you, and the glory of the LORD will be your rear guard. Then you will call, and the LORD will answer; you will cry for help, and He will say: Here am I" (Isaiah 58:8-9).

Day 287 | KINGDUIT

"Your people will rebuild the ancient ruins and will raise up the age-old foundations; you will be called Repairer of Broken Walls, Restorer of Streets with Dwellings."

Isaiah 58:12

Meditate on Isaiah 58 to see how the bible portrays the way the Lord moves in response to people's actions. "If you do away with the yoke of oppression, with the pointing finger and malicious talk, and if you spend yourselves in behalf of the hungry and satisfy the needs of the oppressed, then your light will rise in the darkness, and your night will become like the noonday" (Isaiah 58:9-10). When people do things the Lord's way, the Lord will MOVE!

Jesus explains how Holy Spirit brings to mind what you need to work on as it relates to trauma/sin removal. "But the Advocate, the Holy Spirit, whom the Father will send in my name, will teach you all things and will remind you of everything I have said to you" (John 14:26). Holy Spirit comes alongside you to help you, remind you and teach you how to obey Christ. It's another picture, like legal counsel, that prepares you to be blameless against the accuser of the brethren. When the accuser blames you before God, but you have done the healing work with Holy Spirit to sanctify your mind, then you are clean, and God will not judge that part of your testimony.

It's part of the good fight to overcome old thoughts with good thoughts, to think excellent things post healing. It's accomplished by hard mental work and faith. Although sad, emotional, and difficult, there is a beauty like a sunset on the top of a mountain that makes the challenge of the healing path tremendously rewarding. Post healing actions, like singing praises, can fill, renew, and soothe the mind.

I had a deeply embedded traumatic memory in my soul that I never understood about myself. I prayed for years to get to the bottom of my breach. Meanwhile, I kept reading the bible then obeying truths and commands while I waited for help. One day, Holy Spirit invited me to open a mental door in which He showed me exactly what had happened when I was a child to create that gap in my psyche. That week, I got information that confirmed the revelation. I was committed to seeking Him until the process and healing was sealed by His power and love. God gave me a miracle!

"So Jesus again said to them: 'Truly, truly, I say to you, I am the door of the sheep."

John 10:8

When that faith door was presented to me by Holy Spirit helper while I was seeking the Lord for mental healing, I had no idea the door was Jesus himself. The all-knowing, Almighty God knew I was ready and had the faith to follow Him on a journey of revelation, response, trauma healing, and deliverance.

From the day that door opened, and I walked through, it was like a light switch turned on. I somehow knew something went wrong when I was very small. I started grieving a loss, so knowing that the bible says to "grieve, mourn and wail" in James 4:9, I decided to keep on crying until the Lord showed me more. I took time off work to be alone. A few days later my mom called me out of the blue with a trembling voice. She felt like she needed to tell me a story about my past. We cried together. I told her I would forgive the situation, thanked her, and said I loved her.

I knew in my soul that this was what created the crack in my mental walls for the enemy to sow lies into my being regarding my identity. Jesus softly and tenderly gave me the grace to be willing to process my story. The crying and tears were like a release valve. "You have collected all my tears in your bottle. You have recorded each one in your book" (Psalm 56:8). I felt like every drop represented unspoken words of pain over my lifetime. Jesus was so near, carefully collecting my tears as if they meant so much to Him. It was such a sour and sweet time when I experienced the counsel of the Son of God. Jesus was my "Wonderful Counselor, Mighty God, Everlasting Father, and Prince of Peace" (Isaiah 9:6), my friendly warrior!

My broken walls were being repaired while my mind was completely blown away by the Spirit of wisdom, understanding and counsel.

ART THERAPY DRAW: Draw a shepherd's rod next to the gate of a sheep fence.

Day 289 | KINGDUIT

"As the Father has loved Me, So have I loved you. Remain in my love. If you keep My commandments, you will remain in My love, just as I have kept My Father's commands and remain in his love. I have told you this so that my joy may be in you and that your joy may be complete. My command is this: Love each other as I have loved you."

John 15:9-13

My first traumatic processing experience took about a week to go through. It happened when there was little talk about mental healing or trauma, so the whole situation took me many days to figure out intellectually, experientially, and emotionally (mind, will, emotions).

All these parts of the soul needed to be addressed. If you just cry without identifying in your mind why you are crying, that can lead to excessive sorrow or depression. If you just intellectualize things without grieving and mourning with emotion, then you won't release the traumatic feelings/ memories which can lead to circling thoughts or obsessive/compulsive thoughts. If you are not willing to experience the pain or hug the cactus, then the door to healing will simply not open.

Even a child can cry and release emotions and therefore go through this process. If someone they trust, who is safe, will listen to them, a child can explain why they are upset. Then that child can have an opportunity, if willing, to remedy the pain. Basically, it's about emotional safety and trust. Every child should have at least one safe harbor in mommy, daddy, granny, or grandpa. As for the adults and young adults, Jesus is the safest anchor for every living soul!

I was so grateful and relieved when Jesus showed me how to remove trauma and sad memories, that I told Him I would pass on the blessing and try to be a helper in our broken world. That prayer led me to lead a faith-based therapy group, centered on seeking Jesus the Healer. I showed my sisters in Christ how to find the Jesus door in their soul and encouraged them to open it.

ART THERAPY DRAW: Draw a heart with a door in the middle of it.

KINGDUIT | Day 290

"We have this hope as an anchor for the soul, firm and secure. It enters the inner sanctuary behind the curtain, where our forerunner, Jesus, has entered on our behalf. He has become a high priest forever, in the order of Melchizedek."

Hebrews 6:19

Everyone that came to the faith-based group therapy course felt called by God to seek healing. Most of them were frustrated that the faith journey in the church didn't provide for the need of mental and emotional healing. We all seemed to have an awareness that pain led us to the group and there was respect for other people's emotions. The men processed with the men and the women processed with the women.

Since I led the group away from my home, I didn't know anyone personally. One lady in the group had been seeking the Lord for many years, faithfully processing grief from a traumatic loss. She never mentioned any detail about the loss but said she needed to seek the Lord in a new way to help her along her journey. She told me she read many books about grief, but something was still missing.

When each group member learned to walk to Jesus by faith and then enter the tabernacle of their soul, they got major breakthroughs of wisdom, understanding, emotional release and perfect shalom. After eleven weeks of gathering, the one lady in the group who struggled with grief was not willing to open the Jesus door to her inner sanctuary.

Because I respect the human will, when I gently asked her if she wanted to seek the Lord and she nodded no, I backed off. But during the last ten minutes of the last meeting, all our phone alarms simultaneously blasted an Amber Alert - Beeeeep! Beeeeep! The lady started physically shaking and said out loud, "I'm ready to find Jesus!" We all silently prayed while I tenderly told her Jesus was ready too! Whatever the Lord showed her in that few minutes created a floodgate of emotional release that answered her questions from years of seeking.

A few weeks later she sent me a picture of a cactus and said being willing to hug it and feel the raw paint was the choice that set her free!

Christ - Repairer of Broken Walls

*SPEAK OUT LOUD & DECLARE

I am willing to partner with Helper Holy Spirit and Jesus, the Repairer of Broken Walls to activate victorious healing in my life (Isaiah 58). I will rebuild ancient ruins in my time and raise up the age-old foundations. I will prepare the way for the Lord in my mind. By my willing spirit, I will make a straight path for Him (Mark 1:3). If I struggle along the way, I will pray that the Lord grant me a willing spirit, to sustain me (Psalm 51:12). Jesus said, "the Advocate, the Holy Spirit, whom the Father will send in my name, will teach me all things and will remind me of everything Jesus has said to me" (John 14:26). Surely God is my help; the Lord is the one who sustains me. I wait patiently for the Lord; He hears my cry, He lifts me from every pit of despair, out of the miry clay; He sets my feet upon a rock and makes my footsteps firm (Psalm 40). I am blessed as I trust the Lord. Nothing can compare to the plans the Lord has for me as I delight to do His will. He will be merciful, loving, and faithful while guarding my life. If any seek my life, they will be ashamed and confounded. If any wish me harm, they will be repelled and humiliated. If any try to trick me, they will be appalled at their own shame. The Lord is my deliverer and will not delay in thinking of me. Praise the Lord, O my soul. I will praise the Lord all my life; I will sing praises to my God while I have my being (Psalm 146). The Lord sets me free from mental prisons, opens my eyes and takes away my spiritual blindness, lifts me up when I am weighed down, and He loves me and my righteous pursuit. My soul longs and thirsts for the living God. The LORD decrees His loving devotion by day, and at night His song is with me as a prayer to the God of my life. I put my hope in God, for I will yet praise Him, my Savior, and my God (Psalm 42). Send out Your light and Your truth; let them lead me. Let them bring me to Your holy mountain, and to the place where You dwell. Then I will go to the altar of God, to God, my greatest joy. I will praise You O God (Psalm 43).

Your throne, O God, endures forever and ever, and justice is the scepter of Your kingdom. You have loved righteousness and hated wickedness; therefore God; my God; has anointed me above my companions with the oil of joy. I daily enter the heavenly throne of the palace of the king (Psalm 45).

"The person with the Spirit makes judgments about all things, but such a person is not subject to merely human judgments for, 'Who has known the mind of the Lord so as to instruct him?' But we have the mind of Christ."

1 Corinthians 2:15-16

As we continue to address the idea that the Lord is the trauma counselor and redeemer of the mind, we come into this understanding for our mental healing through the Spirit, the Holy Spirit.

The secular mental health community or even the religious community might not agree with biblical healing. Modern therapy has been in the forefront of healing for over a hundred years and has become mainstream. These groups could lack knowledge regarding biblical mental healing or simply don't believe in Jehovah Rapha or Christ the burden bearer. They also might not believe the bible is flawless and the infallible word of God. That means they don't believe the Word of God is God and every word is directly inspired without errors. "All scripture is God-breathed" (2 Timothy 3:16). Through the years, hundreds of prophecies have been fulfilled and history has validated its text.

You will have to wrestle for yourself to anchor in this truth, but as for obtaining trauma removal and the resilience to thrive in this life, you must believe that the Lord can totally heal your mind, body, soul, and spirit.

"What no eye has seen, what no ear has heard, and what no human mind has conceived' - the things God has prepared for those who love him - these are the things God has revealed to us by his Spirit."

1 Corinthians 2:9-10

Day 293 | KINGDUIT

RESILIENCE

The way to counteract trauma is to be resilient. It is a lifelong practice of creating a place of stability in the mind, so that if life gets chaotic, you know how to quickly bounce back to perfect peace.

Truly one can posture themselves before the Lord in the secret place of soul refuge, in the midst of the Rock of Christ. The bible calls this the shelter of the Most High. One who worships the One true creator God, above all, is the one who hides in the shelter of the Most High, the Supreme maker of heaven and earth.

What would you find in the secret place of the Most High? Psalm 91 makes clear promises of the divine refuge like a fortress. It's an amazing place with divine security and tender communion with the Lord. All the traps of this life can't capture the one who has divine protection physically and emotionally.

When you look to the Lord, he says that your face is lovely, and your voice is sweet. Christ, the loving bridegroom, wants to hear you, fully redeem you and has already given you the mind of Christ. He wants you to be equipped with capabilities to possess peace that surpasses understanding which will guard your heart and mind.

"He who dwells in the shelter of the Most High will abide in the shadow of the Almighty. I will say to the LORD, 'You are my refuge and my fortress, my God in whom I trust."

Psalm 91:1-2

KINGDUIT | Day 294

"But if serving the LORD seems undesirable to you, then choose for yourselves."

Joshua 24:15

"But you are a chosen people, a royal priesthood, a holy nation, God's special possession, that you may declare the praises of him who called you out of darkness into his wonderful light. "

1 Peter 2:9

Due to the increase of traumatic experiences and traumatic stress manifesting in many lives, the need for an escape or relief from trauma is great. Some therapeutic trends use drugs to treat a variety of stressors.

The word pharmacy comes from the Greek word pharmakeia which is defined as using medicine, drugs, or spells. It is a drug-related sorcery or the practice of magic arts (Strongs 5331).[26] Psychedelic Therapy uses powerful natural and synthetic drugs to process traumatic memory. Even a tiny dose of pharmekia can lead to mind-altering experiences.

Here we find another contrast between secular therapeutic remedies and biblical remedies for emotional pain. One is flesh centered and the other is Spirit centered. According to Galatians 5:19-20, pharmekia is a work of the flesh. They conflict with each other, which can force the user to choose either a flesh-based remedy or a Holy Spirit centered remedy. As for psychedelics, they will lead you out of your mind, which is opposite of the biblical goal of having a sound mind.

This picture is a stark contrast from the security the Lord provides. The psychedelic drugs take you to a place of wild movement, color, and other worldly visions with a hope to liberate you. It is a risky hope, and many testify to a very dark side to the mind-altering drugs.

Nonetheless, the Lord still gives everyone the choice to choose for themselves which god/God they want to serve.

YouTube: -Bob Dylan - Gotta Serve Somebody

Day 295 | KINGDUIT

Soldier's Protection

The United States of America has a long history of finding refuge in the shadow of the Almighty, especially during times of tremendous threat of life. The military has claimed Psalm 91[27] as the Soldier's Psalm. There is legend that a brigade of army soldiers was led by a devout Christian who gave them each a Psalm 91 card, with a request that they recite the psalm daily. They engaged in three of the war's bloodiest battles. By the end of World War 1, the other United States units had ninety percent casualties and the 91st Brigade did not have a single combat related casualty.

Another testimony is of a soldier receiving a bible from his mother prior to heading to the jungles of Vietnam. She taught the young man to respect the Word of God because it is a Holy Book.

He found the bible as a source of comfort, protection, and deep emotional security. Even through heavy fire of bullets spraying the air, the soldier survived to pass the same small bible on to seven other US soldiers from 1967-2019.[28] It was carried through eleven combat tours around five countries and always protected each man who believed its promise. "Whoever dwells in the shelter of the Most High will rest in the shadow of the Almighty" (Psalm 91:1). Surely God commanded the angels to guard the men in all their ways. Surely, they fought the good fight of faith with their personal "sword of the Spirit, which is the word of God" (Ephesians 6:17). There were physical safety and mental protection. The promises cover sleep and emotional rest, freedom from paralyzing anxiety, night terrors, day warfare, field pestilence, animal threats and the devastating loss of life that surrounded them.

As for their mental state, they testified that "God was everywhere at work over their individual fate." This amazing testimony of the power of a bible that was kept close to their person, proves the faithfulness of God.

It's worth the time and effort to find a personal bible that is meaningful to you. Cherish it by reading its promises. It will save your life!

ART THERAPY DRAW: Draw a picture of an angel blowing a long trumpet. Put a small banner with the number 91 hanging from the trumpet.

"We do not want you to be uninformed, brothers and sisters, about the troubles we experienced in the province of Asia. We were under great pressure, far beyond our ability to endure, so that we despaired of life itself. Indeed, we felt we had received the sentence of death. But this happened that we might not rely on ourselves but on God, who raises the dead."

2 Corinthians 1:9

As we review different ways to counteract trauma with resilience, we must address suicide, the taking of one's own life or self-murder. God said we should not kill people in the ten commandments, that includes killing ourselves. Our life is so valuable that the Lord even numbers the hairs on our head. Our life is so valuable that our Father in heaven sent His only Son Jesus to take on all the sin of this world so that we might have a superabundant life. Jesus wants us to have both a wonderful life in this world and for all eternity.

Yet Jesus knows how life itself can be extremely difficult at times. Paul describes it well in the verse above. Trouble will come along that is beyond our ability to endure and it will be so bad that we despair of life. However, when life closes in hard and the pressure feels beyond our grasp, that is the time when we must cling to God.

The devil is a "thief who comes only to steal and kill and destroy" (John 10:10). In John 8:44 the devil is a murderer, and he speaks lies to try to get people to kill themselves. When this demonic plot is set against us or someone else, you must call on the name of Jesus to destroy the spirit of death. Say out loud, "I command all lying spirits to leave ______________________ (name/names) in Jesus Name!"

Find Psalm 91 and recite the whole psalm out loud placing the name of the one who struggles above in the text. Claim God's protection!

If you struggle with suicide, you are not alone, the Lord is nearby. Ask Jesus to rescue you or your loved one NOW! Act, call 911 or 988. The National Hopeline Network is 1-800-SUICIDE. Alert help nearby so you are not alone during your time of distress.

PROXIMITY

"Blessed is the man who does not walk in the counsel of the wicked, or set foot on the path of sinners, or sit in the seat of mockers" (Psalm 1:1).

A simple way to maintain resilience in mental health is to steer clear of walking or being close in relationship, either physically or virtually, to wicked environments. The bible describes it as the difference between being in a dry windy desert versus being like a tree planted by refreshing streams of water with fruitful bounty. There is a good reason why people flock to watery, lush, natural destinations. People find soul refreshment in nature, God's creation. Many don't even realize that the Lord's natural beauty is gracing them with peace.

"For the LORD guards the path of the righteous, but the way of the wicked will perish" (Psalm 1:6).

Proximity adjustments will bless you!

ASK: Spend time resting with the Lord today. Ask Holy Spirit if there are any relationships in your life that are keeping you away from the super abundant life of God. Write down the wisdom.

KINGDUIT | Day 298

FAITH ACTIONS

GOD'S PROMISE + YOUR WILLINGNESS

"Is anyone among you sick? Let them call the elders of the church to pray over them and anoint them with oil in the name of the Lord. And the prayer offered in faith will make the sick person well; the Lord will raise them up. If they have sinned, they will be forgiven."

James 5:14-15

Sometimes simple actions create a lifestyle of resilience that can deliver you and your loved ones from a multiplicity of mental health threats. If we are willing to activate our faith to utilize the promises of abundance, including mental and physical healing, then surely God will be faithful to keep His promises.

If you are sincerely seeking to have a sound mind and be strengthened unto victory, pray to find a group of believers that love to pray and watch the Lord heal people. One prayer can change your life. One time of surrounding yourself with godly faith action-based people can teach you a lifetime of blessing actions that can heal all things.

And yes, find some oil and anoint yourself, your home, your car, and anything that you want to mark as property of the living God. It may seem silly to you, but the invisible dark forces know who the Most High God is and that oil represents God's mark of healing and protection. It is a no trespassing sign in the spirit world. If God says that prayer offered in faith will make you well, then it will, if you are willing to believe and step out with action.

There is a bible story where a king needed help. He went to a man of God and was told to get arrows, calling them the "Lord's arrows of victory." He was told to strike the ground with the arrows to represent victory over his enemies. The king did the action three times but was rebuked by the man of God for not striking the ground multiple times to represent total victory.

ASK: Ask Jesus if He has any unique or specific strategies to help you get an epic victory.

Day 299 | KINGDUIT

FAITH ACTIONS

GOD'S PROMISE + YOUR WILLINGNESS

"Submit yourselves, then, to God. Resist the devil, and he will flee from you."

James 4:7

Perseverance is an action that you must practice, thus finding and hold peace every day. There is no such thing as passive Christian. If there was, then Jesus Christ would have never given you all authority with His mighty power to be equipped to overcome the enemy to possess abundant victory.

The action is to take your stand, be ready and strong, fear not, stand your ground, do everything to keep your position, hold your peace, wield your Spirit sword, be alert, and always keep praying. From your willingness to act in faith, the promise from the lips of Jesus is: "NOTHING WILL HARM YOU" (Luke 10:19)!

As you sit in the heavenly places with Christ, you will have a strategic high position. This place of authority that Christ died to give you, is the victory. It is Christ in us. We submit to God first, humbling ourselves to be reminded of what Christ did to empower us for victory. We never get a power trip or think we can boast about the dynamite power. Christ in us is hope. It is the hope that God's glory really does cover us every day if we use it. The devil must flee from you when you position yourself in this way and act, as a result the enemy is paralyzed!

Unfortunately, many don't pay attention to these promises. That's why they suffer unnecessarily. They suffer from depression which is a form of oppression. They suffer from lack of healing, negative emotions, and many other psychological inflictions that can be extinguished by a time of solution-centered prayer.

You may be thinking, I don't have time to pray like that. I work and have responsibilities. I can't be on my knees all the time. It's not like that. Yes, it is wise to start your day with holy meditation, but your sword is your tongue, it is a supernatural sword in your mouth. That's what the devil does to torment, he lies all day. Well, there is authority in your mouth that can make demonic lies release, cease, and desist.

"I am sending you out like sheep among wolves. Therefore, be shrewd as snakes and as innocent as doves."

Matthew 10:16

Wolves and snakes are merciless. They jump fences of private property and slither into areas they don't belong to steal, kill, and destroy. These animals in the bible represent the dark side, "the ruler of the kingdom of the air, the spirit who is now at work in those who are disobedient" (Ephesians 2:2). We use the sword of the Spirit to defeat demonic creatures like wolves and snakes from attacking us.

Would Jesus send out his sheep disciples defenseless? Never! His sheep disciples have great power since Shepherd Jesus healed and equipped them for victory. That equipping includes having a sound mind to outwit the serpent while staying innocent as doves. Therefore, we must go up to the high position by faith!

HEAVENLY REALMS
INCOMPARABLY GREAT POWER FOR US WHO BELIEVE

FAITH ACTIONS

GOD'S PROMISE + YOUR WILLINGNESS

"Endure hardship as discipline; God is treating you as his children. For what children are not disciplined by their Father? If you are not disciplined - and everyone undergoes discipline - then you are not legitimate, not true sons and daughters at all. Moreover, we have all had human fathers who disciplined us and we respected them for it. How much more should we submit to the Father of spirits and live!"

Hebrews 12:7-9

Jesus sent out the disciples like sheep among wolves because He taught them how to defend themselves. Abba Father disciplined them and allowed trials to come into their lives to teach them how to overcome. When you understand holy discipline, you welcome it! Jesus sternly rebuked a great champion of faith one day. "Jesus turned and said to Peter, 'Get behind me, Satan! You are a stumbling block to me; you do not have in mind the concerns of God, but merely human concerns" (Matthew 16:23). That seems shocking, but Jesus knew what Peter had to face when He went back to heaven. Jesus didn't want Peter to fall under the hardships of propelling the gospel, either psychologically or physically, from that point going forward.

So, what did Peter do that made Jesus so upset? Peter told Jesus that he shouldn't ever have to suffer or be killed! Jesus could have said something like, "Heck no! Without my death all my children would go to hell!" But instead, Jesus name-called Peter "Satan".

Peter soon understood the message and became willing to suffer for the gospel just like Jesus suffered. In fact, Peter was crucified but insisted on being turned upside down out of reverence for Christ. Peter's devotion and love made him willing to trust and obey until his last breath.

CONSIDER: How do you view discipline? Were you disciplined as a child? Why or why not?

"They disciplined us for a little while as they thought best; but God disciplines us for our good, in order that we may share in his holiness. No discipline seems pleasant at the time, but painful. Later, however, it produces a harvest of righteousness and peace for those who have been trained by it.

Therefore, strengthen your feeble arms and weak knees. 'Make level paths for your feet,' so that the lame may not be disabled, but rather healed,"

Hebrews 12:10-13

Hopefully the discipline your parents instilled was designed to keep you growing towards health, security and personal growth leading to a productive life. Your parents had good motives, but they are made of flesh and blood. Like you, they have weaknesses.

God is your Father in heaven. He is "the Father of the heavenly lights, who does not change like shifting shadows" (James 1:17). Even when someone had unloving and unkind parenting that felt like shifting shadows, there is still no good reason to project those disappointments on Abba Father in heaven. He is holy and our prayer is "His kingdom come, and His will be done, on earth as it is in heaven" (Matthew 6:10).

Have you ever considered that prayer to be for you personally? That prayer is not just for a church, religious purposes, or a nation, it is for you! Your Abba Father of heavenly lights desires heaven to come down to illuminate your personal bodily temple (body/soul/spirit). He has a will for you that goes from good to pleasing, and then to perfect, if you are willing to trust and obey Him. Your paternal Father in heaven provides bread for your physical needs, forgiveness for your spiritual needs, and protection for your psychological needs.

I had an absent earthly father that made trusting God difficult. It kept me from many blessings. In 2009, on Father's Day, my heavenly Father orchestrated an epic and shocking blessing for me when I was alone and far away. It led to a revelation of my divine father. I could never again deny the love of my Abba Father in heaven!

Day 303 | KINGDUIT

Jesus said, "A good man brings good things out of the good stored up in him, and an evil man brings evil things out of the evil stored up in him. But I tell you that everyone will have to give account on the day of judgment for every empty word they have spoken."

Matthew 12:25-26

Jesus walked around town healing people while some Pharisees (Jewish church leaders) witnessed his healing ministry. They protested Jesus, claiming he was breaking the law by "working" on the Sabbath. Jesus kept healing while walking to the synagogue area as the Pharisees kept fault-finding. The work intensified from physical conditions to psychological problems, like demon-possession. As the psychological problems intensified, the judgment and accusations from the people intensified against healing. They said Jesus was a servant of Satan.

Jesus fearlessly took his stand to defend the Kingdom of God, saying his power came from a higher source than Satan. Jesus clarified that judgment day would certainly come for every single person and every single word spoken by each person. Whoa! This is serious!

You might be asking, "How can I even remember every empty word I ever spoke over my lifetime?" This is a great and valid question for someone who truly loves God and wants to give an account for good in their life. This is where the brain merges into the faith equation.

Your brain is a memory bank holding every single event, word, and thought stored in your body. The body or the flesh can block and suppress things like trauma and memory. Your will and spirit can open soul doors to Jesus the Healer.

Denial, repression, delusion, duplicity, double-mindedness, suppression, and subconscious are some of the ways the soul deals with memories. The unconscious/inaccessible part of the mind often blocks memory. The mental health community tries to help people with these issues, but they are limited!

Conversely, God is never limited! Jesus and Helper Holy Spirit know every detail about you. Biblical mental healing is a lofty way to access self and brain memories so wisdom can bring out treasuries in your soul before the Healer.

"Where are you?"

Genesis 3:9

If God cares about every word, then he cares about the effects of every word spoken over your life. He knows they can become a burden on your mind and in your heart. Trauma removal from a biblical perspective is allowing Holy Spirit Helper to show you how to remove words and memories from circling in the mind. Remember, Christ is the burden-bearer, and Jesus takes things in your life and carries it for you. Burdens are not meant to be carried by Christians.

Some Christians believe if they pursue mental healing, it might be perceived that something is wrong with them, or they are storing up evil. Soul level healing doesn't have to be about being labeled, it's about your story before the Lord, the one who loves you with an everlasting love. It's a love that gives redemption from this troublesome worldly life so that you are sanctified on the inside and ready for a glorious eternal life.

The Lord knows that life and death are in the power of the tongue. He knows the fruit of words spoken over lives gets digested in the human soul and can change one's life trajectory. When we seek the Lord with all our heart, mind, soul, and spirit in order to search our souls, the revelations needed for victory will arrive with divine wisdom!

There was a perfect relationship between God and man in the Garden of Eden. It was a paradise of holy communion. But soon after Adam and Eve got bamboozled by the serpent, the Lord called out to Adam. The serpent's lies caused Adam and Eve to sin, so they stopped talking and started hiding.

ART THERAPY DRAW: "But the LORD God called out to the man, 'Where are you?" Genesis 3:9. Draw a picture of God playing hide and seek with Adam & Eve

MONTH 11 - Holy Spirit Helper

DAY 305 | KINGDUIT

TRAUMA REMOVAL

SPEAK OUT LOUD & DECLARE

Lord, you can sprinkle clean water on me and make me clean. You can cleanse me from all my impurities and from all my idols. You can give me a new heart and put a new spirit in me. You can remove my heart of stone and give me a heart of flesh. You can put Your Spirit in me and move me to follow Your decrees being careful to keep Your laws. You will be my God (Ezekiel 36:25)!

I put my trust in you; I lift my soul to you. Lord, you are forgiving and good, abounding in love to all who call on you. You hear my prayer, you listen to my cry for mercy, you answer me. Among the gods there is none like you. Lord, no deeds can compare with yours (Psalm 86)!

Help me Lord to understand my soul, help me learn how to love you with my soul, to bless you with my soul and glorify you with my soul.

Lord, when I call on you, come to you, and pray to you, you will listen to me. When I seek you with all my heart, I will find you. When I call you, you will answer me and tell me great and unsearchable things I do not know (Jeremiah 33:3).

I come to you, Jesus, in all my toiling and being burdened. Your yoke is easy, and your burden is light. You will give me rest. I take your yoke in exchange for my burdens. You are gentle and humble, and I will find rest for my soul (Matthew 11:28-30). You are the deliverer who turns godlessness away and takes away sins.

Search me, God, and know my heart; test me and know my anxious thoughts. See if there is any offensive way in me and lead me in the everlasting way. (Psalm 139). In Your presence is light, shine on me until my secret sins are set before you. All-consuming fire, refine me, purify me.

As I am willing to work out my salvation with fear and trembling, it is God who promises to work in me to fulfill his good purpose (Philippians 2:12).

As I am willing and obedient, so the Lord's work will be shown, His splendor will shine, His favor will rest upon me.

I will be satisfied every morning with the Lord's loving devotion. I will sing for joy and be glad all my days. The Lord will make me glad despite the afflictions of the past (Psalm 90:14-15).

God will create in me a pure heart. God will renew a steadfast spirit within me (Psalm 51:10). My mind is alert and fully sober. My hope is set to grace!

KINGDUIT | Day 306

"Hear, O Israel; The Lord our God, the Lord is one. Love the Lord your God with all your heart and with all your soul and with all your mind and with all your strength."

Mark 12:29-30

A teacher of the law asked Jesus about the most important commandment. Jesus told Israel to listen as He spoke about loving God. Although this passage describes love, it involves human elements connected to mental healing. Your holes (Strongs 3650), yes, the Greek word for all is holes: the whole, entire and complete being of a person, even the gaps, cracks, and broken places.

Your heart in this passage is Kardias (Strongs 2588). It is not your physical heart with all its chambers and blood pumping mechanisms; it is the thought and emotional center of your being that feels like it can surge through your body like the live flow of blood through the heart. When someone says, "I love you with all my heart," it is implied that strong emotion goes through their whole being.

Your soul is psyches (Strongs 5590). From psucho; breath, spirit, abstractly or concretely. Your soul is eternal, so when people say, "You are my soulmate," it has another worldly implication, like something from the universe made it happen.

Your mind is dianoias (Strongs 1271). It is thought, properly, the faculty, by implication, its exercise. Faculty is a word commonly used for an educational team, but it is also the intrinsic intellect tied to the human mind. It is inborn, empowered and directs physical movement. Often people use thoughts to change their surrounding circumstances. That's the mind power God made for humans. Now imagine Christians possessing the unsearchable riches of the "mind of Christ" (1 Corinthians 5:16) and the possibilities motivated by the love of God.

Your strength is ischyos (Strongs 2479). Strength, power, might, force, and ability, from a derivative of forcefulness. When someone says something like, "be strong," the implication is to be strong mentally which is meant to move into our body and the physical world. As the religious teacher heard this passage, he affirmed to Jesus that loving God was greater than religious activities like burnt offerings and sacrifices. Finally, Jesus found a kingdom leader in Israel!

DAY 307 | KINGDUIT

"The teacher of religious law replied, 'Well said, Teacher. You have spoken the truth by saying that there is only one God and no other. And I know it is important to love him with all my heart and all my understanding and all my strength, and to love my neighbor as myself. This is more important than to offer all of the burnt offerings and sacrifices required in the law."

Mark 12:32-33 (NLT)

Loving God > Religious Activities

"When Jesus saw that he had answered wisely, he said to him, 'You are not far from the kingdom of God.' And from then on no one dared ask him any more questions" (Mark 12:34).

There are many leaders who have been in church for a long time. They have lived sacrificial lives doing religious things with good intentions. They serve their Father in heaven, however understanding the kingdom of God is a foreign idea.

When devotion for God consists of religious activities and meetings that lack engagement with Holy Spirit, the One sent specifically for the purpose of teaching disciples/leaders all things, something is missing. If a church has just as many mental and physical health issues as the secular world, something is missing. When the church is and has been powerless to overcome vast demonic cultural influence, something is missing. When the church has an appearance of godliness that's just religiosity, yet lacks power for healing unto redemption, something is wrong.

On the contrary, when religious leaders' demonstration of God's power radically changes hearts, souls, and minds then no one can deny the kingdom of God. Then we know they are anointed by Holy Spirit. It's time to receive the goal of our faith, soul salvation. Loving God with all heart, soul, mind, and strength must become more important than religious activities.

ART THERAPY DRAW: Draw eight different sized vertical rectangles with triangles on top to represent a kingdom castle. Draw rays of light beaming out behind this castle. Label: KINGDOM OF GOD!

"For Zion's sake I will not keep silent, for Jerusalem's sake I will not remain quiet, till her vindication shines out like the dawn, her salvation like a blazing torch."

Isaiah 62:1

Despite the staggering rejection Israelites imposed on Jesus, the Messiah, he still loved/loves them. There is a golden age for Jerusalem that has yet to be revealed to the world. Jerusalem will be saved, and the glory of God will blaze in the Holy City once again!

When Jesus himself comes back to earth to set up the kingdom of God, He is coming back to the hill in Jerusalem called "Mount Zion, the city of the living God, the heavenly Jerusalem" (Hebrews 12:22-24). There will be thousands of joyful angels assembled there along with God, the Judge of all and the perfected church.

Before this happens, the Gentiles who have been grafted into the olive root of the Lord have an opportunity to provoke the Jewish people to jealousy. A Gentile who would provoke envy would be one who radiates the glory and wonder of the presence of Almighty God. A regular experience of the power and presence of God in the sanctuary would be a cause for holy jealousy, but the story isn't over, and God is still on His throne. Thankfully, the global Ekklesia is praying like never before, revival is breaking out and it will continue, and God will pour out his Spirit as promised.

This is still the season of grace to seek the Lord and find Him with heart, understanding and strength starting within. That will surface and healing will overflow with love for others.

The inmost being, or soul level healing will surely bring total forgiveness, complete mental and bodily healing, redemption from life's pits, supernatural strength, redeeming love for self and others, compassion, obedience, and high praises. These are all traits that show off the power and dominion of the Lord Most High. Let it be!

WRITE AN HONEST REVIEW: What do you think the church looks like to the Jewish people?

"The person with the Spirit makes judgments about all things, but such a person is not subject to merely human judgments, for, 'Who has known the mind of the Lord so as to instruct him?' But we have the mind of Christ."

1 Corinthians 2:15-16

The secret sauce on the banqueting table the Lord prepares for us is Holy Spirit. Holy Spirit gives divine wisdom, not earthly ideas. A good counselor can try to understand you, but Holy Spirit knows every detail and every motivation of your entire life.

You already have the mind of Christ; therefore you have all the abilities to utilize any information needed to reveal the truth about yourself. When you love the Lord with all your mind, your intellect will enable your will to cause your heart to obey and align with God's ways. Then you can use each day's mercy and strength to love God.

Holy Spirit Helper was a guaranteed deposit marked and sealed on your day of salvation. God doesn't lie, when He guarantees a love for you higher and deeper than all creation, greater than angels, demons, history, and any power in the universe, it's a done deal!

Hallelujah, praise, and glory to the Lord, now and forevermore!

ART THERAPY DRAW: Draw the word HOLY SPIRIT in big letters. We will spend time understanding our Jesus appointed Helper.

Counterfeit Cautionary Tale

Right before I met godly friends, a counterfeit friend arrived. She was fun but didn't want to talk about Jesus. She led me away with a smile. The ones that helped me grow in faith, that encouraged me to love and do good deeds, came after the test. Sometimes friend love is deceiving because it is cool, but activities of the relationship can often lead you on a path away from the Lord. "Do not be misled, 'bad company corrupts good character" (1 Corinthians 15:33).

Have you asked Holy Spirit if the activities you partake in with your friends are blessed by Jesus? Are there family members that you feel an obligation to that leave you feeling low? Are your companions foul mouthed, perverse, and controlling? Are your relationship choices just good choices but not the highest and best choices? Are your friend circles helping you improve your mental health? Is your time inspiring or depressing? Spirit led or fleshly? "Do not be yoked together with unbelievers. For what do righteousness and wickedness have in common? Or what fellowship can light have with darkness? What harmony is there between Christ and Belial? Or what does a believer have in common with an unbeliever? What agreement is there between the temple of God and idols? For we are the temple of the living God. As God had said: 'I will live with them and walk among them, I will be their God, and they will be my people" (2 Corinthians 6:14-16).

Cultural Christianity is not biblically centered. Many mention the name Jesus in one breath and use His name as a curse word in another breath. Therefore, they don't know Him, honor Him, or live according to the Word of God. Ask Jesus about each friend and get wisdom.

Searching the soul for divine healing often leads to time alone with God. "Come out from them and be separate," says the Lord. "Touch no unclean thing, and I will receive you. And I will be a Father to you, and you will be my sons and daughters, says the Lord Almighty" (2 Corinthians 6:17-18).

As a young Christian, I was trying to honor God and wanted a friend. She invited me to the beach, but when we arrived, she only wanted to hang out in godless clubs. Holy Spirit inside felt sad, so I left the beach friendless.

DAY 311 | KINGDUIT

"Therefore, since we have these promises, dear friends, let us purify ourselves from everything that contaminates body and spirit, perfecting holiness out of reverence for God."

2 Corinthians 7:1

A sound environment is peaceable and loving (even through the challenges). A toxic environment looks for mistakes in others, then corrupts and exposes them to the dark world.

It's wild to imagine, but the Lord is truly tabernacling or walking inside us. Where we go, He goes. When we partake in godless activities or bow down to idols by proxy, it grieves Holy Spirit. "Do not let any unwholesome talk come out of your mouths, but only what is helpful for building others up according to their needs, that it may benefit those who listen. And do not grieve the Holy Spirit of God, with whom you were sealed for the day of redemption" (Ephesians 4:29-30).

"Do everything without grumbling and arguing" (Philippians. 2:14). Our words are meant to be so inspiring that God can speak through us. Because Christ dwells in us, the potential for power speaking is great. We are willing to make the meditations of our mind and thoughts good, pleasant, and pleasing. From our thoughts come our words. We choose to speak life and blessings, not death, curses, and destruction. This includes our thoughts about self. Even if it takes a lot of practice, working hard at changing internal dialogues will make life better.

It may seem weird, but devil loves when Christians are negative because it creates a crack in our mental walls that devil finds opportunistic. He plants weed seeds into our minds with lies like anger, resentment, bitterness, judgments, critical thoughts, gossip, and fault-finding. The negative ideas fester the emotions of the soul.

"The tongue has the power of life and death, and those who love it will eat its fruit" (Proverbs 18:21). An intentional effort can produce great value. Pursuing pure thoughts will not only lead to peace and mental rest, but it will also set the stage for having a mind able to receive divine revelation. The hard work and moments of weakness or suffering pays in sweet mental fruit!

KINGDUIT | Day 312

<u>HE KNOWS MY NAME</u>: by Tommy Walker

I have a Maker, He formed my heart

Before even time began, My life was in His hands

He knows my name, He knows my every thought

He sees each tear that falls

And hears me when I call

-

I have a Father, He calls me His own

He'll never leave me, No matter where I roam

He knows my name

I'm so glad I can say, He knows my every thought

He sees each tear that falls. And hears me when I call

He knows your name

He knows your every thought

He sees all those tears that fall

And He'll hear you when you call

-

https://www.tommywalkerministries.org

WORSHIP: YouTube-Tommy Walker - He Knows My Name

"But I tell you the truth, it is to your advantage that I go away; for if I do not go away, the Helper (Comforter, Advocate, Intercessor - Counselor, Strengthener, Standby) will not come to you; but if I go, I will send Him (the Holy Spirit) to you [to be in close fellowship with you]."

Jesus in John 16:7 AB

JESUS' RESILIENCE PLAN

One obvious reason the disciples were successful is because they had Jesus, the One and only, the Rabbi King of the Jews by their side during his short three-year earthly ministry. Jesus taught them about the Kingdom of God. He also modeled the life and power of God before their eyes. The disciples witnessed Jesus' healing ministry for themselves and for other people in Jerusalem. They also witnessed Jesus' spiritual, prayer-centered relationship with his Father in heaven.

Jesus told them he wasn't doing anything on his own, but that he was listening to his Father. Jesus stayed close to the love of his heavenly Father to complete God's will. He kept His Father's commands with much joy. He told the disciples that He learned everything from his heavenly Father. This beautiful heavenly relationship is described in John 15 & 16.

Then Jesus turned a corner and began to explain to the disciples how they would survive in the world post crucifixion. He told the disciples to their face that Abba Father was sending the necessary help they needed after Jesus went back up to heaven. "When the Advocate comes, whom I will send you from the Father - he will testify about me. And you must also testify, for you have been with me from the beginning. All of this I have told you so that you will not fall way" (John 15:26-27/16:1).

Jesus knew the disciples would be devastated with grief from witnessing the trauma of his murder, death, and resurrection. Then they would be persecuted for their faith and kicked out of church. Jesus also knew things about their lives that were going to be unbearable, so he explained the resilience plan necessary for 24/7 access to divine love, power, and mental stability so they could combat anxiety. Jesus' psychological plan for disciples still works for you today!

Jesus said, “I will send Holy Spirit to you.” John 16:7

Jesus said that if he didn't send Holy Spirit to the disciples, they would fall away. Jesus had just spent three years under great pressure to fulfill his divine mission. He said he wasn't doing anything on his own, but under the constant loving companionship of his Father in heaven. Therefore, Jesus was clearly warning the disciples that their mission apart from Jesus would result in a falling away if they did not fully depend on the coming Holy Spirit.

We will consider the many ways Holy Spirit gives the disciple/believer the advantage of divine assistance in the same way human Jesus got divine assistance from Abba Father. We will learn about the role of Holy Spirit in our daily devotional and practical life of faith. Our response to Holy Spirit for mental healing leadership, along with moment-by-moment obedience, will give us strength to stand strong in the Lord for the coming challenges of these times.

When Jesus was warning the disciples about the reality of falling away on account of him, Peter replied in Matthew 26:33, "I never will." Go ahead and shake your head and look down, because you know Peter fell hard and got Satan-sifted.

This is the part of a life of devotion that we must heed the scriptures, be sober-minded and take this life of faith seriously. It is not a joke or a walk in the park. Our life of faith today is about a kingdom that is being intensely debated in the natural and spiritual world. Even though Jesus finished the work on the cross and our lives are fully forgiven and redeemed, there is much kingdom work to be done inside our souls and in the outside world. If it were not so, Jesus would not have given us all the authority in heaven and on earth. Getting out of the house to fulfill the great commission can only be done under (or submissive to) the power of Holy Spirit.

If you want to walk in love, power, and sound-mindedness to live in liberty and fruitfulness for yourself, your mission, your family and the generations to follow, you need Holy Spirit! I am not talking about a small dose of dedication, but a daily filling to overflow your life. It looks like joy and power!

ART THERAPY DRAW: Draw a dove in flight, wings stretched out, with an olive branch in beak.

DAY 315 | KINGDUIT

Jesus said, "Holy Spirit will not speak on his own; he will only speak what he hears and will tell you what is yet to come."

John 16:13

Jesus wasn't on a solo mission; He was willing to seek his Abba father daily. Holy Spirit does not speak on his own either, His information comes from Jesus. This is an example of the Godhead Trinity at work in heaven via Holy Spirit. When we listen and obey Holy Spirit, we fulfill the part of the Lord's prayer that says: "Your kingdom come, your will be done, on earth as it is in heaven" (Matthew 6:10).

Our connection to the vine of Christ gives us access to the Godhead (Father, Son, and Holy Spirit). Three in one work together inside the temple of a willing believer. All the tools came into us by the power of salvation and the promised seal of Holy Spirit. That first step of obedience, called baptism, crucified us with Christ's death, burial and resurrection and raised us to new life in Christ with a new Spirit. We were born into the Kingdom of God and from that point our job was to get our soul "transformed by the renewing of your mind" (Romans 12:2). Surely that verse clearly points to biblical mental health.

That's why a foundation of bible reading will help us have the faith to find and walk on the path of righteousness. Grasping the bible through study will confirm these truths. If we boiled down the idea of mental health and healing to its simplest biblical concept, it can be expressed like this: "Do not conform to the pattern of this world but be transformed by the renewing of your mind. Then you will be able to test and approve what God's will is - his good, pleasing and perfect will" (Romans 12:2).

The brain and the mind are highly complex organs in the human body. Everything that happens in the body connects to the brain through the central nervous system. The structures and skills of the brain are automatic like vision, temperature, appetite, breath, along with other complex functions. Yet still, the intellect/will part is autonomous or free to govern itself. God says we are going to have to get involved with mind transformative work to find God's highest and best results for our human experience. What a hope we have in this life, God's glory!

ART THERAPY DRAW: Draw an olive branch. Find out what it represents.

Jesus said "The wind blows wherever it pleases. You hear its sound, but you cannot tell where it is going. So it is with everyone born of the Spirit."

John 3:8

Because of the uncertainty of these times, as well as the increase of evil and obvious departure from godliness, many are getting very serious about their faith. They realize that unless the Lord shows up, darkness might move in. In many families, darkness has overtaken their loved ones, destroyed lives, and stolen treasures.

The Jewish community knows all about this because evil leaders have taken over throughout history with their godless agendas and destroyed the Israeli people and possessions time and time again. Each time the nation got restored and redeemed, it was by the mercy, prophecies, and loving devotion of Jehovah.

As New Testament believers, we are fully equipped with all power and every resource for total mental healing. Still, many put the brakes on Holy Spirit. Jesus told us Holy Spirit would be invisible like the wind and unpredictable, yet with a breath that has the power to give us incredible confidence and hope. Jesus went as far as saying in Mark 9:28 that "everything is possible for one who believes."

Holy Spirit wind can move around your body, soul, or spirit and inspire action in your being. Holy Spirit will do this without any word, command or even confirmation, you will just know. It takes a willing spirit to have faith to step out and follow that divine wind. I find Holy Spirit spontaneous and delightful, yet fearsome and convicting at the same time. If I sense that wind, I try to stop everything and respond. Often it doesn't make any sense, it's pure faith. Since I've been praying for mental healing for decades, I know Jesus is going to help me, so it's no surprise that wind will blow grace and mercy my way. When you pray for Holy Spirit to come, get ready for a gentle wind to swirl. The step out and obey must happen at once. Don't have a meeting, follow God! "And without faith it is impossible to please God, because anyone who comes to him must believe that he exists and that he rewards those who earnestly seek him" (Hebrews 11:6).

ART THERAPY DRAW: Draw a person walking by a stop sign, draw lines to represent wind.

DAY 317 | KINGDUIT

Jesus said, "But when he, the Spirit of truth, comes, he will guide you into all truth."

John 16:3

A hot debate topic of our time is the war about truth. What is truth? Some say they determine truth for themselves by claiming truth to be a fluid concept. On the other hand, the bible says truth is a person named Jesus.

"Thomas said to him, 'Lord, we don't know where you are going, so how can we know the way?"

Jesus answered, 'I am the way and the truth and the life. No one comes to the Father except through me'" (John 14:5-6).

The Godhead trinity embodies truth, so when Jesus went back up to heaven with his Father, the promised Holy Spirit would then be available to guide you into the truth needed to navigate life on a steady path.

Certainly, there are a lot of lies and falsehoods today, even from the most trusted institutions and people. The devil, the father of lies, roams around seeking to devour people with false information, leading to troubled responses. "You, dear children, are from God and have overcome them, because the one who is in you is greater than the one who is in the world" (1 John 4:4).

Jesus promised to guide you in all truth, and He is faithful. "For who knows a person's thoughts except their own spirit within them? In the same way no one knows the thoughts of God except the Spirit of God. What we have received is not the spirit of the world, but the Spirit who is from God, so that we may understand what God has freely given us. This is what we speak, not in words taught us by human wisdom but in words taught by the Spirit, explaining spiritual realities with Spirit-taught words. The person without the Spirit does not accept the things that come from the Spirit of God but considers them foolishness and cannot understand them because they are discerned only through the Spirit" (1 Corinthians 2:11-14). As you seek Jehovah Rapha, God the Healer, you are seeking Father, Son and Holy Spirit. The Spirit of truth has all the answers you need.

Jesus said, "Which of you fathers, if a son asks for a fish, will give him a snake instead? Or if he asks for an egg, will give him a scorpion? If then, though you are evil, know how to give good gifts to your children, how much more will your Father in heaven give the Holy Spirit to those who ask him?"

Luke 11:11-13

For many conservative Christians, stepping out in faith to trust the invisible wind of Holy Spirit is a frightening concept. Church attendance, bible reading, service and good deeds feel right, but trusting the Lord to lead you along an unfamiliar path of soul level discovery seems weird or maybe even dark. Snakes and scorpions are symbolic of the dark side of the evil realm.

There are no demons in heaven, there never have been nor will there ever be there. Rebellious angels are cast out of heaven. The Father in heaven is holy, pure, radiating with light and no shadows. Ask and trust the Father's gift of Holy Spirit!

Subconsciously, some mistake or compare our Father in heaven to an earthly father. There is absolutely no comparison because God the Father is eternal. He is not a mere mortal man of dust.

Despite the truth, many still doubted and accused Jesus of getting power from Satan's kingdom. His awesome power came from Abba alone and with that power he resisted Satan's kingdom.

"Trust in the Lord and do good; dwell in the land and enjoy safe pasture. Take delight in the Lord, and he will give you the desires of your heart. Commit your way to the Lord; trust in him and he will do this: He will make your righteous reward shine like the dawn, your vindication like the noonday sun. Be still before the Lord and wait patiently for him; do not fret when people succeed in their ways, when they carry out their wicked schemes" (Psalm 37:3-7).

ART THERAPY DRAW: Draw a fish, snake, egg, and scorpion. Circle the two food items a child might desire if he/she asked their father for a meal.

DAY 319 | KINGDUIT

Jesus said, "But the Advocate, the Holy Spirit, whom the Father will send in my name, will teach you all things and will remind you of everything I have said to you."

John 14:26

The help Holy Spirit gives is in the form of guidance. Like a still small voice, He shows and reveals truth in a gentle manner. It is often a recalling of scripture, a story, or the sounding memory of a worship song that comforts you. The more you read, meditate, memorize, and ponder the scriptures, the easier it is to get acquainted with Holy Spirit. When you remember scriptures or hear with your spiritual ears the stories and passages of the Bible, you will realize the Lord is speaking to you as Holy Spirit teaches and reminds you about godly things.

The still small voice and presence of Holy Spirit proves to be spot-on in guidance, continues to comfort, and is truthful and honest. Soon, that voice becomes noticeable in your heart. It has a tone, a gentleness, and an undeniable conviction. Holy Spirit wisdom is matchless and excellent, worthy of responding with praise and thanksgiving.

When I started my healing journey, I felt emotionally vulnerable. My struggle was often met with a negative response. Trusting others, even Christians, made me unsure if they were going to judge and criticize me. I realized people meant well, but they still said things and acted out in ways that kept me from liberty.

One friend was seeking healing at the same time but was using another holistic method that was different from my biblical pursuit. She really wanted me to try her soul remedy, but I was reluctant. I asked Holy Spirit for help and was strongly impressed to offer hospitality and listen to her. She shared her healing testimony and we enjoyed fellowship. Later I sought the Lord and asked specifically for topical bible wisdom regarding her soul remedy. Immediately, a biblical passage popped in my mind. I read it to find detailed confirmation of the wisdom she was sharing with me. I applied it and the Lord gave me profound revelation and the best breakthrough.

ASK JESUS FOR SPECIFIC WISDOM: Remind yourself to pay attention and listen, then act.

"The Spirit told Philip, 'Go to that chariot and stay near it.' Then Philip ran up to the chariot and heard the man reading Isaiah the prophet. 'Do you understand what you are reading?' Philip asked.

'How can I,' he said, 'unless someone explains it to me?' So he invited Philip to come up and sit with him."

Acts 8:29-31

Philip was a spirit-filled and spirit-led disciple. He operated in the power of the Gospel, the authority of the kingdom and was led by Holy Spirit. He was joyfully and fully equipped to deal with salvation, baptism, unclean spirits, healing, witchcraft and the demonic.

One day Philip was led to go on a walk and found an Ethiopian court official on the side of the road in a chariot reading Isaiah the prophet. In a moment, Holy Spirit winded around Philip and the Ethiopian, telling one to offer biblical help and the other to ask for spiritual guidance. In that same moment, both men responded to the Spirit and a great work of the Lord transpired.

Read Acts 8:26-40. You will sense the swift movement of Holy Spirit. There was no time to stop and think, there was only time for immediate obedience. God moved mightily because both men had a willing response to the things of God. This is a divine example on how the Holy Spirit moves swiftly in believers' lives.

"People of Zion, who live in Jerusalem, you will weep no more. How gracious he will be when you cry for help! As soon as he hears, he will answer you. Although the Lord gives you the bread of adversity and the water of affliction, your teachers will be hidden no more; with your own eyes you will see them. Whether you turn to the right or to the left, your ears will hear a voice behind you, saying, 'This is the way; walk in it" (Isaiah 30:19-21). Holy Spirit can be fast like the wind!

MEDITATE: Ask Holy Spirit to remind you of a time you stepped out in faith without exactly understanding what was happening. Write that experience down in detail. Circle the parts of the story when Holy Spirit led you. Put a rectangle around your faith response. Underline the blessing.

DAY 321 | KINGDUIT

"Praise be to the God and Father of our Lord Jesus Christ, the Father of compassion and the God of all comfort, who comforts us in all our troubles, so that we can comfort those in any trouble with the comfort we ourselves receive from God."

1 Corinthians 1:3-4

In the King James Bible, one of the names for Holy Spirit is the Comforter. Holy Spirit is also the one sent by Abba Father to teach us all things, reminding us of the truth from Jesus, the Word of God.

In your journey for mental health, if you ever question why you should trust God, the above verse will confirm. It's like a soul balm, the God of all comfort! What type of comfort, you ask? The comfort that carries you through all your troubles. Yes, all!

The help is so full of compassion and the comfort from God is so complete that there is a tremendous compulsion by the Spirit of the living God to extend that same comfort to those in any trouble. In other words, God's comfort and compassion is so amazing that it must be shared.

Cry out or extend your hand to heaven, He will help you. "God is not human, that he should lie, not a human being, that he should change his mind. Does he speak and then not act? Does he promise and not fulfill" (Numbers 23:19)?

So, what exactly is comfort from God's perspective? Is it a hug, a song, money from heaven? Nope, it is the best, blessed comfort in heaven and on earth. It is the comfort that draws near, talks to you, and calls out to invite you over during troubling times of distress, tribulation, affliction, or pressure (Strongs 2347 troubles). If Jesus were sitting nearby, he'd say, "Come to me, all you who are weary and burdened, and I will give you rest. Take my yoke upon you and learn from me, for I am gentle and humble in heart, and you will find rest for your souls" (Matthew 11:28-29).

Try calling out to the Lord the next time you feel hard pressed and pray for divine comfort and compassion to draw near.ASK FOR COMFORT: Think of your most difficult challenge. Ask Holy Spirit to comfort you.

"I will ask the Father, and he will give you another advocate to help you and be with you forever - the Spirit of truth. The world cannot accept him, because it neither sees him or knows him. But you know him, for he lives with you and will be in you."

John 14:16-17

Remember that Holy Spirit reminds you about the truth in the Bible. This means when you experience some of the hard times connected to mental health issues, Holy Spirit will advocate for you by reminding you that Jesus Christ already paid the price for your mistakes. He paid the price for the mistakes of everyone in the entire world: past, present, and future.

When the accuser of the family of God tries to judge, condemn, and throw shame on you with demonic lies, Holy Spirit will be your witness in heaven before the throne on High and plead your case. The throne of God has righteousness and justice at its foundation. When Holy Spirit advocates on your behalf, even regarding your sin, it is done with faithful love.

God knows that much of the trouble, pressure, and distress we experience often comes from some type of root issue. In the case of mental health issues, sometimes we get so perplexed by life that we can't even figure out why we are so upset. Are the distressing issues from personal fault or others? Are they root issues that trigger emotions or false belief in the mind? Are they oppressive night terrors or evil arrows flown by day that come for no reason?

No matter the situation, Holy Spirit Advocate is always there with the Father to represent us before the throne of God. As you seek to understand and heal, redemption stays at the center of all circumstances. Even though you might not feel it, the blessing is in being willing to believe and act while gratefully exulting His righteous throne. This is Jesus' promise: "If you love me, keep my commands. And I will ask the Father, and he will give you another advocate to help you and be with you forever-" (John 14:15-16).

ART THERAPY DRAW: Draw a throne or judge's bench. Draw a heart next to it with your name inside.

DAY 323 | KINGDUIT

"In the same way, the Spirit helps us in our weakness. We do not know what we ought to pray for, but the Spirit himself intercedes for us through wordless groans. And he who searches our hearts knows the mind of the Spirit, because the Spirit intercedes for God's people in accordance with the will of God..."

Acts 8:26-27

One of the many lies some believe is that they are not worthy to approach God. The truth is that God's throne exists for you! You are one of God's people, an heir. His righteous, loving, faithful and just ways serve to help you govern your journey from death to life, from flesh to Spirit.

Holy Spirit is interceding for you to grow in revelation, liberty, redemption, and glory. That's the blessing God has in mind for his children, regardless of human weakness. Holy Spirit prayer is a powerful help! The best remedy in any situation can start with prayer or even a groan if you are perplexed or in distress.

If we don't actively make the shift to praying during the difficult times, we can find ourselves in a place of weakness that could lead to other sin and more trouble. If I am around others during a weak situation, my first prayer is "Lord, be the watchman over my lips." The tongue can be a flame according to the bible, so I cover that first. Often pressured times or times of trouble can create a temptation to lash out at others because of repressed pain, lack of self-control or heartaches that flare up.

On the other hand, many people that get hit with hard times run right out to see a professional because they need someone with a sound mind to sort things out for them. Wise counsel is biblical, but don't deny Holy Spirit, for he is already interceding for you. Those prayers always align with God's will. In addition, if you run to the closet to pray in secret with the Father, there is a promised reward available for you (Matthew 6:6).

ASK FOR GOD'S COUNSEL: Pray specifically for wisdom to understand something perplexing in your mind, your emotions, your body, or your spirit.

"I will praise the Lord, who counsels me, even at night my heart instructs me. I keep my eyes always on the Lord. With him at my right hand, I will not be shaken. Therefore, my heart is glad and my tongue rejoices; my body also will rest secure."

Psalm 16:7-9

Of all the leaders of the bible, King David had no problem looking to the Lord for counsel. He said his eyes were always on the Lord as his heart welcomed divine counsel even through the night.

Since the salvation of our souls is our faith goal, pursuing soul-level healing covers all parts of life: mind, will, emotions, and body. As the mind goes, so does the body.

A paradigm shift is necessary to turn from self-ways to setting the Lord's ways overall. It takes a humble heart to confess and believe that the Lord can lead you down all areas of life. Even the Jewish community struggled to follow God as a nation. They didn't want to follow God, they preferred to follow a man.

When Israel was just a family, they followed a father. As they grew into a nation, they became oppressed under a satanic Pharaoh. After hundreds of years of crying to God in distress, Moses was provided as their leader. The desperate circumstances caused a dependence on Moses, who became responsible for seeking God for counsel. As time moved forward, the Jews struggled with God's presence and continued to follow human leaders, priests, and prophets.

Israeli elders could discern whether new leaders followed God's ways and soon they asked the prophet Samuel to find a king. This hurt the Lord because after all his faithfulness to Israel, they rejected his counsel. "Listen to all that the people are saying to you (Samuel); it is not you they have rejected, but they have rejected me as their king. As they have done from the day, I brought them up out of Egypt until this day, forsaking me and serving other gods, so they are doing to you" (1 Samuel 8:6-8). Can you imagine God feeling rejected because you won't see His counsel?

LOOK HONESTLY AT YOURSELF: Where or who do you go to for advice?

DAY 325 | KINGDUIT

"Then his people recalled the days of old, the days of Moses and his people — where is he who brought them through the sea, with the shepherd of his flock? Where is he who set his Holy Spirit among them, who sent his glorious arm of power to be at Moses' right hand, who divided the waters before them, to gain for himself everlasting renown, who led them through the depths like a horse in open country, they did not stumble; like cattle that go down to the plain they were given rest by the Spirit of the Lord. This is how you guided your people to make for yourself a glorious name."

Isaiah 63:11-14

The Spirit of God was present at the creation of the world and with God's people from the beginning. It is often said that Holy Spirit is the most neglected person of the Trinity. Did you know that Holy Spirit guided the Hebrews out of Egyptian slavery?

This passage gives credit to Holy Spirit for shepherding the flock of God's people by the power of his glorious arm. Holy Spirit led them through a deep journey without stumbling and gave them rest. Holy Spirit guided them all the way to becoming a nation of everlasting fame that was led by God. We can only imagine how Holy Spirit strengthened them for the Exodus, stood by them, sustained them, and guaranteed their victory.

Based on your faith/church experience, do you think Holy Spirit has been a neglected Person of the Godhead? Who do you relate to most in your life of faith: Father, Son, or Holy Spirit? Can you describe why you prefer one over the other?

ART THERAPY DRAW: Draw a symbol you will remember for FATHER GOD. Draw a symbol for JESUS CHRIST. Draw a symbol for HOLY SPIRIT.

Who do you relate to most in your life of faith: Father, Son, or Holy Spirit? Some people talk to God as Father when others have never prayed to the Father in heaven. Some only talk to Jesus in their conversational prayer life because they identify with Jesus through their salvation experience.

Write down why you think you prefer one person of the Godhead over the other?

DAY 327 | KINGDUIT

Jesus. said, "The Holy Spirit . . . will remind you of everything I have said to you."

John 14:26

One of the wonderful attributes of Holy Spirit is the way He works to remind us of important things. For example, things that are spiritual like words from the bible or songs of comfort and even practical earthly natural things that we need or care about.

Countless are the testimonies of prayers over lost practical items that could not be found, and soon a plea goes out to the Lord and suddenly the information is revealed. Numberless are the times when worship songs spring up from God in our souls, bringing comfort and spiritual exhortation. When that beautiful music pops up in our soul/mind, we sing out and the atmosphere around our emotions can easily shift.

The word "remind" is all through the bible, often with a feeling of the maternal comforting nature of our God. The Passover story was to be told year after year as a reminder of the mighty hand of God, able to deliver people from slavery.

In the Old Testament, the Lord used countless physical objects to serve as reminders of God's ways. Abraham's tree, Jacob's well, tabernacle features, Joshua's river stones, and a scarlet thread.

Then in the New Testament, writers were often putting reminders in print to direct others to stay on the path of God's ways as a means of encouragement. Things like, "Don't argue, submit, be ready to do good, fan into flame the gift of God, be stimulated into wholesome thinking" and on and on. That's how Holy Spirit will help you!

"So, I will always remind you of these things, even though you know them and are firmly established in the truth you now have. I think it is right to refresh your memory if I live in the tent of this body, because I know that I will soon put it aside, as our Lord Jesus Christ has made clear to me. And I will make every effort to see that after my departure you will always be able to remember these things" (2 Peter 1:12-14). Even Peter's written tone sounds maternal, with a heart full of love and care for the body of Christ in his time. I wonder if Peter knew he'd be reminding billions throughout the ages.

"For anyone who speaks in a tongue does not speak to people but to God. Indeed, no one understands them; they utter mysteries by the Spirit. . . Anyone who speaks in a tongue edifies themselves."

1 Corinthians 14:2/4/14-15

The bible teaches that Holy Spirit helps us to pray to God. It is another gift of the Spirit given to believers as a way to edify ourselves. God's ways are much higher and beyond the ways of man, therefore praying in Holy Spirit is a blessed resource, especially in the area of mental healing.

Even if you didn't belong to a church or have grown up with Christians who practiced praying in tongues, that doesn't disqualify the gift. Paul was grateful that his devotional life consisted of praying in tongues so he would be built-up to complete his mission.

I understand this well because of my agnostic upbringing and conservative introduction to faith. I rolled my eyes about it for a long time. Then I came into a season of suffering that I might be conformed into the image of Christ and my attitude changed. I prayed to the Lord for help, saying I was willing to follow Him. The next thing I know the help God provided is someone telling me I need more Holy Spirit and more prayer in my life. I couldn't argue that my need for personal edification was great because the Lord knew I was about to walk through a dark valley. Having a strong prayer life has always been the secret to my closeness to God, so I prayed about it and studied the Bible.

If you are struggling with mental health issues, increase your prayer life and watch the Lord bless you with better mental health. If you don't feel comfortable with praying in tongues during your private devotional life, talk to Jesus more. Ask Holy Spirit to lead you to a safe Christian mentor, book, or helper in this area of your life that needs tender loving care and hope for the future.

"And hope does not put us to shame, because God's love has been poured out into our hearts through the Holy Spirit, who has been given to us" (Romans 5:5).

EDIFY YOURSELF: Ask the Lord for the gift of praying in tongues.

"In the same way, the Spirit helps us in our weakness. We do not know what we ought to pray for, but the Spirit himself intercedes for us through wordless groans. And he who searches our hearts knows the mind of the Spirit, because the Spirit intercedes for God's people in accordance with the will of God."

Romans 8:26-27

Some of you reading this devotional have stories and experiences that are so overwhelming and horrific that you can't even talk about it. Perhaps you tried to get professional help, and it made matters worse or you tried to reach out to the faith community, and they were not equipped to handle your case.

One day I spoke with an old veteran pilot whose plane was shot down and then captured as a prisoner of war in Vietnam. I asked him if he ever shared the details of his traumatic airplane crash and captivity. He told me that his soldier companions did not speak about it, mostly because they were publicly scorned upon their return to the USA. The political anti-war movement created too much hostility for them to feel emotionally safe. Nonetheless, I tenderly asked him to tell me something about being a prisoner of war. At the least, someone who is compassionate, interested and a good listener can help.

Corrie Ten Boom was a holocaust concentration camp survivor. The Nazi Party wiped out her family and she miraculously survived. She was compelled to dedicate her life to proclaiming that God forgives as a result of forgiving others. One day she saw the death camp soldier in town who murdered her family, and her heart was filled with hate. The pain was too deep, but Holy Spirit reminded her of Romans 5:5 that says, "For we know how dearly God loves us, because he has given us the Holy Spirit to fill our hearts with his love." Listen to her tell the story: YouTube: Corrie ten Boom forgives guard concentration camp (English with Dutch subtitles).

Holy Spirit can help you through life, shower the love of God on you and give you hope to get through life's painful perplexing mysteries.

"I have told you these things, so that in me you may have peace. In this world you will have trouble. But take heart! I have overcome the world!"

Jesus in John 16:33

What things did Jesus tell us to have peace in our earthly life? Jesus told the disciples first, then John recorded the instructions in his gospel book so that we would have the secret to overcoming life's trouble.

The summary of the Jesus resilience plan centers completely around the trinity: Father, Son and Holy Spirit. The plan includes help, love, fellowship, and divine provision that includes comfort, spiritual defense, prayer, counsel, strength, and close help. Another name for Holy Spirit is "the Spirit of truth." "But when he, the Spirit of truth, comes, he will guide you into all the truth" (John 16:13). Jesus is "truth" because he said, "I am the truth" in John 14:6. Therefore Jesus truth and Holy Spirit of truth partner together to life-guide disciples.

The bottom line is, life on planet earth can be troublesome, but the Prince of Peace not only gives you peace but also has provided a solution. He cares about every burden put upon humanity and is willing to carry everyone. Jesus doesn't want you to be anxious about anything, so if you are willing to do your part to cast the cares of your heart on him, he will overcome them. Then he will give you the peace that passes your understanding along with the blessing of a guarded heart.

Secular counselors are trained to diagnose, number, tag, document and provide a place for you to keep talking about your troubles. Jesus, the Prince of Peace, has overcome all world troubles and wants to give you peace by removing burdens that cause anxiety.

<u>Personal Troubles Jesus Will Help Overcome</u>

- ____
- ____
- ____
- ____
- ____
- ____

DAY 331 | KINGDUIT

"Jesus replied, 'Very truly I tell you, no one can see the kingdom of God unless they are born again.'

'How can someone be born when they are old?' Nicodemus asked. 'Surely they cannot enter a second time into their mother's womb to be born!'

Jesus answered Nicodemus, 'Very truly I tell you, no one can enter the kingdom of God unless they are born of water and the Spirit. Flesh gives birth to flesh, but the Spirit gives birth to spirit. You should not be surprised at my saying, you must be born again. The wind blows wherever it pleases. You hear its sound, but you cannot tell where it comes from or where it is going. So it is with everyone born of the Spirit.'

John 3:3-8

Understanding the work of Holy Spirit in a believer's life will help you get along on your healing journey. There are many books out there that further explain the work of the Holy Spirit. I have highlighted how Holy Spirit specifically reveals the truth about yourself to receive divine counsel for mental healing. Jesus called Holy Spirit the Spirit of truth in John 16:13 and explained how you will be guided by the truth that sets you free. When Jesus talked about the flesh and the spirit of mankind, flesh is of the natural man. whereas spiritual birth comes from Holy Spirit.

Understanding Holy Spirit can be challenging. Sometimes I wonder if the Lord purposely keeps wisdom hidden so that we seek Him with all our heart in. to receive understanding. Our willingness to seek the Lord shows the Lord how much we care about His promise of super abundance in our soul.

Nicodemus was willing to pursue Jesus to understand the concept of being born again. This process involves someone willing to fully commit to the Lord. When they do, they will be born again, brand new with a new spirit, the HOLY SPIRIT. This is the game changer in the life of a believer. They supernaturally move from being human spirit centered to Holy Spirit led. Then, the powerful wind of God blows into their willing life with power for mental healing. Truly Holy Spirit is the key to Biblical Mental Healing!

"Jesus found the place where it was written: 'The Spirit of the Lord is on Me, because He has anointed Me to preach good news to the poor.

He has sent Me to proclaim liberty to the captives and recovery of sight to the blind, to release the oppressed."

Luke 4:17-18

There was no hiding the ministry of Jesus during his time on earth. He went to the synagogue in Nazareth and read the Isaiah prophecy about himself. He said something like, "it's Me the anointed One! I am going to preach good news, proclaim liberty, heal, and release the oppressed!" His mission was clear, documented in Isaiah and the scroll was open before Jesus. He willingly declared the fulfillment of the prophecy in real time, then went about doing exactly what the prophecy said. What a great example of biblical obedience!

Many Christians respond to Jesus out of a need for salvation from eternal punishment, and then stop short of the freedom and deliverance needed to survive on this earth. Abba Father made sure New Testament believers had eternal and earthly salvation.

Salvation is not just about heaven; it's about receiving heaven on earth via the guaranteed deposit of Holy Spirit. It's about bringing heaven down to earth before going up to heaven for eternity. That process is called sanctification and it is only the beginning of a glorious life of liberty, love, and power. In reading the original passage from Isaiah 61, freedom from oppression or mental redemption is the Lord's specialty, including recovery from spiritual blindness. He proclaims liberty, but as you keep reading, the prophecy switches to our willing response. Oppressive thoughts and spiritual blindness must be released.

"Then your light will break forth like the dawn, and your healing will quickly appear; then your righteousness will go before you, and the glory of the LORD will be your rear guard. Then you will call, and the Lord will answer; you will cry for help, and He will say: Here am I" (Isaiah 58:8-9).

DAY 333 | KINGDUIT

"To comfort all who mourn and provide for those who grieve in Zion - to bestow on them a crown of beauty instead of ashes, the oil of joy instead of mourning, and a garment of praise instead of a spirit of despair. They will be called oaks of righteousness, a planting of the Lord for the display of his splendor."

Isaiah 61:2-3

The Lord is a comforter to the broken hearted. He is an ever-present help in time of need and when there is mourning and grief, He is there! When there is no other who understands the heart and soul, God does. He knows and He cares.

That is comforting enough, but the Lord goes further. He can turn the mourning into dancing and give praise while in the middle of despairing pain. It doesn't stop there; the Lord can redeem the most painful seasons of life and turn the grief stricken one into a strong and mighty tree of splendor.

That was the mission of Jesus, the anointed One. He was filled with the Spirit of the Lord and lived to fulfill the message of redemption. As each person's life gets redeemed by the Spirit of the Living God, strength comes into their life like an oak tree. The tree is mighty and strong, able to withstand the storms of life and stays rooted and grounded.

ART THERAPY DRAW: Draw a mighty oak tree. Put your name on the tree trunk. By faith, thank God for blessing you with the ability to overcome all things.

"They will rebuild the ancient ruins and restore the places long devastated; they will renew the ruined cities that have been devastated for generations."

Isaiah 61:4

Bible stories teach us how the Lord raised up the Jewish people and families repeatedly. Those who sought the Lord for redemption, comfort, liberty, and vision got the provisions from God. All the trouble and ashes of the hard times eventually turned to beauty. All the mourning and despair from being overtaken by the enemies of God's people eventually turned to praise and joy.

This happened in the life of Joseph, Moses, Joshua, Caleb, David, Daniel, Ruth, Hannah, Esther, Mary, Elizabeth, Peter, Paul and many more. When the Spirit of the Lord came upon them to carry them through and out of the hard times, overwhelming joy and spontaneous erupting praises burst forth from their hearts and mouths. That's what divine deliverance and healing did for them and millions more.

The Lord's help made them so grateful that a natural desire formed in their souls to magnify God. Then came a willingness to turn back and help other people. They rebuilt, restored, and renewed physical cities and communities until they prospered with housing, agriculture, and commerce.

Today in Jerusalem as the Jewish community works diligently to rebuild the Temple in Jerusalem. It's called the "Temple Movement of the Messianic Age." Since the destruction of the Second Temple in 70AD, Jerusalem still longs for the temple restoration including divine features, furnishings, priestly duties, and worship as recorded in the bible. Biblical prophecies guide them as the Jewish community rebuild and collect all the divine components.

As the Jews (still not believing Jesus the Messiah) work on the physical temple, the Gentiles are working on their bodily temples. The Gentiles are rebuilding their souls, seeking to love God with a transformation and renewing of their minds so that they can find God's will and bless their generation.

LOOK UP: YouTube search: "BREAKING NEWS: Third Temple Rebuilt ANNOUNCEMENT in Jerusalem."

MONTH 12 - You A Living Temple Stone

"And you will be called priests of the Lord, you will be named ministers of our God. You will feed on the wealth of the nations and in their riches you will boast."

Isaiah 61:6

"But you are a chosen people, a royal priesthood, a holy nation, God's special possession, that you may declare the praises of him who called you out of darkness into his wonderful light."

1 Peter 2:9

The evidence of what God has done and continues to do in our times is extraordinary. Right now, there is a simultaneous rebuilding of the temple of God. While Israel is collecting the elements for rebuilding the third Temple, the Gentiles are pursuing the healing of the mind, will and emotions to present themselves before the Lord as a glorious body of Christ. Gentiles are offering their bodies as a living sacrifice to fulfill the priesthood of the believers.

Israel has obtained the divine geographic land in Jerusalem, perfect red heifer animals for temple sacrifice, specifically trained priests to conduct temple worship, and even the King's harpists are ready.

These are just a few activities that the Lord is blessing in our time to create a symphony of divine fulfillment. Jews and Gentiles all around the world are being inspired by the Holy Spirit with their praises and beautiful display of the Lord's splendor.

The more biblical mental healing you experience in your life, the more you will witness for yourself what it is like to live in your divine identity as God's special possession. We are chosen, royal, and holy to declare God's high praise and live the glorious light of Christ!

"Great are the works of the LORD; they are pondered by all who delight in them. Glorious and majestic are his deeds, and his righteousness endures forever. He has caused his wonders to be remembered; the LORD is gracious and compassionate." Psalm 111:2-4

Day 336 | KINGDUIT

"Once you were not a people, but now you are the people of God; once you had not received mercy; but now you have received mercy."

1 Peter 2:10

I know it sounds wild, but if you are taking part of this devotional and engaging the Lord for mental health and healing, then you belong to Him and are one of God's people. It's not a religious thing to the Lord. You are like a living stone being strategically placed into the house of God. This spiritual house is composed of many living stones and other people being built up by God with the intent goal of a holy priesthood. As you offer the sacrifices of a surrendered life, being crucified in Christ, born again by Holy Spirit, and willingly pursuing the things of God, you will live in His marvelous light. This is all happening by the mercy of God over your life paired with obedience to Holy Spirit.

The more you fight the good fight, refusing to partake in the things of the flesh and the world, the more you will identify with God's house, people, nation and God's kingdom come. You will become more and more aware of Jesus, the cornerstone that supports this spiritual house you belong in. You will realize that He is the solid Rock that is immovable, steadfast and abounding with love for you. As you submit more and more to His holy word and His ways, you will live with a heart fully believing, submitting, doing good, and being aware of the presence of God in your life. Soon an overwhelming gratitude for His mercy, healing and grace will grow into a loving devotion that is willing to even suffer.

When thanksgiving isn't enough praise to offer God, then living to serve the King and the royal priesthood becomes the glorious life you desire. Worthy is "The Lamb of God who takes away the sin of the world" (John 1:29)!

"Like living stones, you are being built into a spiritual house to be a holy priesthood, offering spiritual sacrifices acceptable to God through Jesus Christ."

1 Peter 2:5

You are God's Temple

SPEAK OUT LOUD & DECLARE

"Don't you know that you yourselves are God's temple and that God's Spirit dwells in your midst" (1 Corinthians 3:16)? "I am a chosen person, a royal priesthood, a part of God's holy nation, God's special possession." I will "declare the praises of God who called me out of the darkness and into his marvelous light" (1 Peter 2:9). I will "live such a good life among the pagans that, though they accuse me of doing wrong, they may see my good deeds and glorify God on the day he visits" (1 Peter 2:12). God will be faithful to build me into a spiritual house. God will empower me to be holy. May the grace of God be over my healing season. May my will align to God's will so I will be so complete in Him, that I will serve the Lord.

When I serve the Lord, I will do so with the strength God provides, so that in all things God may be praised through Jesus Christ. When I speak, God's grace will enable me to speak the very words of God. God will get all the glory as I use my gift to serve others, stewarding God's grace (1 Peter 4:11). The more I heal, the more love abounds in my life. I will love others deeply from the heart.

Thank you, God, you always lead me in Christ's triumphal procession. You use me to spread the aroma of the knowledge of him everywhere I go. Even to you God, my life is a pleasing aroma of Christ since Christ is in me. I have hope for glory over my life. Even those who are lost and without hope will see the light of Christ in my life (2 Corinthians 2:14). Even though my physical body is formed from dust and like a clay vessel, there is a treasure inside full of all-surpassing power from God (2 Corinthians 4:7). God's light will shine in my heart to glorify God. Even when the days are evil and the nights are long, Jesus will never leave me, and His life will keep manifesting the goodness of God in my mortal body.

No matter what age I am, no matter what weaknesses I have, no matter how perplexed I feel or where I am being pressed by others, I will always carry Jesus with me and the power of Holy Spirit all the days of my life. My God's kingdom is unshakable no matter what happens in the universe, the heavens, on the earth, or in my life. I will be thankful and worship the King with honor, humility, 1st love devotion, reverence, and awe! May the living God inside me be honored and glorified by me!

Day 338 | KINGDUIT

"Dear friends, I urge you, as foreigners and exiles, to abstain from sinful desires, which wage war against your soul."

1 Peter 2:11

The downside of healing and liberty is the season when the spiritual world wages against you to resist your changing for the good. Often the temptation to sin gets worse right before you get better. And then, as you begin to get cleaner in your mind and body, there might be a season of demonic resistance pressing in on you until you flee and keep pursuing liberty. As your liberty bell rings, so will some persecution, but Jesus says you are getting more blessed.

Perseverance is necessary the more you pursue God. The more you pursue biblical mental healing, people might find fault with you, even godly and wonderful people. The more healing you receive, the more people might say you are crazy. The higher your praises are and the louder you sing, the more annoyed the enemy will get and those close to you might despise your worship. The more you pray, others might say you are lazy with little work ethic. The more you forgive, the more the enemy will taunt you with lies about how others are not worth the effort to forgive. The more you pursue purity and holiness, the more people will accuse you of being a worthless human being or even a shame to the cross of Christ. The more you selflessly give, the more people will say that you are cheap. The more that you choose to love no matter what people do, the more people might hate you. The more you try to be selfless and help others, the more people might accuse you of having a Savior complex.

It's weird, but it seems like when you stay away from the sinful parts of life, the greater the battle is to keep you off the righteous path. Hold fast, because soon you will surely be steadfast, free, and immovable.

"But you, man of God, flee from all this, and pursue righteousness, godliness, faith, love, endurance, and gentleness. Fight the good fight of the faith. Take hold of the eternal life to which you were called when you made your good confession in the presence of many witnesses."

1 Timothy 6:11-12

"I love you, Lord, my strength. The Lord is my rock, my fortress, and my deliverer; my God is my rock, in whom I take refuge, my shield and the horn of my salvation, my stronghold."

Psalm 18:1-2

The upside of mental healing and liberty is when seasons change, the freedom bells rings clearly in your heart and the living waters of eternal life splash. The hard work to willingly change for the good pays off with abounding joy and the amazing shalom of God. The longings for the presence of the Lord become greater than the temptation of the flesh. The reality of being human will exist, but Holy Spirit's voice on the inside becomes more valuable than soulish emotions. The desire for righteousness increases along with an understanding of the role of suffering and obedience. As a result of human frailty like weakness, getting off track, being distracted, or a biblical rebuke becomes refreshing or welcoming.

Before I experienced biblical mental healing, I struggled with the difficult and shameful parts of my testimony. I just couldn't understand how to rejoice when trials came along. When the bible says in James 1:2 to consider it pure joy when you face trials of many kinds, I could trust the flawlessness of the word of God. I kept asking Jesus to help me embrace that verse with true joy in my heart. Little by little the Lord showed me why I should be joyful about bad stuff from the past.

Once, a godly friend confronted me about some negative words I was confessing about my past. It was a relief that she cared enough to sharpen me in a humbling way. I agreed and stopped being in denial about what I was confessing and why I was speaking stupid things about my perspective when the Lord clearly told me that I was blessed in my suffering. I quickly asked the Lord to give me new words to put in place of that stupid phrase I repeated. He did and I truly believe that the sovereignty of the Lord is real, and that God has reigned over all my life. I could be like Job and say, "The Lord gave, and the Lord has taken away; may the name of the Lord be praised" (Job 1:21).

My healing journey has brought me to the place where I know the Lord really loves me. It's true in my soul, not just in the bible. He loves me and I finally believe it!

Day 340 | KINGDUIT

"By day the LORD directs his love, at night his song is with me - a prayer to the God of my life."

Psalm 42:8

I traveled to Athens, Greece to inspire my writing. I wanted to stand where Paul stood on his mission. He found the city full of idols, as it remains today. Remarkably, the literal grounds and temples of the Aeropagus are stunning and still stand stately pillared and tall on top of Ares Rock. The mountain is lightly touched by time, human intervention, natural disaster, or greed. I felt so impassioned and moved by the testimony of Paul in Athens written in the word of God:

"Paul then stood up in the meeting of the Areopagus and said: 'People of Athens! I see that in every way you are very religious. For as I walked around and looked carefully at your objects of worship, I even found an altar with this inscription: TO AN UNKNOWN GOD. So, you are ignorant of the very thing you worship—and this is what I am going to proclaim to you.

The God who made the world and everything in it is the Lord of heaven and earth and does not live in temples built by human hands. And he is not served by human hands, as if he needed anything. Rather, he himself gives everyone life and breath and everything else. From one man he made all the nations, that they should inhabit the whole earth; and he marked out their appointed times in history and the boundaries of their lands. God did this so that they would seek him and perhaps reach out for him and find him, though he is not far from any one of us. 'For in him we live and move and have our being.' As some of your own poets have said, 'We are his offspring" (Acts 17:22-28).

The truth that sank deep in my soul was that Jesus does live in me and move with me. His glorious being has been with me, inside the temple of my body, guarding my whole life and yours. With heart soaked in grace, I spent hours taking in the ancient biblical site and considering the Apostle Paul's extraordinary life of suffering, glory, obedience, and faithful service.

Then day turned to evening with a bright full moon and glorious azure sky. I sat at a rooftop cafe with cool wind blowing from the Aegean Sea while old-school music loudly played in the background. I gazed at the ancient architecture illuminated with spotlights in glorious display.

"By the rivers of Babylon, we sat and wept when we remembered Zion. There on the poplars we hung our harps, for there our captors asked us for songs, our tormentors demanded songs of joy."

Psalm 137:2

The Return of the Harp

The soothing sounds of a harp instrument is universally associated with the Kingdom of God and heaven! Did you know the bible remedied evil and torment with harp music?

"Saul's attendants said to him, 'See, an evil spirit from God is tormenting you. Let our lord command his servants here to search for someone who can play the harp. He will play when the spirit from God comes on you, and you will feel better" (1 Samuel 16:15-16).

Young David happened to be a harp worshiping sheep shepherd who found companionship in the Lord. God knew his gift of worship would lead him to the palace, Kingship, and to the design-build for the Temple and the Kingdom. David was so in awe that God chose him to set up the divine temple, being that he was just a mere human, that he often would burst forth in spontaneous praise.

Later, when David became king, he ordered harpists to play joyfully in the presence of God. The gentle sound of harps promotes peace and reverence. David's Psalm writing often mentions stringed music to be played before the Lord and further added night and day continual worship.

The Temple Institute in Jerusalem is dedicated to bringing all the elements of the Jewish Holy Temple back into modern day service. One element, harp worship, has been prepared by the King's Harpists. The anticipation for the Messiah's return has inspired the heavenly sounds for worship in the temple.

Day 342 | KINGDUIT

"This is what the Sovereign Lord, the Holy One of Israel, says: "In repentance and rest is your salvation, in quietness and trust is your strength, but you would have none of it."

Isaiah 30:15

Don't deny the promise of salvation and strength the Lord provides. Don't be like King Saul who rebelled against the voice of the Lord. Seek to have a heart like King David, who devoted his imperfect life to the glory of the Lord and Kingdom of God. He was also determined to bring sweet and glorious worship before the Lord.

Give time to rest before the Lord. Write Jesus a heart-felt letter of your thoughts, concerns, and questions about your life. Listen and write down the thoughts in your mind and the meditations of your heart. Record the wisdom Holy Spirit brings in response to the mysteries of your circumstances.

Watch the testimony below from outside the Western Wall. You will see the fruit of decades of temple preparation and practice from people all over the world who delight in the praises of the King of Glory from the instrument of the harp!

YouTube: The Kings Harpists: The Blessing

KINGDUIT | Day 343

HEAVENLY HARPS

"I saw in heaven another great and marvelous sign: seven angels with the seven last plagues - last, because with them God's wrath is completed.

And I saw what looked like a sea of glass glowing with fire and, standing beside the sea, those who had been victorious over the beast and its image and over the number of its name. They held harps given them by God and sang the song of God's servant Moses and of the Lamb:

'Great and marvelous are your deeds, Lord God Almighty. Just and true are your ways, King of the nations. Who will not fear you, Lord, and bring glory to your name? For you alone are holy. All nations will come and worship before you, for your righteous acts have been revealed.'

After this I looked, and I saw in heaven the temple - that is, the tabernacle of the covenant law - and it was opened."

Revelation 15: 1-5

ART THERAPY DRAY: Draw a heavenly harp.

Day 344 | KINGDUIT

MY	GOD's
<u>Willingness</u>	<u>Redemption</u>

<u>Biblical Redemption Stories</u>

"Give thanks to the Lord, for he is good; his love endures forever. Let the redeemed of the Lord tell their story - those he redeemed from the hand of the foe, those he gathered from the lands, from the east and west, from the north and south."

Psalm 107:1-2

Sometimes the best way to approach the Bible is to just do exactly what it says. This simple step of faith will bring about the wonders of God in your life - so say and tell your beautiful stories! Psalm 107 above says that the redeemed should tell the story of the enduring goodness of God. I will start and then it's your turn to speak out for the love of God.

I was born into an agnostic family. There was no claim to God or even a claim against God. I have no memories of a bible being seen or read in my childhood home. Somehow, one simple nursery rhyme from the eighteenth century got into my mind and out of my mouth as a bedtime routine:

"Now I lay me down to sleep | I pray the Lord my soul to keep

If I should die before I wake | I pray the Lord my soul to take."

I've often struggled to recall childhood memories, but these words got stuck in the mind part of my soul. I can only thank God that an unredeemed child's innocent words would be answered down the road by Jesus. A high-school classmate shared the gospel with my brother, and he became a Christian. Years later he led me to Christ when I was far from home and completely lost. Even though I attended a High School zoned next to a large Jewish community, I had no exposure to biblical history or biblical thought. When the gospel light was beaming in my college bedroom, I saw a vision of Jesus. His holiness terrified me, so got on my knees, burst into tears, and asked Jesus to forgive and receive me. That Thanksgiving Day Jesus gathered me up in His love!

KINGDUIT | Day 345

Psalm 107: Redeeming God

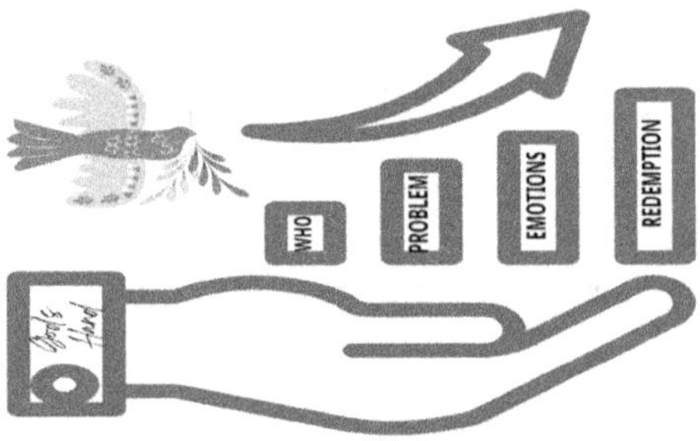

Some of the best bible teacher's markup the bible precept by precept. They dissect the text, pull it apart and review each idea, action, exhortation, or command. Psalm 107 is a poem of thanksgiving to God for the many stories of divine deliverance. It starts with praise to God and then has an exhortation for the redeemed to say so or tell their story. Then verses 4-42 give examples of different ways the Lord lovingly rescued people. The last verse tells the reader how wise they would be if they pondered the vast rescue blessings of God and honored His request for meditation and proclamation.

If you read the whole psalm, you will see a pattern form: 1. Who=The Lord/ People 2. What happened=The Problem 3. The Response = Related Emotions 4. God's Rescue = Redemption

Day 346 | KINGDUIT

THEIR GOD's

Willingness Redemption

Biblical Redemption Stories

Here is a sample of how to write out bible texts that list the who's, the problem, the emotions, and the redemption stories in categories.

WHO	WHAT HAPPENED	RESPONSE	GOD'S RESCUE
verses 4-9 Some wandered in desert wastelands	They were hungry and thirsty, almost dead	They cried out to the Lord in trouble and distress	Led them by a straight way to settle in a city, satisfying them
verses 9-16 Some sat in prison darkness suffering and chainedways	Rebellion against God, bitter to His	They cried out to the Lord in trouble and distress	He brought them out of darkness and broke chains
verses 17-22 Some fools rebellious, suffering, afflictions	Loathed all food and drew near to the gates of death	They cried out to the Lord in trouble and distress	He sent out His word and healed them, rescued them from the grave
verses 28-32 Went out to sea on ships, water merchants	Stormy seas, mighty winds & perilous waves, at wits' end	They cried out to the Lord in their trouble courage melted	He stilled the storm to whisper, haven guide
verses 33-38 Wickedness of residents orchard salt	Rivers turned to deserts, springs dried up, bad leadership	God lifted the needy out of afflictions from ground into wasted	Turned deserts into pools, parched springs

KINGDUIT | Day 347

YOUR	GOD's
Willingness	Redemption

Your Redemption Story

"Let the one who is wise heed these things and ponder the loving deeds of the LORD."

Psalm 107:43

Sometimes the Lord will attach blessings to the reading and consideration of the bible. "For the word of God is alive and active" (Hebrews 4:12). Psalm 107 is an example of a blessing of wisdom for those reading the redemption stories to think about how loving and kind the Lord is. He is not just emotionally loving and kind but greatly moving on behalf of those who cry out to Him with tangible results.

I didn't chart out everything in Psalm 107, but exercises like charting out of the redemptive works of the Lord prove to be fruitful, especially if you do the simple human response of crying out to the Lord.

A father had a job offer and brought his family with him to the United States. The job fell through, and the young family went broke with rent due. They cried out to the Lord in their trouble. They needed food, medical care, household objects, and a job, so they prayed in their great need. The Lord came through to supply every need. Today, they are a God worshiping family with tremendous blessings.

The book of Job tells the story of a man in utter distress. "And this man was blameless and upright, fearing God and shunning evil. . . Job was the greatest man of all the peoples of the East" (Job 1:1, 4). Even if you love and serve God faithfully, times of distress can come. Job went from being amazing, to looking like a total loser in the eyes of his community. Even his wife gave up on him. Yet through his hard times, he told the story of redeeming love when Job said, "I know that my redeemer lives, and that in the end he will stand on the earth" (Job 19:25). Job talked to the Lord in the dark night of his soul and God spoke back. Are you willing to ponder the works of the Lord? Are you willing to read stories to find out the wondrous works of the Lord's redeeming love that endures forever?

Day 348 | KINGDUIT

"A psalm of David. The LORD is my shepherd, I lack nothing. He makes me lie down in green pastures, he leads me beside quiet waters, he refreshes my soul."

Psalm 23: 1-3

David was the warrior king who understood the soul. Time and time again he composed psalms that referenced his soul. He figured out that aligning his soul to the Lord and His kingdom was a strategy for victory, worship, mental health, and divine protection.

Despite family rejection, multiple war attacks and the relentless resistance that tried to keep him from building something glorious for God's kingdom, David took command of his soul. Even all the way to the day of his death, David persevered! He figured out how to refresh, rest, and earnestly seek God with his soul.

It has taken many years of seeking the Lord, personal contemplation, and biblical study to grasp the concept of soul. The more I read and understand, the more I realize how critically important our souls are to God.

How have we neglected such a vital part of our being? Perhaps because the soul is invisible and only God can see it. Although the soul might be challenging to explain, that doesn't mean we can't learn about it. If the bible says that the goal of our faith is soul-level salvation, then we are all meant to have soul victory just like King David.

Jesus warned us that worldliness could cause us to lose our soul when He said, "What good will it be for someone to gain the whole world, yet forfeit their soul? Or what can anyone give in exchange for their soul. For the Son of Man is going to come in his Father's glory with his angels, and then he will reward each person according to what they have done" (Matthew 16:26-28).

It might take some seeking and practice, but we must master our own soul. Our will is the tool needed to complete this work. We must seek, thirst, wait, rest, hope, speak gracious words, and fear God.

"I wait for the LORD, my soul waits, and in his word, I put my hope."

Psalm 103:5

The Invisible Soul

SPEAK OUT LOUD & DECLARE

PRAY: I won't be afraid of those who kill the body but cannot kill my soul. Rather, I will fear the One who can destroy both soul and body in hell. If God cares for sparrows, then I won't be afraid because my life is worth more than many sparrows (Matthew 10:28-31).

Give me happiness, O Lord, for I give my soul to you (Psalm 86:4). I will love the Lord my God with all my heart and with all my soul and with all my mind and with all my strength (Mark 12:30).

I will praise the Lord, my soul. My God, you are very great; you are clothed with splendor and majesty. Let all that I am praise the Lord (Psalm 104:1).

I bless the Lord, O my soul, and I will not forget all your benefits - you forgive all my sins and heal all my diseases, you redeem my life from the pit and crown me with love and compassion, you satisfy my desires with good things so that my youth is renewed like the eagle's (Psalm 103:2-5).

Truly my soul finds rest in God; my salvation comes from him. Truly he is my rock and my salvation; he is my fortress; I will never be shaken (Psalm 62:1-2).

As the deer paths for the streams of water, so my soul pants for you, my God. My soul thirsts for God, the living God. When can I go and meet with God? My tears have been my food day and night, while people say to me all day long, "Where is your God?" These things I remember as I pour out my soul: how I used to go to the house of God under the protection of the Mighty One with shouts of joy and praise among the festive throng. Why, my soul, are you downcast? Why so disturbed within me? Put your hope in God, for I will yet praise him, my Savior, and my God (Psalm 42:1-5).

I pray that I may enjoy good health and that all may go well with me, even as my soul is getting along well (3 John 1:2).

For you created my inner being you knit me together in my mother's womb. I praise you because I am fearfully and wonderfully made; your works are wonderful; I know that full well (Psalm 139:13-14).

I will speak gracious words over myself and others that are like a honeycomb, sweet to the soul and healing to the bones. (Proverbs 16:24).

Day 350 | KINGDUIT

"Jesus said, 'And when He (Holy Spirit) comes, he will prove the world to be in the wrong about sin and righteousness and judgment: about sin, because people do not believe in me; about righteousness, because I am going to the Father, where you can see me no longer; and about judgment, because the prince of this world now stands condemned."

John 16:8-11

Many faith-based people express no desire to examine the sin problem they have when living in the flesh. They lean so heavily on the finished work of the cross that they neglect taking responsibility for their worldly, godless lifestyle.

I knew this to be true, but one day I listened to a co-worker delight in a party lifestyle, then later proclaim the gospel while repeating Jesus' words in John 19:30, "It is finished" to prove grace.

Even though grace alone provides salvation, we still need to work out our salvation. Our hearts are deceitful, wicked, and double-minded. "Who can understand it? I the Lord search the heart and examine the mind, to reward each person according to their conduct, according to what their deeds deserve" (Jeremiah 17:9-10).

Since it is difficult to save our own soul and even God says it's hard to understand, we need help. Jesus explained exactly how Holy Spirit helps by convicting and rebuking our wrongs. The healing will flow to those willing to listen and respond to the work of Holy Spirit in our soul.

"The coming of the lawless one will be in accordance with how Satan works. He will use all sorts of displays of power through signs and wonders that serve the lie, and all the way wickedness deceives those who are perishing. They perish because they refuse to love the truth and so be saved. For this reason, God sends them a powerful delusion so that they will believe the lie and so that all will be condemned who have not believed the truth but have delighted in wickedness" (Thessalonians 2:9-12).

Run to the throne of grace and pursue Holy Spirit! Don't let this world shock you by the coming judgment.

"And this is the testimony: God has given us eternal life in his Son. Whoever has the Son has life; whoever does not have the Son of God does not have life. I write these things to you who believe in the name of the Son of God so that you may know you have eternal life. This is the confidence we have in approaching God: that if we ask anything according to his will, he hears us."

1 John 5:11-14

Have you ever wondered how you can have confidence for mental healing, total forgiveness, and full redemption? Your confidence is not based on yourself, your family, your spouse, your therapist, your pastor, or your church. You can fully lean on the Lord your God, your Creator and "the Maker of heaven and earth" (Psalm 115:15) because Jesus came to earth for you to have a super abundant life. The one who knit you together in your mother's womb, who formed your inmost being (Psalm 139) has the power to heal your body, soul, mind, and spirit.

Jesus gave you ALL authority to overcome anything and everything that sets itself against the knowledge of God's power in your precious life. This includes an enormous spectrum of things that you haven't had the right opportunity to deal with using that authority. Therefore, you don't feel free in your soul.

You must utilize your God given authority to apply His power by faith over each problem in your life that needs healing!

SPEAK OUT: "Thank you Jehovah Rapha for healing my soul!"

Day 352 | KINGDUIT

"O Lord, if you heal me, I will be truly healed; if you save me, I will be truly saved."

Jeremiah 17:1

Samuel Trevor Francis lived in London in the 19th Century and became so ill that he moved in with a doctor for a year. A man took him to a baptismal service where he heard the gospel of the Lord Jesus. Later he confessed privately to Jesus, "I do believe!" and at once was healed. He then wrote poems of worship and served God for seventy-three years until his death. His song "O the deep, deep love of Jesus" proclaims God's love and is still sung today. "O the deep, deep love of Jesus | Vast unmeasured, boundless, free | Rolling as a mighty ocean | In its fullness over me."

It's true, if the Lord heals you, you will be truly healed. If you seek salvation, you will be truly saved from anything. Learning about the biblical Jewish testimonies is fascinating because we see the Jews had absolutely no way to escape Satanic Pharaoh, especially after four hundred years of generational oppression, but Almighty God is mighty!

That four hundred years to me represents an ancestral line of people that cannot possibly be traced so we can address all the errors from past godlessness. It's impossible to cover all the wrongs and make them right, but God knows it all and if God did it for the Jews, He can do it for the Gentiles too! How do I know?

"If God is for us, who can be against us? He who did not spare his own Son, but gave him up for us all - how will he not also, along with him, graciously give us all things? Who will bring any charge against those who God has chosen? It is God who justifies. Who then is the one who condemns? No one. Christ Jesus who died - more than that, who was raised to life - is at the right hand of God and is also interceding for us. Who shall separate us from the love of Christ? Shall trouble or hardship or persecution or famine or nakedness or danger or sword? As it is written: 'For your sake we face death all day long; we are considered as sheep to be slaughtered. 'No, in all these things we are more than conquerors through him who loved us. For I am convinced that neither death nor life, neither angels nor demons, neither the present nor the future, nor any powers, neither height nor depth, nor anything else in all creation, will be able to separate us from the love of God that is in Christ Jesus our Lord" (Romans 8:31-39). O the deep healing love that covers us all!

"There is a time for everything, and a season for every activity under the heavens; a time to be born and a time to die, a time to plant and a time to uproot, a time to kill and a time to heal."

Ecclesiastes 3:1-3

Your Father in Heaven already wrote the story of heaven and earth. He lives in eternity, that means God the Father lives outside of time. Eternity has no time, it is endless, so there is no need to measure time because eternity goes on forever.

I wonder if people realize when they say "I love you forever" that it literally means for all eternity and on and on. But when the Lord Jesus says that He loves you with an everlasting love, He truly understands it because Jesus came from living in the eternal heaven with his Father and then entered time as a human baby. Jesus became man and lived within the limited lifespan of time.

Time started in Genesis 1 after God took a dark, formless, and void planet earth and spoke light into it (light measures time). It's like God turned on the lights and started time. He made the garden in the natural world along with the first human, Adam.

The book of Ecclesiastes explains some of the things God designed inside of time. One of them is a time to heal. It's interesting that the world is focusing on mental health in this season of history while the whole creation itself is groaning with all sorts of natural disasters. You can be sure God has a plan to heal the earth and restore it back to the beauty of the Garden of Eden.

For us, we are invited to jump into a time to heal and find the health and vitality necessary to overcome dark days that the bible calls "the last days" (2 Peter 3:3).

When God created earth's story and the natural world, He designed it with purpose, provision, intention, and redemption. "Even the stork in the sky knows her appointed seasons, and the dove, the swift and the thrush observe the time of their migration. But my people do not know the requirements of the Lord" (Jeremiah 8:7).

The Lord criticized the Jewish people for not understanding his ways. We are not exempt from divine judgment. We will regret overlooking the appointed times we have been given to appropriate the wonder of divine health.

Day 354 | KINGDUIT

"There is a river whose streams make glad the city of God, the holy place where the Most High dwells. God is within her, she will not fall; God will help her at break of day. Nations are in uproar, kingdoms fall; he lifts his voice, the earth melts. The Lord Almighty is with us; the God of Jacob is our fortress."

Psalm 46:4-7

Is there anyone in your life that you see as a role model in the subject of mental health? Someone who is resilient during hard times and filled with joy in the day-to-day life of responsibility and work? Do you know anyone who refuses to conform to the world systems and lives peacefully with humble confidence in the goodness of God? Have you witnessed the full balance of emotional health, from mourning to dancing and everything in between?

The bible describes it like someone with a river running through them right to the holy place of the Most High. The joy within them splashes out all the way up to heaven. Even when things get deep or the waters roar, foam, and surge, the Lord Almighty never leaves. Even with all the movement that life brings, God is the fortress.

With biblical mental healing, the promises of God are a sure thing! Endless are the tools for refuge, peace, help, understanding, wisdom, forgiveness, and hope. Even weakness is strength.

Even on sad days, it's okay. A bad day, a weary day, tempting day, perplexed day, an oppressive day, a confusing day, a troublesome day, hard pressed day, day in need of perseverance, day when you want to give up and let go, can always be met with the love and grace of God. That's when setting the will to the "HOLD ON" mode, embracing the humility to deal with low feelings, oppression, and mental struggles.

A young man grew up in a home void of encouragement and lacked emotional intelligence, so he often struggled alone. He had a Christian roommate in college, which was a new experience in his home life. A troubled day came, and he couldn't hide his distress. Without asking questions, the roommate said, "It's okay to have a bad day. Permission granted to take the day off! Rest all day! Do nothing! No responsibility, just be still."

"Though you have not seen Him, you love Him; and though you do not see Him now, you believe in Him and rejoice with an inexpressible and glorious joy, now that you are receiving the goal of your faith, the salvation of your souls."

1 Peter 1:8-9

Every day you choose the pure way of God's love and righteousness, your soul travels on a highway leading to the things of God. "Since then, you have been raised with Christ, set your hearts on things above, where Christ is, seated at the right hand of God. Set your mind on things above, not on earthly things. For you died, and your life is now hidden with Christ in God" (Colossians 3:1-3).

The more you choose, as an act of your will, the beautiful life filled with the riches God has given you in Christ, the more you will rejoice. Receiving God's ways will take you higher and higher, into a place of inexpressible and glorious joy. It might sound like pride, but it is the opposite. As you humble yourself in grateful celebration for the matchless blessings of the gift of God, the Lord lifts your soul!

As you do the work, keep forgiving, and continue to seek Jehovah Rapha so that you will be renewed. When the glorious joy comes, there is your confirmation that it's happening, you really are hitting the center mark, you are experiencing soul salvation.

"The human will, that force unseen, The offspring of a deathless soul,

Can hew a way to any goal, though walls of granite intervene."

James Allen, AS YOU THINK

Day 356 | KINGDUIT

Redemption & Glory

SPEAK OUT LOUD & DECLARE

"And we all, who with unveiled faces contemplate the Lord's glory, are being transformed into his image with ever-increasing glory, which comes from the Lord, who is the Spirit" (2 Corinthians 3:18).

Lord you are the Potter, I am the clay. Thank you for making the riches of your glory known to me, an object of mercy. Thank you for preparing glory for even Gentile's by calling us your people, the children of the living God (Romans 9:23-26).

Thank you, God, "for choosing to make known among the Gentiles the glorious riches of this mystery, which is Christ in Me, the hope of glory" (Colossians 1:27).

I will proclaim Christ, admonishing and teaching everyone with all wisdom, so that I may present others fully mature in Christ. I will work towards this end with great effort, contending with all the energy Christ so powerfully works in me (Colossians 1:28-29).

"Help us, God our Savior, for the glory of your name; deliver us and forgive our sins for your name's sake" (Psalm 79:9).

You are the God of glory. Your voice is over the waters, Your voice thunders, the Lord thunders over the mighty waters. The voice of the Lord is powerful; the voice of the Lord is majestic. The voice of the Lord breaks the cedars, the Lord breaks in pieces the cedars of Lebanon. The voice of the Lord strikes with flashes of lightning. The voice of the lord shakes the desert; the voice of the Lord twists the oaks and strips the forests bare. And in his temple all cry, "Glory!" (Psalm 29:3-5/7-9).

"Even if our gospel is veiled, it is veiled to those who are perishing. The god of this age has blinded the minds of unbelievers, so that they cannot see the light of the gospel that displays the glory of Christ, who is the image of God. For what we preach is not ourselves, but Jesus Christ as Lord, and ourselves as your servants for Jesus' sake" (2 Corinthians 4:3-5). Thank you, Lord, for making Your light shine in my heart to give me the light of the knowledge of God's glory displayed in the face of Christ (2 Corinthians 4:6).

"I offered My back to those who struck Me, and My cheeks to those who tore out My beard. I did not hide My face from scorn and spittle. Because the Lord GOD helps Me, I have not been disgraced; therefore, I have set My face like flint, and I know that I will not be put to shame. The One who vindicates Me is near."

Isaiah 50:6-7

This is the testimony of Jesus, how he kept the resilience plan even when life was difficult, and suffering was painful. He set his face to be like a stone wall by refusing to believe the lie that God would fail to be faithful or leave his side without providing vindication.

That famous saying, "to set your face like flint," comes from the bible. The flint stone can be found in the Judean wilderness. It is a hard mineral that can ignite a spark when struck against steel.

Jesus lived thirty years as a normal boy and man before he started his God-mission of redemption. His father in heaven used his young life to prepare Jesus for an epic three-year mission. Right before John the Baptist started trumpeting his voice to call out in the desert to prepare the way for the Lord, Jesus was led out into the Judean wilderness to be tested with fasting and trials.

Of course, Satan showed up to offer Jesus' power, material things, and food. He leveraged the things he could since his garden takeover fueled his pride. Jesus knew fully well that by resisting Satan, he would welcome suffering. Nonetheless, Jesus set his soul to be like a stone, refusing to be set ablaze by the god of this world.

A mentally strong believer will do the same, knowing that "the god of this age has blinded the minds of unbelievers, so that they cannot see the light of the gospel that displays the glory of Christ, who is the image of God" (2 Corinthians 4:4).

"THE MIND GOVERNED BY THE SPIRIT IS LIFE AND PEACE."

ROMANS 8:6

ART THERAPY DRAW: Draw a big stone with eyes and a smile. That's you, the living stone.

Day 358 | KINGDUIT

"I run in the path of your commands, for you have broadened by understanding. Teach me, Lord, the way of your decrees, that I may follow it to the end."

Psalm 119:32-33

The only way to broaden your understanding is by the Lord. This world system is not designed to make you wiser than the darkness. A sure way to outwit the dark invisible forces that influence evil, and corruption is to run on the Lord's path.

The biblical heroes got their victorious directives and help from the Almighty. Even hero Jesus was given every understanding by Abba Father to overcome in his day. The current biblical plan is for Jesus to give the Holy Spirit the plan for every believer in their day since the battle of good and evil still exists. If you don't seek the Lord, you won't have necessary insight.

"Therefore, he can completely save those who come to God through him, because he always lives to intercede for them. Such a high priest meets our need - one who is holy, blameless, pure, set apart from sinners, exalted above the heavens" (Hebrews 7:25-26).

We focus on things above as we run this race of faith. Jesus will always be the good one, the faithful one, the one with perfect love, the forgiving one, the holy one, the rest giver and thank God, the one who ALWAYS LIVES TO PRAY FOR US. Even if the road is long and our humanity finds itself at its wits end, we set our hearts to finish. We place our souls in God's hand and trust in his mercy and grace to carry us around like the good Shepherd always does for the sheep.

We can humble ourselves and honestly say: "I'm hurting today, I'm weary today, I'm not feeling it today, so I will stay quiet and find my peace in God." Even if there is a reason to complain, argue or back bite, we hold our tongue. As an act of our own will, we refrain and guard lips, mouth, tongue, hand gestures and eye rolls.

If the natural world blows wind and lightning from a storm, people run inside to protect their physical bodies. In the same way, we must run to the shelter of the Most High and take cover from emotional gusts or heat waves until the emotions pass over. Jesus is the safe harbor when we are feeling tossed, mishandled, or disheveled. We can call out to Holy Spirit for help, a friend, wisdom, and divine protection until we make it to the end.

KINGDUIT | Day 359

"I will praise the Lord, who counsels me; even at night my heart instructs me. I keep my eye always on the Lord. With him at my right hand, I will not be shaken."

Psalm 16:7-8

I can't think of a better time to be strong in the Lord and his mighty power than during the holidays. Get up in the night to simply worship and praise the Lord to adore Jesus and beautify your temple within. Pray up the walls of peace and blessing!

These are the times many people gather with friends, family, and young ones. The season filled with lights, special decor, special food, and time off dedicated to connecting with others is the time to let your own light shine. Share the healing love and glory of God. Bless big and little children with a word of encouragement, a smile, a silly time of laughter, a meaningful hand-written letter, a spoken word of respect, a deeply thoughtful gift, a real pure heart-infused hug, or two big ears and a zipped mouth..

Behold a tiny son was born in Bethlehem that day.

The child of God in pure delight, to free us all of sin - no pay.

This baby grew to be a man, no other could compare.

He walked earth without fault: no wrongs, no lies, even in a childhood dare.

So as this season reaches height, I ponder this man Jesus.

His Father God we shan't deny, who made us, loves us, & sees us.

He gave free will, He gave choice, so we would be the one,

to take a gift of heaven & peace on earth to come.

In all He gives to me, I motive write to you.

The season stirs me to express a love that's always new.

Christmas, Christmas, Fa La La,

Christmas, Christmas, yeah!

I urge you friends to take this time to know the reason for the day!

Phebe 1992

Day 360 | KINGDUIT

"Then David said, 'The house of the Lord God is to be here, and also the altar of burnt offerings for Israel. . .

. . . Now devote your heart and soul to seeking the Lord your God. Begin to build the sanctuary of the Lord God, so that you may bring the ark of the covenant of the Lord and the sacred articles belonging to God into the temple that will be built for the Name of the Lord."

1 Chronicles 22:1 & 19

1 Chronicles 22 is when King David prepares for the Temple before his death. He knew his son Solomon would be responsible for the building project, but David made sure the vision of his heart's desire to see the glory of God would be secured. David said he took great pains to translate his resources into material provisions for the temple of the Lord. David also prepared the leaders in Israel to stand ready to support the build.

Read the stunning account of King Solomon's Temple Build in 1 Kings Chapters 6-9 and 1 Chronicles Chapters 9-13 in the context of value, architectural design, beauty, and wealth. When David sought a plan to physically manifest the glory and beauty of the Lord, he pursued the greatest achievement known to man.

Even though that physical wonder was destroyed in the natural world, God longs for that same glory to manifest in our hearts. As we meditate and reflect on the exquisite building project, we can imagine the honor and splendor that resides in our soul because Christ is in us today, so, God's tabernacle is with us! Hallelujah! Christ is the hope of glory. Since God chose us to be like precious living stones of the spiritual house of God, then we have every spiritual blessing provided in the glorious light, love and splendor of the King of Kings and Lord of Lords.

KINGDUIT | Day 361

"By wisdom a house is built, and through understanding it is established; through knowledge its rooms are filled with rare and beautiful treasures."

Proverbs 24:3-4

Only you have the keys to your soul. What does your key look like? Only God has the glorious design for your life. Are you willing to seek divine wisdom to get the plans for your personal tabernacle?

"O Lord, you have searched me and know me. You know when I sit and when I rise; You understand my thoughts from afar. You search out my path and my lying down. You are aware of all my ways. Even before a word is on my tongue, you know all about it. O Lord. You hem me in behind and before; You have laid Your hand upon me. For You formed my inmost being. You knit me together in my mother's womb. I praise You, for I am fearfully and wonderfully made. Marvelous are Your works, and I know this very well. My frame was not hidden from You when I was made in secret, when I was woven together in the depths of the earth. Your eyes saw my unformed body; all my days were written in Your book and ordained for me before one of them came to be.

How precious to me are Your thoughts, O God, how vast is their sum" (Psalm 139:1-5,13-17)!

No matter what has transpired in your life from the past, you are God's treasured possession. Are you willing to seek after divine understanding so that you seek to establish your glorious temple within?

The specific masterplan designs of your personal stone for God's temple are accessible via Holy Spirit, conceived by the vast thoughts of the Almighty. He says if you seek his wisdom, understanding and knowledge, you will come to know about the rare and beautiful treasures that the Lord hopes you are willing to fill in your living temple stones.

Will you seek God for these marvelous and lofty designs?

ART THERAPY DRAW: Draw a special glorious golden key.

"Now if the ministry that brought death, which was engraved in letters on stone, came with glory, so that the Israelites could not look steadily at the face of Moses because of its glory, transitory though it was, will not the ministry of the Spirit be even more glorious? If the ministry that brought condemnation was glorious, how much more glorious is the ministry that brings righteousness! For what was glorious has no glory now in comparison with the surpassing glory. And if what was transitory came with glory, how much greater is the glory of that which lasts!"

2 Corinthians 3:7-11

Jesus knocked on the door of your heart with the gift of salvation. He carried a treasure trove of riches for you inside the bible. As you stood on the seashore among the sands of humanity, he invited you to come and receive.

That first weighty step of sin conviction followed by confession led to the divine pardon and hurling your iniquities into depths of the sea (Micah 7:19). As you opened the door to receive His blessings, unquenchable love washed over you with overwhelming and immeasurable power. You cried out for mercy and a hope to be sealed with love forever. Jesus proved it with a literal, invisible sealed stamp of Holy Spirit inside your soul, unseen by others, but fully known by the Lord to mark you as belonging to the family of God.

Abba Father in heaven adopted you and said, "Come up here to visit my throne!" It wasn't a joke, it was real and when you finally decided to run swiftly to approach God's throne, the door was open. You knew you would find grace, mercy, and help, but when you opened that kingdom door, there was much more!

The treasures, sounds, and atmosphere were breathtaking. Though unspeakable, your spirit leapt in spontaneous praise when you found the One sitting on a glorious throne encircled in emerald. The surround sound of trumpets, thunders, and flashes of lightning in front of the crystal sea stirred awesome reverence in your spirit. Although you weren't alone, you joined the elders and heavenly creatures to cry out words of holiness, worthy, glory and honor to your Lord and God forever and ever. Amen (Revelation 4)!

"I press on toward the goal to win the prize for which God has called me heavenward in Christ Jesus. All of us, then, who are mature should take such a view of things. And if on some point you think differently that too God will make clear to you. Only let us live up to what we have already attained."

Philippians 3:14-16

It's all up from here: higher and higher we are all called to ascend to our heavenly home in Christ along with our Father in heaven. Perfect peace, perfect love, with our perfect Father, and His perfect law and perfect gifts. His perfect Son Jesus was made perfect by His sacrifice so that we would be perfect forever. When God's time of healing is complete, the perfect will arrive when we shall see Him face to face.

In the meantime, our mortal brains have too many nooks and crannies to count, hiding the deep things in a neural circuit board that only God can compute. A lifetime in therapy can't untangle the tapestry of feelings, memories, triggers, emotions, and thoughts present in the soul. Yet fear not, because they are all fully known well by the God who created your inmost being. He wove together your frame in secret places and counted precious your thoughts during your time on the earth. He longs for you to ask, seek, and knock for Him to heal and help you. His ears are tuned to the unique sound of your voice. His hand is still upon you in faithfulness to complete the work He started.

You are made in the image of a high, lofty, and unstoppable force of unconditional love. God will make everything clear to the one who seeks Him. Jesus is the way. Holy Spirit is the Helper.

Because we are being transformed by His perfecting holiness, the goal of a heavenly prize is drawing near. The upward call of Christ Jesus, the high calling heavenward, is upon us in this "NOW" season of life and history. Look, can you see the view in your spirit? Can you hear what the Spirit and the bride are saying? Listen to the eternal encouragement of Lord Jesus and Father God!

"May our Lord Jesus Christ himself and God our Father, who loved us and by his grace gave us eternal encouragement and good hope, encourage your hearts and strengthen you in every good deed and word" (2 Thessalonians 2:16-17).

PSALM 145

SPEAK OUT LOUD & PROCLAIM GOD'S PRAISES!

I will exalt you, my God the King; I will praise your name for ever and ever. Every day I will praise you and extol your name for ever and ever. Great is the Lord and most worthy of praise; His greatness no one can fathom. One generation commends your works to another; they tell of your mighty acts.

They speak of the glorious splendor of your majesty - and I will meditate on your wonderful works. They tell of the power of your awesome works—and I will proclaim your great deeds. They celebrate your abundant goodness and joyfully sing of your righteousness.

The Lord is gracious and compassionate, slow to anger and rich in love. The Lord is good to all; he has compassion on all he has made. All your works praise you, Lord; your faithful people extol you. They tell of the glory of your kingdom and speak of your might, so that all people may know of your mighty acts and the glorious splendor of your kingdom.

Your kingdom is an everlasting kingdom, and your dominion endures through all generations. The Lord is trustworthy in all he promises and faithful in all he does.

The Lord upholds all who fall and lifts up all who are bowed down.

The eyes of all look to you, and you give them their food at the proper time.

You open your hand and satisfy the desires of every living thing.

The Lord is righteous in all His ways and faithful in all He does. The Lord is near to all who call on Him, to all who call on Him in truth He fulfills the desires of those who fear him; He hears their cry and saves them. The Lord watches over all who love him, but all the wicked He will destroy.

My mouth will speak in praise of the Lord. Let every creature praise His holy name for ever and ever.

"Having purified your souls by your obedience to the truth for a sincere brotherly love, love one another earnestly from a pure heart"

(1 Peter 1:22).

"Look, I am coming soon! My reward is with me, and I will give to each person according to what they have done. I am the Alpha and the Omega, the First and the Last, the Beginning and the End.'

Blessed are those who wash their robes, that they may have the right to the tree of life and may go through the gates into the city. Outside are the dogs, those who practice magic arts, the sexually immoral, the murderers, the idolaters and everyone who loves and practices falsehood.

'I, Jesus, have sent my angel to give you this testimony for the churches. I am the Root and the Offspring of David, and the bright Morning Star.'

The Spirit and the bride say, 'Come!' And let the one who hears say, 'Come!' Let the one who is thirsty come; and let the one who wishes take the free gift of the water of life.

I warn everyone who hears the words of the prophecy of this scroll: If anyone adds anything to them, God will add to that person the plagues described in this scroll. 19 And if anyone takes words away from this scroll of prophecy, God will take away from that person any share in the tree of life and in the Holy City, which are described in this scroll.

He who testifies to these things says, 'Yes, I am coming soon.' Amen.

Come, Lord Jesus. The grace of the Lord Jesus be with God's people. Amen."

Revelation 22:12-21

The above words have seriously motivated my will to persevere. There is so much to look forward to and the rewards start immediately.

Thank you for joining me on this biblical mental healing journey. I bless you to experience the presence, power, and peace of your Wonderful Counselor every day! May His love inspire you to run this race of life and win big for the Kingdom.

Endnotes

1. Chabad.org. "Rosh Hashanah: What's It Really All About?" YouTube, uploaded by Chabad.org 02,SEP,2021

2. https://www.psychiatry.org/psychiatrists/practice/dsm

3. https://www.biblestudytools.com/bible-study/topical-studies/reasons-to-praise-god-as-el-roi.html

4. https://bcmj.org/back-page/symbols-medicine

5. James Strong, *The New Strong's Exhaustive Concordance of the Bible* (Nashville, TN: Thomas Nelson Publishers, 1990), ref. no. 7495

6.https://www.verywellhealth.com/an-overview-of-the-dsm-5-5197607#:~:text=DSM%2D5%20 Diagnoses,%2D%20and%20 stressor%Related%20 disorders.

7. Jewison, N. (Director) (1999). *The Hurricane.* Universal, Touchstone

8. https://kidshealth.org/en/parents/central-nervous-system.html

9. Sounart, C. (2013). Origins: "*What Happens in Vegas . . .*", *Coloradan Alumni Magazine*, Spring 2014. Coloradan.edu

10. James Strong, *The New Strong's Exhaustive Concordance of the Bible* (Nashville, TN: Thomas Nelson Publishers, 1990), ref. no. 5590

11. Duguay, C. (Director) (1999). *Joan of Arc.* Artisan Entertainment

12. https://www.hearing-voices.org/wp-content/uploads/2013/05/HVN-Position-Statement-on-DSM5-and-Diagnoses.pdf

13. https://www.britannica.com/biography/Saint-Joan-of-Arc/Character

14. "diagnosis."Merriam-Webster.com.2023. https//www.merriam-webster.com (22 October 2022).

15. https://www.britannica.com/topic/International-Classification-of-Diseases#:~:text=History%20of%20the%20ICD,-Some%20of%20the&text=The%20International%20Statistical%20Institute%20adopted,statistician%20and%20demographer%20Jacques%20Bertillon.

16. https://www.psychiatry.org/psychiatrists/practice/dsm/about-dsm/history-of-the-dsm

17. James Strong, *The New Strong's Exhaustive Concordance of the Bible* (Nashville, TN: Thomas Nelson Publishers, 1990), ref. no.. 1108

18. https://www.psychiatry.org/psychiatrists/practice/dsm/about-dsm

19. https://www.poetryfoundation.org/poems/46550/the-new-colossus

20. https://www.thegospelcoalition.org/article/6-ways-jesus-joshua/

21. James Strong, *The New Strong's Exhaustive Concordance of the Bible* (Nashville, TN: Thomas Nelson Publishers, 1990), ref. no. 5331

22. James Strong, *The New Strong's Exhaustive Concordance of the Bible* (Nashville, TN: Thomas Nelson Publishers, 1990), ref. no. 5590

23. https://www.nbcc.org

24. Worthington, E.(2004, Sept 1). Greater Good Magazine. The New Science of Forgiveness.

25. American Psychiatric Association (1980). Diagnostic and Statistical Manual of Mental Disorders. (3rd ed.). Washington D.C.Commonly known as the DsM-III. http://traumadissociation.com/ptsd/history-of-post-traumatic-stress-disorder.html#dsm-iii

26. James Strong, *The New Strong's Exhaustive Concordance of the Bible* (Nashville, TN: Thomas Nelson Publishers, 1990), ref. no. 5331

27. http://gadsdenmessenger.com/inspiration-from-gods-word-psalm-91-the-soldiers-pslam

28. https://www.christianitytoday.com/ct/2021/may-june/bible-battle-army-gideon-soldiers-vietnam-iraq-afghanistan.html

www.ingramcontent.com/pod-product-compliance
Lightning Source LLC
LaVergne TN
LVHW052223200926
848481LV00001B/196
9798989275526